IS IT POSSIBLE
FUTURE? DOES
DESTINY? IS AMERICA MENTIONED ANYWHERE
IN PROPHECY? SHOULD THE U.S. JOIN IN WITH
THE NEW ONE WORLD GOVERNMENT SYSTEM?
SHOULD WE CONVERT TO THE METRIC SYSTEM?

Prophets
and
Frauds

by Edward Oliver

WHICH IS CORRECT, EVOLUTION OR CREATION?
DID NOSTRADAMUS PREDICT THE 9/11 ATTACK?
WHAT IS THE TRUE CAUSE OF LYME DISEASE
AND WEST NILE VIRUS?   WHEN WILL THE
ANTICHRIST APPEAR?   DID THE EXODUS
REALLY HAPPEN? WHEN WILL JESUS RETURN?

INTRODUCTION

Is it possible for man to see into the future? Modern scientists tell us that it is not possible for man to see through time, but for nearly 6000 years the ancient Hebrew prophets have been trying to warn us about future world wars and other calamities. This ongoing battle between science and religion has been going on for many centuries, and has never been settled to anyone's satisfaction.

Many of the world's greatest scientific minds, like Sir Isaac Newton, Johannes Kepler, and Louis Pasteur, never saw any conflict between science and religion. They only observed conflicts between the men of science, and the men of religion.

Even today, the battle between science and religion still rages on in America's courts over such matters as Evolution and Creation. Many of the world's most respected scientists have now in fact become avowed atheists who consider belief in God to be a "pointless delusion."

In the year 1555, the great prophet and astrologer Nostradamus accurately predicted that in the late 1880's a man named "Pasteur" would come along to discover what was "long hidden" from the eyes of man, and that Pasteur would be honored as a "demi-god" for his discovery. When Nostradamus' famous prediction finally did come true in the late 1880s, the members of the scientific community refused to acknowledge Nostradamus for this incredible prophetic feat.

Likewise, when the great scientist Galileo announced in 1616 that the Earth revolved around the Sun, instead of the reverse, the Pope ordered Galileo placed under arrest for heresy. For the following three centuries the Catholic Church stubbornly refused to admit its error in this matter until the year 1992, when Pope John Paul II finally apologized to the scientific community for the Vatican's unfortunate "mistake."

It is often difficult for scientific and religious authorities to swallow their pride and admit when they are wrong, and it may have been this fact more than any other that is responsible for the present state of hostile relations between the religious and scientific communities. Unfortunately, the confidence of the general public in their religious institutions has been steadily declining over the last half century, resulting in the closure of many churches across America.

In this book we will attempt to examine the scientific and religious aspects of both modern technology and ancient prophecy, to see if we can determine exactly who are the genuine prophets, and who are the frauds. I hope you will enjoy reading these strange but true stories about our historic past, and hope they might raise some questions in your mind about the role destiny may have played in mankind's bumpy ride through history. Most of us live in the world of the seen, but constantly wonder about the world of the unseen. Perhaps this book will raise some questions in your mind about that unseen world.

Author

CONTENTS

CHAPTER 1

THE WORLD TRADE CENTER

"Great promontories on fire in the center of the mainland. There will be a trembling in the Towers in New York City. Two great rock monoliths will be continuously attacked. This is when air-vessels will turn-round to a new course."

Nostradamus Quatrain #1-87

On the morning of September 11th, 2001, American Airlines Flight 11 left Boston's Logan Airport, bound for LA International Airport in California. It was just another Tuesday for most of the passengers on board Flight 11, just three more days until a restful weekend.

About a half hour into the flight, Boston air traffic controllers suddenly noticed that Flight 11 had turned around to a new course. They desperately tried to contact the pilot to find out what was going on aboard the plane, but received no response.

The airplane, originally westbound, was now headed in a southerly direction toward New York City. Air traffic controllers immediately instituted standard emergency procedures, but no one was able to determine what was going on aboard Flight 11.

When American Airlines passengers originally boarded the airplane at 7:45 AM that morning, they had no idea that they were in the company of a group of Arab terrorists who were planning on hijacking the flight. Mohamed Atta and four other men were planning to take over the Boeing 767 and crash it into the World Trade Center in New York City. Flight 11 had a total of 92 passengers on board, including the aircraft's crew, and the five hijackers.

At approximately 8:15 AM the hijackers, using box cutters as weapons, took control of the airplane's cockpit and turned the aircraft around to a new southerly course. The hijackers did not know how to navigate such a large jet, but they did know how to steer one, and intended to visually follow the Hudson River all the way to their New York City destination. They had trained for this mission for over a year at numerous flight schools in the U.S., and had carefully planned every detail of the flight. Later investigations would reveal that the hijackers had made a number of dry runs in advance of their deadly mission.

James Woods, a famous Hollywood actor, had taken an earlier flight from Logan to LA International during one of these dry runs, approximately one month prior to the attack. On that flight, Woods was sitting in first class accompanied by four Middle Eastern men who were behaving very strangely. They never drank or ate anything during the flight, and were constantly talking to each other in subdued tones, taking notes, and periodically glancing out the windows of the airplane. Woods had the distinct impression that these men were preparing for a future hijacking of this flight. He reported his suspicions to the pilot and crew, and federal authorities were notified when they landed in LA. The FAA was also notified.

These dry runs proved to be very valuable to the hijackers. It was later found out that on one flight, the hijackers gained easy access to the pilot's cabin by telling the pilots that they were flight students and wanted to know what a jet cockpit looked like. They were also able to calculate the exact timing of their hijacking to coincide with the plane's passing over New York's Hudson River Valley in upper New York State. The hijackers planned to follow the Hudson River all the way to New York City.

On the morning of September 11th, 2001, the citizens of New York City were in a state of shock when an airplane suddenly crashed into the north tower of their World Trade Center. Workers in the south tower called home to reassure their families that they were OK, and would soon be evacuated so New York firefighters could deal with this terrible accident.

News bulletins flashed across television screens all over the world, as live coverage of the incident took over regularly scheduled programming on all major television networks. Viewers all over the globe witnessed a flaming hole in the side of the World Trade Center's north tower where an aircraft had crashed into it.

When it was announced that the plane was a large commercial jet from Logan Airport, instead of a smaller private plane, some people began to wonder whether this was truly an accident. Then, before their thoughts could congeal, another plane suddenly crashed into the Trade Center's south tower, sending fiery debris crashing down into the streets below.

Unfortunately, the New York Port Authority delayed evacuating the south tower after the north tower was struck, and many people who could have escaped the disaster in the south tower would later die unnecessarily. Now, suddenly, the unthinkable had become a reality. The United States of America was under attack! Attention soon broadened to cover the rest of the nation. What else might follow? Everyone held their breath in anticipation of the frightening events that were now unfolding in front of their eyes.

Suddenly, another report from Washington DC; the Pentagon has been struck by an airplane, and the White House might also be in danger. Soon, a fourth plane was also reported missing. Things calmed down a bit as news reports seemed to indicate that these attacks were confined to the hijacking of commercial airliners. All air traffic in the continental United States was immediately halted at all major airports in order to deal with the situation.

The World Trade Center towers were apparently designed to withstand the impact of aircraft, since small planes had crashed into tall buildings before, but the towers were not designed to withstand the impact of large jet airliners. Such crashes were considered nearly impossible, since large commercial jets were so closely monitored by air traffic controllers.

The steel superstructure supporting the towers was unable to withstand the intense heat from the huge fire caused by the jet fuel, and ultimately gave way when heat weakened the building's metal supports. To everyone's horror, the World Trade Center's south tower suddenly collapsed on itself, sending clouds of dust and debris into the streets of New York. Although the north tower had been struck first, the steel superstructure of the north tower only had to support the weight of ten floors above the location of that airplane crash. The south tower had to support the weight of 20 floors above its crash site, and therefore collapsed first. Many occupants of the World Trade Center towers were in fact able to successfully escape the disaster. Even some workers on the uppermost floors were able to escape to the streets below by quickly evacuating their buildings. Loss of life in the World Trade Center attack however, was still one of the largest in U.S. history. The shape of the New York City skyline and the security of the American people, were forever altered by this tragic event.

Shortly after the 9/11 attack, the Internet was overwhelmed by claims that this attack had been foretold by the prophecies of Nostradamus. False poems allegedly written by Nostradamus were circulated on the Internet, describing the horrible event in great detail. These poems had been hurriedly pieced together from many different Nostradamus quatrains by Nostradamus fans desperately trying to create a verse to fit the occasion. Most Americans didn't pay much attention to these wild claims, since Nostradamus prophecies were quoted almost every time a major disaster occurred.

Writing over four centuries earlier, Nostradamus had in fact produced some very interesting predictions of future events. One notably accurate prediction concerned the famous French scientist Louis Pasteur. In Chapter 1, Quatrain 25, of Nostradamus' famous book the *Centuries*, he not only included Pasteur's name, but foretold Pasteur's discovery of the long-hidden microbe, giving the date, and also describing the ridicule Pasteur suffered at the hands of his peers in the European medical community. The truly incredible part of this famous prophecy was that it was recorded over two centuries before Pasteur was born!

Nostradamus was a Jewish physician and prophet who claimed to have received hundreds of visions about future events. He was born Michel de Nostradame in the St. Remy province of France in the year 1503 (Old Calendar). He was the eldest of five sons, and his father was the town notary. His family had converted from Judaism to Christianity a year before his birth in order to avoid persecution by the Holy Roman Church of Europe.

Nostradamus received his Bachelor's degree from Mont Pellier medical university in France, and later earned a PHD. He eventually traveled to Agen, where married Adriete de Loubejac, who bore him two children. But in 1538, a local epidemic of the pneumonic plague killed his entire family, and Nostradamus left home and wandered the cities of Europe for many years tending to the sick and the destitute. In 1554 he married his second wife, Anne Gemelle, and published his famous book the *Centuries*, a collection of prophecies on future events. He recorded his visions in the form of four-line poems called "quatrains."

The first edition of his book contained seven chapters of 100 quatrains each, but the last few pages of the first publication were badly damaged, and only 48 of the original 100 quatrains from Chapter 7 still exist today. Later editions added three more chapters, and then two additional chapters. Of the original 1200 or so quatrains, only about 962 still exist today. Nostradamus quatrains are not recorded in any understandable order, so dating them is very difficult.

Nostradamus also very cleverly disguised some his quatrains in order to confuse anyone attempting to interpret the prophecies before their fulfillment. Nostradamus' quatrains were hand-written in Old French, and are thus very difficult to translate. Nostradamus was also known to anagram names and employ clever word games to further disguise his prophecies. He would also occasionally include a "punch" line in certain quatrains which, when correctly translated, revealed the true meaning of the poem. Through these clever deceptions, Nostradamus was able to keep his prophecies successfully veiled for many centuries.

Among Nostradamus' many poems however, was one that specifically mentioned "towers" that were "trembling" and "on fire" in New York. This poem, recorded in Chapter 1 of the *Centuries*, was Quatrain number 87, and specifically mentioned that the event would take place in New York City. This quatrain had generated quite a bit of interest in the world of prophecy for many years. When the basement of New York's World Trade Center was bombed in 1993, many Nostradamus fans thought this was the fulfillment of the prophecy, and therefore retired the quatrain from their list of active prophecies. But when the World Trade Center was attacked for a second time on September 11th, 2001, interest in the prophecy was once again renewed. The last line, or "punch" line, of the poem had never been successfully translated. A rough English translation of the prophecy yields the following result:

Chapter 1, Quatrain 87 (English translation)

Great symbols on fire in the center of the island,
Will cause trembling in the towers of New York City;
Two great skyscrapers will be continuously attacked,
Then Arethuse turn-round to a new course.

In this quatrain, Nostradamus refers to the World Trade Center towers as the "Enno-sigee" (*enno* – great ones, *sigee* – standing silent,) or great "ensigns" of the New York skyline. The World Trade Center towers were indeed the great ensigns, or symbols, of American capitalism, and were repeatedly referred to as such during media coverage of the 9/11 event.

Another key word in this prophecy was the French word "Arethuse." Its exact spelling is very difficult to determine, since the original prophecy was hand-written in Old French, but the word "Arethuse" does in fact exist in the modern French language. It is a class of submarines and other sea going vessels. Some prophecy interpreters therefore thought that someone might try to hijack a submarine, and use it to attack New York City.

Another possible spelling for the word "Arethuse" is "Aerthuse." This word in Old French simply means "air-tubes" ("air" from the Old World "aer" and "tube" from the Old World "thuse," a surveyor's metal sighting tube used for measuring land). Could it be that Nostradamus' use of the word "air-tubes" was actually an attempt to describe the tube-shaped metal vessels in his vision that had the ability to fly through the air? If the word "aer-thuse" does in fact mean "air-planes," then the prophecy would suddenly make sense.

But hold on! This would mean that Nostradamus was actually able to see through time! That's impossible of course! All modern scientists and astrophysicists agree that it's impossible for men to see through time. The ability to see through time however, is indeed the basis for all prophecy, including Bible prophecy.

There's been a long-standing controversy going on for many centuries between the scientific and religious communities over this exact issue. The prophecies of Nostradamus have always been a thorn in the side of modern science. Most scientists just can't understand how people living in a modern, technologically advanced society such as ours, could still hold on to silly fantasies about men seeing into the future. In this world of technological miracles like space travel and cloning, how could anyone still believe in the prophecies of an obscure 16th century Jewish prophet?

Nostradamus had often been accused of being vague in his prophecies, but Quatrain #87 seemed to be quite specific in its description of the World Trade Center attack. Unfortunately the last line of the prophecy could not be accurately interpreted until after the event took place. As with most other Nostradamus prophecies, the prophecy was not recognized for what it was until after its fulfillment. Foreknowledge of the event therefore, could not be scientifically demonstrated.

Could it be possible that the fate of the World Trade Center was locked in destiny? That's silly, there's no such thing as destiny! We all determine our own destiny, don't we? In this modern scientific world, the idea that human destiny is predetermined by some great force beyond our control, should have fallen by the wayside long ago. No one believes in prophetic destiny anymore, in fact, very few people even believe in God anymore, and are actively trying to remove Him from the public arena. But how else are we to explain this uncanny prediction? Could Nostradamus' prophecies actually be true after all, or is this just another case of strange coincidence?

There are more than 960 prophecies in Nostradamus' famous collection. Most aren't dated, and so it's left to the individual to interpret the prophecies on his own. Most modern observers however, do not believe in the accuracy of Nostradamus' predictions, and no Nostradamus prophecy has ever publicly been successfully interpreted before its occurrence.

We'll delve further into the question of Nostradamus' alleged ability to see into the future in some future chapters of this book. For now, there is one thing that cannot be denied, and that is the fact that the following quatrain is printed in numerous books, all of which were published many years in advance of the World Trade Center disaster. It would therefore be difficult for us to deny Nostradamus' foreknowledge of the event if the translation is correct. You can still purchase many of these books in modern bookstores today. The original prophecy #1-87 was written in the Old French language, and so I've included a glossary of definitions for those of you unfamiliar with the Old French and Latin terms.

CHAPTER 1, QUATRAIN 87 (Old French)

Great-ensigns on fire in the center of the mainland,
Enno-sigee feu du centre de terre.
Will shake the towers of the City of New (York);
Fera trembler au tour de Cite' Nuefve.
Two great skyscrapers continuously will be attacked,
Deux grands rochiers long-temps feront la guerre,
This is when air-vessels will turn-round to a new course.
Puis are-thuse rou-gira nouveau fleuve.

OLD FRENCH (O.F.) AND LATIN (L.) DEFINITIONS
Are-thuse – (L. arethuse vessels) air-vessels
Centre – (F.) center, middle
Cite' Neufve – (O.F.) City of New York, (9th empire)
Deux – (F.) two
Enno-sigee – (L.) ensigns, great-promontories, symbols
Fera/feront – (O.F. faire) will make, will be
Feu – (F.) on fire, burning
Fleuve – (O.F.) river, course
Grands – (F.) grand, great
La Guerre – (O.F.) war, warlike attack
Long-temps – (O.F.) long-time, continuous
Nouveau – (F.) new
Puis – (O.F.) then, this is when
Rochiers – (O.F.) rock-monoliths, skyscrapers
Rou-gira – (OF) round-gyrate, turn-round
Terre – (O.F.) land, island, mainland

Tour – (O.F.) towers

Trembler – (F.) trembling, shaking

Prophecy #87 in Chapter 1 of Nostradamus' book, the *Centuries,* is not the only prophecy specifically mentioning New York City. Nostradamus mentions many world cities in his prophecies, but New York City seems to be the only U.S. city he mentions. Nostradamus refers to New York as "Cite' Neufve," or the "City of New." Over its long history, New York City has been variously known as the City of New Netherlands, the City of New Holland, the City of New Amsterdam, and the City of New York. Always however, it was the city of "New."

New York has always been the most important city in the U.S. for many reasons. It is the number one commercial, financial, and entertainment capital of America. When our nation was first formed, New York City was proposed to be our nation's capital, but New York was not a very elegant city at the time, and eventually lost out to Philadelphia, and then to the more stately Washington D.C. area.

New York City however, is still the most important city in America. It's the home of the New York Stock Exchange, the United Nations, the New York Times, and countless other famous institutions. New York City still remains the main business, economic, and trading capital of our nation.

Nostradamus followers have for many years been trying to figure out how his prophecies would affect the United States. Prophecies mentioning New York City therefore were always viewed with great interest by most Nostradamus followers.

Nostradamus' prophecies were first translated many years ago, and unfortunately these original translations were not very accurate. No significant changes in the translations have occurred over the years, and so most Nostradamus books published since that time have merely carried through these original translations unchanged. The overall accuracy of these English translations is therefore still quite poor, so many modern Nostradamus followers must labor under the disadvantage of not having accurate interpretations of his prophecies to work with. The Old French word meanings have also changed quite considerably over the last 450 years, and often no longer directly relate to modern French terms.

Nostradamus followers are certain however, that "Cite' Neufve" does indeed refer to New York City. The term "Cite' Neufve" is used only 3 times in Nostradamus' book the *Centuries*. Prophecy number 1-87, involving the World Trade Center, was originally perceived to be an attack upon New York City's skyscrapers, but there are more prophecies that have also been interpreted as describing attacks upon New York City.

In 1981, author Erika Cheetham published her famous softcover book, *The Man Who Saw Tomorrow – The Prophecies of Nostradamus*. In the index of her book, under the heading "New York City," Ms. Cheetham references specific quatrains that she says foretell future attacks upon "Cite Neufve," or New York City. Quatrain #6-97, describing an "attack" upon New York involving a "bombing," Quatrain #1-87, describing an "attack" involving New York's "towers or skyscrapers," and Quatrain #10-49, describing "New York poisoned through its water supply." Ms. Cheetham's book index listing includes another prophecy, Quatrain #9-92, that might possibly refer to New York City as well, although in this quatrain the name of the city is spelled differently.

These predictions did not seem very plausible in 1973 when Erika Cheetham's book was first published, but now in the 21st century, with the advent of Arab terrorism, these kinds of despicable acts are no longer quite so implausible. Could it be that God was trying to warn us about these horrible events through the Hebrew prophet Nostradamus? If so, it appears that not many people were listening. According to modern scientists and academics, there is no way that Nostradamus could have predicted these events. Scientists still firmly insist that it is impossible for anyone to predict the future, and therefore consider the prophecies of Nostradamus to be utter nonsense.

We may never be able to determine for sure whether Nostradamus is actually one of the 500-year Hebrew prophets sent by God to warn His people about future events, and unfortunately, the future is still unknown to us. No one has yet been able to unlock all the secrets of the ancient prophecies. All prophecy, including religious prophecy, has therefore been relegated to the status of fantasy or myth.

In a rather macabre move, on September 11th, 2002, on the one-year anniversary of the 9/11 disaster, over 5000 people played the number 911 in the New York State Lottery. And believe it or not, 911 actually did come up that evening as the winning number. It has also been shown that the number 11 somehow seems to be intricately woven into many 9-11 related events.

Only time will tell whether the events foretold within the pages of the *Centuries* will ever come true, and liberate the prophet Nostradamus from a rather ignominious fate.

CHAPTER 2

THE CYCLE OF THE PRESIDENTS

He took them both, these two great men
That dark and peaceful night,
To be with Him above the clouds
In His eternal light.

The deaths of Presidents Jefferson and Adams

Do you believe in destiny? In our modern scientific world, the concept of prophetic destiny has now been relegated to the realm of mere fantasy. When amazing historical coincidences do suddenly present themselves, they are generally attributed to chance happenings, and no one becomes overly concerned with their significance. The scientific and religious communities have been arguing over the matter of prophetic destiny for many centuries, but the question has never been settled to anyone's satisfaction.

In U.S. history some very interesting examples of unusual coincidence are recorded for us in the history of the U.S. presidency. The presidency of the United States has always been the subject of much attention by members of the media, who closely follow its many controversies and scandals.

The assassination of an American president is an event that always draws an enormous amount of attention from the news media, and the 1963 assassination of President John F. Kennedy in particular was the subject of much media attention concerning conspiracy theories and the like.

The thought that prophetic destiny might have had anything to do with the fate of any of our presidents has probably never crossed the minds of most people. In this short story however, we're going to take another look at that subject to see if in fact, prophetic destiny might have had something to do with the Kennedy incident, and others like it.

President John F. Kennedy was probably the most popular president of the 20th century. His background was not that of a typical American president. He was the son of Boston millionaire Joseph P. Kennedy Sr., and his mother was Rose Fitzgerald Kennedy, daughter of the late John "Honey Fitz" Fitzgerald, former mayor of Boston. Joseph P. Kennedy Sr. was a clever businessman and politician, who was quite adept at advancing his power and authority within the Boston Irish community, and also within the national Democratic Party.

The elder Kennedy had supported the presidential campaign of Franklin D. Roosevelt, and received the Chairmanship of the Securities and Exchange Commission in return for that favor. Roosevelt later appointed Kennedy to the office of Ambassador to Britain (U.K.). Joe Kennedy enjoyed wielding great political power, but did not particularly enjoy all the attention and public exposure that went along with it. He much preferred to work behind the scenes as the "power behind the throne." Joe Kennedy therefore conceived a clever plan to groom his eldest son, Joseph Patrick Kennedy Jr., for the office of President of the United States.

Kennedy held enough power and influence to successfully carry out this plan, but the plan was nearly thwarted when his son Joe Jr. was unexpectedly killed in a wartime airplane explosion in 1944. Kennedy's favorite daughter Kathleen was also tragically killed four years later in an airplane crash in Europe on the way to meet her father.

Kennedy then decided that his next eldest son, John Fitzgerald Kennedy, would be groomed for the office of President. After WWII ended, Joe Kennedy used his considerable power and influence to run his son John for congressional office. The elder Kennedy took a terrible tongue lashing from the press however, when in the primary race another man with the same name as John's popular opponent mysteriously appeared on the ballot. With dad's help, and his opponent's vote thus split, the younger Kennedy easily won the election.

Young Congressman John F. Kennedy went on to become a U.S. Senator in 1952, and was finally elected to the office of President of the United States in 1960. Joe Kennedy's plans for his son John ultimately did come to fruition, but his own plan for seizing power was short lived. The elder Kennedy suffered a massive stroke on December 19th, 1961, and was left paralyzed and essentially speechless. He died on November 18th, 1969, after living just long enough to see two more of his children die tragically.

President John F. Kennedy was the first member of the Catholic faith to hold the office of President of the United States. JFK was a liberal idealist who championed the twin causes of science and technology. The Kennedy years marked the beginning of a social and moral revolution in America that would continue for many decades, and eventually alter the very fiber of American life. Catholics all over the U.S. were celebrating the fact that the previous reign of conservative White Anglo-Saxon Protestant (WASP) presidents was now over

John Kennedy however, had created many enemies during his brief tenure as President. His failed "Bay of Pigs" attack upon Fidel Castro's communist regime in Cuba, his numerous crackdowns on the Italian Mafia, and his conflict with the USSR over nuclear missiles in Cuba, had earned him many powerful enemies. Kennedy was also hated by many people in America's South because of his stand on civil rights. His efforts to eliminate racial segregation in the South stirred up feelings that had not been experienced since the Civil War when President Lincoln had walked a similar path. Adlai Stevenson, sent on ahead as an advance man for Kennedy's trip to Dallas, Texas, was spat upon by angry southern white supremacists. The stage was thus set for John F. Kennedy's date with destiny.

On November 22nd, 1963, President Kennedy was riding in an open limousine in a political parade through Dallas, Texas, when assassin Lee Harvey Oswald shot him from the sixth floor window of a book warehouse located along the parade route. Oswald fired three shots at the president. The first shot to hit the president struck him in the neck, and the next shot, which proved to be the fatal shot, struck the president in the back of the head.

Oswald made the fatal mistake of running, instead of walking, away from the scene of the crime, and a description of him was immediately dispatched to Dallas police. Oswald shot Dallas police officer J. D. Tippit while fleeing, and was tracked to the Dallas Theater where he was promptly arrested for the crime. Oswald was taken to police headquarters for questioning concerning the shootings, and the Dallas police decided that they had enough evidence to hold him. Threats on Oswald's life however, had been phoned in to the police station, and police therefore decided it would be necessary to move Oswald to a more secure facility.

The next day, while police were attempting to transfer him out of the police station, Oswald was shot and killed by Jack

Ruby, a local night club owner. Ruby gunned down Oswald in the basement of Dallas police headquarters. Rumors about a conspiracy were running rampant, and Oswald, the most important source of information concerning any conspiracy, had now been silenced forever. The assassination of President Kennedy resulted in one of the largest criminal investigations in U.S. history. In addition to numerous private investigations conducted by many national news agencies and professional historians, a special federal government investigative commission, headed by Chief Justice Earl Warren, was set up to thoroughly investigate all aspects of the Kennedy assassination.

Early into the investigation however, federal investigators were struck by the many similarities between the Kennedy assassination and the assassination of Abraham Lincoln that had occurred a century earlier. For instance, both presidents had been shot in the back of the head on a Friday while seated next to their wives, and both assassins were southern white extremists.

These similarities were too unusual to be labeled as mere coincidence, and so investigators started digging more deeply into the assassination of President Lincoln that had occurred a century earlier, to see if there might be some sort of a weird conspiracy going on here. But the deeper federal investigators dug, the stranger things became. For instance, when Abraham Lincoln was first proposed to be run as the Republican candidate for president in 1860, his proposed running mate was a former Secretary of the Navy whose name was, believe it or not, John Kennedy! And the man who protected President Lincoln against the famous 1861 Baltimore assassination plot, was New York Police Superintendent. John Kennedy! The parallels between these two presidencies were truly amazing, for instance:

President Lincoln was shot while sitting in the Ford Theater
President Kennedy was shot while sitting in a Ford limousine, model Lincoln!

The Kennedy's maid, whose name was Mrs. Lincoln, pleaded with him not to go to Dallas.
The Lincoln's maid, whose name was Mrs. Kennedy, pleaded with him not to go to Ford's theater.

Abraham Lincoln was shot in the back of the head while seated next to his wife
John F. Kennedy was shot in the back of the head while seated next to his wife.

President Lincoln's assassin shot him in a theater, and was captured in a tobacco warehouse.
President Kennedy's assassin shot him from a warehouse, and was captured in a theater.

Lincoln's vice president was a former Democratic southern senator named Johnson.
Kennedy's vice president was a former Democratic southern senator named Johnson.

Lincoln was elected President in 1860.
Kennedy was elected President in 1960.

Abraham Lincoln was elected to Congress in 1846.
John F. Kennedy was elected to Congress in 1946.

Vice President Andrew Johnson was born in 1808.
Vice President Lyndon Johnson was born in 1908.

Andrew Johnson died 10 years after President Lincoln.
Lyndon Johnson died 10 years after President Kennedy

Abraham Lincoln lost a son while in office.
John F. Kennedy lost a son while in office.

President Lincoln's assassin was shot before trial.
President Kennedy's assassin was shot before trial.

Abraham Lincoln is pictured on a U.S. coin.
John F. Kennedy is pictured on a U.S. coin.

The names Lincoln and Kennedy each contain 7 letters.

The names Andrew Johnson and Lyndon Johnson each contain 13 letters.

The names John Wilkes Booth and Lee Harvey Oswald each contain 15 letters.

Yes, it goes on and on, but because all these strange coincidences and many others were so popularized in books and magazines after the assassination of President Kennedy, many people are well aware of them.

What many people may not be aware of however, is that these strange coincidences are only a small part of an even larger set of unusual coincidences surrounding the U.S. presidency. Those who study both prophecy and astrology are aware of some other very interesting facts surrounding the question of the prophetic destiny of U.S. presidents. A closer examination of American history reveals the following facts:

> President William Harrison was elected in 1840, and he died in office.

Twenty years later,

> President Abraham Lincoln was elected in 1860, and he died in office.

Twenty years later,

> President James A. Garfield was elected in 1880, and he died in office.

Twenty years later,

> President William McKinley was elected in 1900, and he died in office.

Twenty years later,

> President Warren G. Harding was elected in 1920, and he died in office.

Twenty years later,

> President Franklin Roosevelt was elected in 1940, and he died in office.

Are you beginning to notice a pattern here? American historians also noticed this strange 20-year pattern of U.S. presidents destined to die in office. It was therefore with great interest that they viewed the 1960 election of President John F. Kennedy. The eyes of all historians were firmly fixed upon this young man to see if he would be the first president in history to end the mysterious 20-year death cycle of American presidents. A presidential assassination was considered to be a distinct possibility in this case, since President Kennedy was considered much too young to die of natural causes.

On May 13th, 1956, the famous psychic and astrologer, Jeane Dixon, predicted in a nationally distributed magazine article that the 1960 presidential election would be won by a Democrat who would be assassinated or die in office. When seven years later JFK was assassinated on November 22, 1963, he became the last American president to fall victim to this infamous 20-year presidential death cycle. Unbeknownst to many people however, this mysterious cycle that had run for 120 years from 1840 to 1960, was not actually over.

The public did not know that the 20-year Jupiter/Saturn conjunction astrological cycle of destiny, known to the ancient Greeks as the "Great Chronocrator," was overlain by an even larger 480-year astrological cycle known as the "Cycle of the Elements." The four elements involved in this larger 480-year repeating cycle are FIRE, EARTH, AIR, and WATER, each element holding control of the cycle for 120 years.

The 20-year presidential election cycle that ran from 1840 to 1960 operated under the EARTH portion of the cycle of the Elements. The EARTH cycle, represented by the EARTH substance lead, meant that presidents elected under the 120-year EARTH cycle were destined to meet their fate through assassination, either by a lead bullet, or by using arsenic of lead powder to poison their food.

In the 19th century, one popular method of killing someone was to mix white lead arsenate powder (a paralytic neurotoxin), into their mashed potatoes. After eating this mixture at a meal, the victim would suffer severe abdominal symptoms of food poisoning, and meet with an untimely death. A thorough investigation of presidential deaths that occurred during the EARTH cycle from 1840 to 1960 has never been conducted, so we may never know if any American presidents died in this manner. One fact is certain however; all these presidents were reclaimed by the EARTH while they were still in office.

As previously mentioned, the 120-year EARTH cycle ran from 1840 to 1960. It was preceded however, by another 120-year astrological cycle that ran from 1700 to 1820, known as the FIRE cycle. Presidents elected under the FIRE cycle were not destined to die in office, but were instead destined to meet with an entirely different fate. There were only two U.S. presidential elections that occurred under the FIRE cycle (the Chief Executive in 1780 was John Adams who was appointed by his peers). Adams was the person who borrowed the money from the Dutch to fund the war and convinced the French to aid in our defense against the British Navy. Adams was also the chief signatory of the Treaty of Paris peace agreement with England.

The two public elections occurring under the FIRE cycle were the elections of 1800 and 1820. Thomas Jefferson was the winner of the election of 1800, and James Monroe won the election of 1820.

President Thomas Jefferson's death, believe it or not, actually occurred on America's FIRE holiday. FIRE holiday you say? Yes, you know, that holiday we celebrate with firecrackers, fireworks, bonfires, sparklers, and all sorts of other fiery things. Thomas Jefferson actually died on the 4th of July, America's FIRE holiday! Now there's a nifty coincidence for you!

It's actually a double coincidence however, because Jefferson was also the person who gave birth to the United States of America on this exact same date with his famous hand written document, the Declaration of Independence, signed on July 4th in 1776!

But hold on, it's also a triple coincidence, because Jefferson died on July 4th, 1826, which also happens to be the 50th birthday of the nation he gave birth to by authoring this famous document. Read on folks, it gets better!

President James Monroe, the next president elected under the 20-year Jupiter/Saturn conjunction cycle, won the election of 1820, and also died on July 4th! That's right, it was James Monroe's prophetic destiny to also die on July 4th, America's FIRE holiday, since he also was elected under the FIRE cycle.

Believe it or not, there's a fifth coincidence as well. While drafting America's Bill of Rights, President John Adams wrote a letter to Thomas Jefferson, who was in France at the time, asking him what specific rights he thought should be included in America's new bill. Jefferson sent back a list of individual freedoms that he thought should be included, and America's "Bill of Rights" was born.

Jefferson and his mentor, John Adams, through their two famous documents, the Declaration of Independence and the Bill of Rights, are the two men most responsible not only for the birth of our nation, but also for all the precious God-given freedoms we enjoy today. These God-given rights that all free individuals hold against government tyranny, are what make our nation unique from every other nation on Earth.

Since Thomas Jefferson and John Adams were the true founding fathers of the United States of America, God apparently decided to honor them in a very special way. Believe it or not, He took both Jefferson and Adams from us on the exact same day, July 4th, 1826, which also happens to be our nation's 50th birthday. Jefferson died at his home in Monticello, Virginia, and Adams died at his residence in Quincy, Massachusetts, more than 500 miles away. Neither man knew of the other's passing.

The Cycle of the Elements has now completed both its FIRE and EARTH cycles, and now operates under the 120-year AIR cycle that will run from 1980 until the year 2100. President Reagan, elected in 1980, was the first president destined to suffer a destiny related to the element AIR. But was it breathing AIR, an airplane crash, or some other type of AIR related fate? When Ronald Reagan was shot by John Hinckley in 1981, the bullet lodged in is lung, which may have been a hint as to his ultimate fate. President Reagan died in 2004, and his official death certificate reads "pneumonia," the inability to breathe AIR.

These strange cycles that seem to govern the fate of America's presidents were originally identified more than 2500 years ago, at a time when the Hebrew prophet Daniel ruled over all the wise men and astrologers of Babylon (Dan. 2:48).

In this modern progressive world, the pseudo-science of astrology is not considered to be a significant factor in the destiny of mankind, but the cycle of the Presidents is a haunting example of the many unusual events that helped to shape the destiny of our nation. Most people attribute such events to mere coincidence, but there are others who see a much deeper significance in their occurrence. The history of this strange prophecy is recorded in the chart below:

ELECTION	PRESIDENT	ELEMENT	DIED
1780	Adams	FIRE	(July 4th)
1800	Jefferson	FIRE	(July 4th)
1820	Monroe	FIRE	(July 4th)
1840	Harrison	EARTH	(lead bullet)
1860	Lincoln	EARTH	(lead bullet)
1880	Garfield	EARTH	(lead arsenate)
1900	McKinley	EARTH	(lead bullet)
1920	Harding	EARTH	(lead arsenate)
1940	Roosevelt	EARTH	(lead arsenate)
1960	Kennedy	EARTH	(lead bullet)
1980	Reagan	AIR	(pneumonia)
2000		AIR	???

CHAPTER 3

MOSES AND THE EXODUS

And He said unto Abram, know of a surety that thy seed shall be a stranger in a land that is not theirs, and shall serve them; and they shall afflict them 400 years. And also that nation whom they shall serve, will I judge.

Gen. 15:13

What would you think if one day you went down to the ocean and discovered that it had suddenly and unexpectedly disappeared? Well, believe it or not, this type of mysterious event has occurred many times throughout human history. One of the most famous examples of this sort of occurrence is recorded for us within the pages of the Holy Scriptures.

When we think of epic Bible stories, the one that often comes to mind is the biblical Exodus, with its vision of the waters of the Red Sea parting, allowing the ancient Hebrews to escape Egypt, and then the waters rushing back in to drown the Pharaoh's army.

Many of these stories told in the Old Testament were originally thought to be allegorical in nature, so as to prove a point, and others were sometimes viewed as a combination of myth and fact. The Exodus story is viewed by most modern scientists and historians as a myth, without any basis in either scientific or historical fact.

In our modern scientific world, miracles like the waters of the Red Sea suddenly parting, and the Nile River turning blood red, are just too difficult for most people to accept as true fact.

Recent archeological discoveries however, are beginning to shed a new light upon the Exodus story, and it might now be time for us to take another look at the biblical Exodus, to see whether or not it may have in fact occurred just as the Bible describes.

We must first state that biblical dating is not an exact science. Dates back to the time of Christ are fairly accurate, but dates prior to that time are often prone to many inaccuracies. Most modern archeological evidence now places the date of the biblical Exodus at approximately 1470 BC. In order for us to accurately assess the Exodus story however, it may first be necessary for us to further explore the background of those times.

The 15th century BC was a barbaric time for mankind. Blood sports were a common form of entertainment, slavery was rampant, and morality practically non-existent. In 1470 BC, the barbaric Minoan civilization was thriving on the islands of the eastern Mediterranean Sea. The Minoans were one of the civilizations that preceded the Greeks. They were a seafaring people who often traded with the Egyptians.

The Minoans controlled most of the sea trade in the Mediterranean region. Their ships sailed between Europe and Africa and traded slaves and precious cargoes for money among the many civilizations in that area. Minoan society and culture gradually spread its influence over the entire Mediterranean, and proved to be a dominant force in the region.

The Minoan culture was centered around money and pleasure. The Minoans worshipped the Golden Heifer. This form of cattle worship was very popular in ancient times, and had spread rapidly throughout the Mediterranean basin. Exodus Chapter 32, Verse 4, and Deuteronomy Chapter 9, Verse 16, both tell us that worship of the Golden Heifer had even spread to the ancient Hebrews of Egypt. This form of cattle worship still survives today in India, giving rise to the familiar English expression, "holy cow."

The modern sport of bullfighting also owes its roots to the Minoans. The ancient Minoans practiced a form of bullfighting that differs from the bullfighting of today. In Minoan bullfighting, the bullfighter was an athlete who faced the bull without a cape. When the bull charged, the bullfighter would leap between the horns of the bull, and be vaulted over the bulls back in a graceful leap. This form of bullfighting was called bull vaulting. The bull vaulter had to be very careful to time his leap just right, or he could be caught on the horns of the bull and gored to death, much to the delight of the crowds viewing the event. Such bloody and barbaric sports were very popular in Minoan society.

The Minoans populated many of the islands of the eastern Mediterranean Sea. One of the more interesting islands they inhabited was the volcanic island of Stronghyli (Santorini). Stronghyli boasted many natural hot springs, and the island soon became a vacation paradise for the wealthy upper classes. The island was the site of numerous palatial estates where the rich lived in great luxury, enjoying public steambaths and fresh crops of figs and olives that could be grown year-round in the island's warm soil. Large, elaborately decorated barges, rowed by teams of African slaves, provided scenic tours around the island for its many wealthy visitors.

With so much material wealth, it was not long before Minoan society fell into a state of great moral decay. Stronghyli's many attractions included gambling, bloody sporting events, and all sorts of erotic sensual pleasures.

Paradise can often bring out the worst in human nature, and can also sometimes bring on the wrath of God.

While the Minoans were busy enjoying their island paradise, God's Hebrews were being held as slaves in nearby Egypt. The Hebrews had entered Egypt many years before at the invitation of Joseph, a Hebrew who'd been sold into slavery by his jealous brothers. Joseph was one of the twelve sons of the Hebrew patriarch Jacob. When Jacob bestowed God's special blessing upon his son Joseph, Joseph's jealous brother Reuben stirred up his siblings into kidnapping Joseph and selling him to the Ishmaelites, who carried Joseph to Egypt and sold him into slavery. It was Joseph's destiny however, to eventually rise out of that slavery and achieve a high position in Egypt.

Joseph was blessed by the Lord with the ability to accurately interpret prophecy, and soon found favor with Egypt's Pharaoh by correctly interpreting a vision that Pharaoh had received. This vision foretold a great famine that was about to occur in Egypt, lasting for 7 years. Joseph told Pharaoh that the Egyptians could survive this famine by storing away grain in the 7 good years prior to the famine's arrival.

Pharaoh was pleased with Joseph's accurate interpretation of his dream, and promptly placed Joseph in charge of preparing for the upcoming disaster. Joseph was given full charge of Egypt's granaries, and proceeded to fill the granaries to overflowing in the 7 years before the drought.

When the drought and famine finally did arrive, the Egyptians had plenty of food with which to feed their people. The ancient Hebrews living in the lands to the East however, were not so lucky. They were nomadic sheepherders who relied heavily upon the wild grasses of the field for their existence. When the drought arrived, they were totally unprepared, and in danger of starvation. When word arrived that the Pharaoh's granaries were filled to overflowing, the Hebrews decided to approach the Pharaoh to beg for grain to sustain them through the famine.

The Hebrew patriarch, Jacob, sent his remaining sons into Egypt to beg for grain. When his sons arrived at Egypt's granaries, they did not know that the man they were begging from was their own brother whom they'd sold into slavery many years before. Joseph however, recognized his brothers, and ultimately revealed himself to them. He found it in his heart to forgive them for their treachery, and invited them into the land of Egypt as his guests. His father, Jacob, finally got to meet the son he thought he'd lost forever.

The Hebrews survived the great famine, and prospered in Egypt. Over the many years of their stay in Egypt however, the Egyptian throne eventually passed to a Pharaoh who did not know Joseph, and therefore felt no allegiance to Hebrews. The Hebrews soon found themselves working as slaves for their Egyptian masters. The iniquity of Joseph's brothers was thus repaid unto the fourth generation and beyond (Ex. 20:5). God's vengeance was delivered upon Joseph's brothers for their sinful act of jealousy.

The Hebrew prophets had foretold the birth of a Deliverer who would lead the Hebrews out of their Egyptian bondage. Pharaoh however, wanted no part of any Deliverer, and ordered the death of all male Hebrew children born in Egypt. The wails of dying children and grieving mothers soon broke the silence of many Egyptian nights.

A Levite woman named Jochabed gave birth to a male child, and set him adrift in the Nile River in a basket woven of reeds in order that his life might be spared. The Pharaoh's daughter found the child floating in the river and adopted him as her own son. She named him Moses (drawn-out), because she had drawn him out of the river. And so it was that God arranged for the Deliverer of the Hebrews to be raised up in Pharaoh's own house.

When Moses reached adulthood, he decided to explore his Hebrew roots. He made use of the blanket he was wrapped in as a child to find his family, for it was the custom of the ancient Hebrews to identify their individual tribes in much the same way as the modern Scottish peoples of today. The Hebrews were also known to weave distinctive plaid patterns into their clothing in order to identify their various clans. By using the plaid of the blanket, Moses was successfully able to locate his mother, Jochabed, his brother Aaron, and his sister Miriam.

Moses held a high position in Egypt, and often reviewed the work of the Hebrew slaves. One day, while reviewing a Hebrew work site, he caught an Egyptian taskmaster in the act of beating one of the Hebrew slaves. Moses killed the taskmaster and attempted to hide his body by burying it in the sand. Moses was exposed by the slaves for his act, and was forced to flee into nearby Midian to escape the wrath of Pharaoh.

Moses eventually married the daughter of the priest of Midian, and settled down to raise a family. But the Angel of the Lord appeared unto Moses in a dream, and commanded him to return to Egypt to deliver his people from their bondage. Moses then returned to Egypt and pleaded with the new Pharaoh to release the Hebrews from their slavery.

The pleading of Moses however, fell onto the deaf ears of Pharaoh, who refused to even consider releasing the Hebrew slaves. But the Hebrew God was quick to anger, and soon, from deep within the Earth, a rumbling sound was heard beneath the volcanic island of Stronghyli. The great Stronghyli volcano, asleep for so many years, now suddenly awakened and violently shook the Minoan island paradise.

This great volcano, 7 times larger than any other in recorded history, was about to shake the eastern Mediterranean basin. Tens of thousands of Minoans desperately tried to flee their island in boats in order to escape the giant red clouds of volcanic ash generated by the huge eruption. As the great Stronghyli volcano awakened, thick clouds of red smoke and ash rose high up into the heavens and began moving in the direction of the Egyptian Nile Delta.

These crimson clouds of volcanic ash drifted over the land of Egypt and settled into the headwaters of the great Nile River, causing its waters to turn a bright red. The fish in the river soon died from the acrid water, and millions of frogs were driven onto dry land. The frogs poured into the houses of the Egyptians and perished by the thousands, creating a great stench throughout the Pharaoh's land.

Volcanic clouds of ash darkened the skies over Egypt for three full days, allowing millions of mosquitoes and flies to swarm during the daytime. Violent thunderstorms and hail soon enveloped the Nile Valley, smashing and ruining the crops of the fields. Animals that drank the poisonous river water soon died, and their carcasses drew even more swarms of flies. The flies also bit the Egyptians, causing great boils to appear on their skin, spreading disease throughout the Pharaoh's land. Windstorms then brought clouds of locusts to devour the remainder of the crops in the fields and also the leaves of the fruit trees.

Exodus Chapters 7 through 10 tell us that in spite of all these plagues, Pharaoh still refused to release the Hebrew slaves. The Lord therefore instructed the Hebrews to slay a lamb and splash the blood of the lamb upon the lintels and doorposts of their homes, for the Lord would slay the firstborn of any house without blood on its doorposts. This was the root of the Passover, for the Angel of the Lord "passed over" the homes of the Hebrews.

That night the Angel of the Lord smote all the firstborn of the land of Egypt, including even the firstborn of the cattle. This was the last straw for Pharaoh, who finally yielded to the Hebrew God, and told Moses that he and his Hebrews should leave Egypt quickly.

The Hebrews, at the Lord's direction, had borrowed huge sums of money and jewelry from the wealthy Egyptians prior to their great Exodus. Even Pharaoh herself, in an act of foolish vanity, had allowed the Hebrews to borrow Egypt's treasures without realizing their true plan. When the plot was revealed however, Pharaoh flew into a great rage and sent her army to chase down the Hebrews and kill them all. Moses knew that the Pharaoh would be angry, and as he and his Hebrews embarked upon their Exodus across the desert, he decided to travel by both day and night to keep ahead of Pharaoh's army.

It was difficult to travel in the desert at night without the sun to determine direction, and so Moses used the Stronghyli volcano as his guide. Exodus Chapter 13, Verse 21, and Nehemiah Chapter 9, Verse 19, both tell us that the Hebrews used the visible column of smoke by day, and the volcano's plume of fire by night, to find their way across the Egyptian desert.

When the Hebrews finally arrived at the Nile River Delta, they had to find a way to cross the great canal that in those days connected the Red Sea to the Mediterranean Sea. There were only a few boats available, and it would take many days to cross the canal in this manner.

The Hebrews feared they would be trapped and killed by the Pharaoh's pursuing army, but just then, the sound of a gigantic explosion shook the Mediterranean basin. The volcanic island of Stronghyli, after erupting for so many days, now suddenly exploded and sank beneath the sea. The huge collapse sent a giant wall of water moving out in all directions from the spot that had once been the great Stronghyli volcano.

A few minutes later on a nearby island, the inhabitants noticed the sea level dropping suddenly, as if the tide were going out. But the waters kept receding until they had completely disappeared from view. Where there was once a vast ocean only minutes before, there was now only a dry, sandy seabed. Many villagers rushed down to the beach to witness this strange phenomenon. But the older fishermen on the island had heard the great explosion, and knew from experience that the ocean water was being drawn out to sea to fill the volume of an approaching tidal wave. They immediately shouted a warning for everyone to get to high ground as quickly as possible. Frightened mothers scooped up their children and ran as fast as they could for the center of the island. Time was short, for the tidal wave would arrive in only a few minutes.

Ships on the open sea are unaffected by tidal waves, because these waves travel over open ocean as gentle swells of water only a few feet high. These "tsunami's," or "tidal waves," are thus called because they cause an extremely low tide to occur just prior to their arrival. Large tidal waves can completely empty out harbors, rivers, canals and estuaries just before their sudden arrival. They travel at hundreds of miles per hour, and it is only when these immense waves reach the shallow waters near shore that they slow down and rise up into the air to become the great terror we know as the tidal wave.

As the Stronghyli tidal wave approached each island, it rose up over 200 feet in the air like a giant cobra, and struck the shoreline, destroying fishing villages and smashing ships and small boats against the rocks. Striking island after island, the great wave destroyed everything in its path. The giant wave continued on across the Mediterranean in the direction of the Egyptian Nile Delta, which unfortunately had no high shores to protect it.

Less than an hour after the collapse of the former island paradise of Stronghyli, the waters of the Red Sea Canal were suddenly being drawn out to sea by a strange tidal flow. The Egyptian villagers were frightened by this strange force that was suddenly emptying out their canal, but Moses knew who had sent this, and ordered his people to be ready to cross the dry canal bed quickly. There was high ground on the other side where they could find refuge from what was about to happen.

Dust from the chariots of the approaching Pharaoh's army could now be seen in the distance. There was no time to spare. The Hebrews quickly gathered up their animals and belongings, and rushed to cross the dry canal bed in order to reach the safety of the opposite shore. From the top of a high plateau on the other side, they would at least have a chance of holding off Pharaoh's troops.

The Pharaoh's army charged into the dry seabed in pursuit of the fleeing Hebrews, but when they had gotten only about half way across, they heard a loud roaring sound coming from the North. When they turned their heads to look, they beheld a sight that caused their hearts to stop. A great, thundering wall of water almost 200 feet high was racing down the dry canal bed toward them. There was no time to retreat, and before the troops could even turn their horses, the tidal wave was upon them. With heavy armor and weapons weighing them down, the Egyptians did not stand a chance against the giant wave.

The ancient Hebrews had a bird's eye view of this entire event from the safety of their position on the high plateau east of the canal The Pharaoh's mighty army was completely destroyed in just a few moments right in front of their eyes. The rich lowlands of the Nile River Delta were entirely submerged beneath the salt waters of the great wave. Hundreds of farming and fishing villages along the Mediterranean coast were totally destroyed in this great catastrophe.

Along with the story of Noah and the Great Flood, this story too was destined to become a permanent part of Hebrew literature. In one momentous event, the Lord had destroyed one entire civilization, liberated another, and the great Pharaoh's army was no more.

The devastation caused by this cataclysm was greater than that of any other in recorded history. The Minoans were so traumatized by the event that they decided to relocate what was left of their civilization to the European mainland. There, the high shoreline would prevent any possibility of a tragedy like this ever occurring again. And it was many years before the Egyptians recovered from the damage to their farmland caused by the salt from the seawater. For decades after this disaster, there was famine in the land of Egypt, and much resentment against the Pharaoh Hatshepsut for her great foolishness. When Thutmose III finally achieved the throne of Egypt, he would make every effort to permanently erase his aunt's memory from Egyptian history. Note: the eggheads at the Smithsonian apparently haven't figured this out yet (see: Smithsonian magazine - Sept. 2006).

The story of the fate of the barbaric and sinful Minoan civilization, and the sinking of the island of Stronghyli, eventually became a part of ancient Egyptian folklore. The story was passed down through the tales of many civilizations inhabiting the Mediterranean region. Many centuries later, the Greeks picked up the story from the high priests of Egypt, who recorded these great "cleansings" by the gods of societies that had turned carnal in their interests.

The Greeks promptly inflated the story by a factor of ten to make it worthy of Greek mythology, and the story eventually found its way down to the Greek philosopher Plato, who recorded it for us in his ten-book piece, *The Republic*. The story of the island of Stronghyli is still told today as the mythical tale of the doomed island of Atlantis.

To this very day, a layer of bright red volcanic ash still coats the Mediterranean seafloor, testifying to the truth of this ancient tale. The path of this red ash leads directly from the remains of the volcanic island of Stronghyli, to the Egyptian Nile Delta. The crimson cliffs of the island of Thera, and the other small islands surrounding the former crater of the old Stronghyli volcano, still color the seawater a bright red even today.

Archeologists are slowly beginning to uncover more scientific evidence of this ancient Bible event that was until recently regarded as fiction. The Bible has now become a useful tool that modern man can use to reveal much about his historic past.

Many scientists no longer view the Bible as they once did. It has now become a useful source of information for historians and archeologists alike, concerning the history of mankind, and man's prophetic destiny as revealed by God through the Hebrew prophets. Now that the seventh millennium of man's civilized existence on Earth has finally arrived, scientists and archeologists everywhere are beginning to discover more information about the many prophetic events that governed the destiny of God's blessed people.

CHAPTER 4

THE GREAT PYRAMID

In that day, shall there be an altar to the Lord in the midst of the land of Egypt, and a pillar at the border thereof to the Lord.

Isaiah 19:19

It is still the most amazing structure on the entire face of the Earth, and although archeologists have been studying it for many centuries, no one has yet been able to determine who built it, or exactly what it stands for. It is the Great Pyramid, and the only thing we know for sure about it, is that it was not designed or built by the Egyptians. That's right, contrary to everything you learned in school, the Great Pyramid was not built by Egyptians (just as the Mayan pyramids were not built by the Mayans).

Who built it then? In order for us to answer that question, it will first be necessary for us to review what modern science has thus far been able to reveal about this truly incredible structure. First of all, we know that the Great Pyramid has been standing in its present location for more than four thousand years, and in spite of the fact that the pyramid is over four thousand years old, it still holds the world's record for being the most massive stone structure ever built by mankind. This fact alone makes it one of the most unique objects on Earth. Of the original Seven Wonders of the World, the Great Pyramid is the only one that is still standing today.

The Great Pyramid was originally constructed from over 2,000,000 hand-cut stone blocks weighing anywhere from 2 to 20 tons apiece. Every single one of these massive stone blocks had to be hand-quarried, cut into a perfect geometric shape, and then finely honed with such a degree of accuracy, that to this day a credit card cannot be fit between any two of them.

When the Great Pyramid was originally built over four thousand years ago, its exterior was completely covered in white polished limestone that shined so brightly, sailors on the Mediterranean Sea often used the pyramid to chart their courses.

In the second millennium before Christ, the Great Pyramid was a truly breathtaking sight to behold. Its polished limestone exterior made it appear as if an object from heaven had somehow mistakenly fallen to Earth. Around 1300 AD however, this beautiful white limestone exterior was stripped off by Arab raiders who used the blocks to build their religious mosques.

Archeologists have since determined that the Great Pyramid contains no hieroglyphics. This is an extremely unusual fact, for it places the structure in sharp contrast to all other pyramids in the area. Nowhere on the Great Pyramid are there any markings that would identify it as being Egyptian in origin.

In the 1700's, European archeologists discovered some other very interesting facts about this massive stone structure. They were able to determine through precise measurements, that the geometric shape of the Great Pyramid indicated its builders possessed an advanced knowledge of both mathematics and geometry. Archeologists uncovered the surprising fact that the Great Pyramid's height was in relation to the distance around its base, in the same proportion that the radius of a circle holds to the circumference of a circle. This was a truly shocking discovery, for it clearly demonstrated that that the builders of the Great Pyramid possessed an understanding of the pi relationship. It was not previously thought that any early civilizations were aware of the value of pi.

When this amazing discovery was first announced to the world, most European scholars absolutely refused to believe it was true. Teams of archeologists were immediately dispatched to the Middle East to further examine the Great Pyramid and take more precise measurements of its dimensions, in order to dispel this wild theory.

When these archeologists attempted to determine the smallest common measuring unit used to build the pyramid, they found this measurement recorded on the top of a decorative boss located in the interior of the structure. This basic measuring unit turned out to be exactly equal to the modern day British inch! This shocking discovery presented scientists with an even more difficult puzzle to explain. How could the British inch have possibly survived unchanged for more than four thousand years?

When archeologists then sought to determine the next largest unit of measure used to build the pyramid, they found the measurement recorded in the so-called "Queen's Chamber," located at the 25th level of the structure. This measuring unit was found to be exactly equal to 25 British inches. Archeologists labeled this new measure the "Sacred Cubit" since the ancient Hebrew cubit was known to be about this length (actually 25.025025 inches). When archeologists measured the length of one side of the pyramid's base using this measurement, they were shocked to find out that it measured exactly 365.242 of these sacred cubits in length, representing the exact length of Earth's solar year! But how could the builders of the Great Pyramid have possibly known the exact length of Earth's solar year? This discovery sent yet another shock wave through the European scientific community. More expeditions were sent to Egypt to further investigate these claims.

European religious leaders were also now beginning to express an interest in this ancient monument, originally built in biblical times, for the Bible had said that in the Last Days there would be an altar to the Lord still standing in the midst of Egypt (Isaiah 19:19). As with many other investigations into prophetic matters, it seemed that the deeper investigators dug into the subject, the more incredible their findings became. As more and more of these amazing revelations came to light, the fame of the pyramid steadily grew. Even the great Sir Isaac Newton had expressed an interest in the pyramid. Newton had always held that the length of the ancient Hebrew cubit was somewhere between 23 and 26 inches. Newton was therefore quite anxious to find out whether the pyramid accurately recorded this ancient measure.

When it was finally determined that the pyramid set the ancient cubit's length at exactly 25 English inches, it was soon afterwards determined that this length also held a direct relationship to the size of the planet itself. The Sacred Cubit turned out to be exactly equal to one 10,000,000[th] part of the distance between the North Pole and the center of the Earth, meaning that at the time of the inception of this measurement, the Earth was exactly 500,000,000 inches tall! This shocking revelation meant that the builders of the Great Pyramid were also aware of the exact size of the Earth! Their measurement was so precise that it even reflected the subtle effects of Post-Glacial Rebound, which slightly increased this measurement over time, due to the melting of the Earth's polar ice caps. How could all this be possible?

More archeological expeditions were immediately dispatched to Egypt to see if the Great Pyramid held any more revelations for mankind. More accurate measurements needed to be taken. As the development of man's technology advanced, more and more of the pyramid's secrets could be revealed.

Mapmakers also noticed that the Egyptian Nile Delta extended into the Mediterranean Sea in the shape of a semi-circle. When the full arc of this circle was inscribed upon a map of Egypt, the Great Pyramid stood at its exact center! But how could the ancient Egyptians have possibly determined this precise location without the use of modern satellite mapping techniques?

Modern science had always taught that human evolution resulted in the advancement of mankind out of an ignorant and aboriginal past, but now the Great Pyramid was revealing past knowledge far in advance of that of the present. Could there have been a past civilization on Earth more advanced than our own? And what other secrets might this incredible repository for information contain for mankind?

It was not long before the world's greatest minds were focusing their full attention upon this massive stone object that did indeed seem to be a source of previously unavailable information concerning our planet and the greater solar system. Men like Charles Piazzi Smyth, Royal Astronomer of Scotland, and a host of others, undertook detailed studies of the Great Pyramid to see if any more information could be gleaned from it. They soon became convinced that this structure had been built by a source of inspired knowledge in the far distant past, and that the pyramid was specifically designed to serve as some sort of time capsule for other information on the history and the destiny of mankind. The amount of information available from the Great Pyramid seemed to be limited only by man's ability to accurately measure and interpret it.

As modern technology advanced, the improved accuracy of measuring instruments allowed scientists to determine that the sides of the pyramid not only recorded the exact length of Earth's solar year, but also the anomalistic and sidereal years as well. It was also found that the two diagonal measures of the base of the pyramid produced a combined pyramid inch total of 25,827 inches, or the exact period of the Precession of the Equinoxes, recording Earth's 25,827-year wobble in space. This information was recorded again at the King's Chamber level of the pyramid. The distance around the exterior of the pyramid at the King's Chamber level was exactly 25,827 inches!

The pyramid's height when complete with its original tall capstone, was found to be equal to one 1,000,000,000[th] part of the mean distance from the Earth to the sun (4500 years ago). And the empty coffin found inside the King's Chamber had an internal volume exactly equal to that of the ancient English chaldron. The chaldron's quarter part is still recorded for us today in an English "quarter" of wheat.

Scientists also determined that the Great Pyramid was not only located at the exact center of the arc of the Egyptian Nile Delta, but it was also exactly oriented to the four cardinal points of the compass. It is also located at the exact point where all the area above that latitude exactly equals all the area below that latitude on Earth's northern hemisphere. The pyramid was then found to be located on the world's longest longitudinal and latitudinal land contact meridians as well. In other words, if all the world's land masses originally broke away from one large landmass as scientists now suspect, then the Great Pyramid was located at its exact center. The Great Pyramid also divides Upper Egypt from Lower Egypt, thus fulfilling the prophecy of Isaiah 19:19 that in the last days there would be an altar to the Lord standing in the midst of Egypt and also at the border thereof. All these revelations were more than modern scientists could rationally explain.

The many mysteries of the Great Pyramid are truly mind-boggling. The floor of one of the interior anterooms for instance, is 116.26 inches in length, with 103.33 inches of it being constructed of red sandstone. This again records the magic relationship between the circle and the square, as the area of a circle with a diameter of 116.26 inches, is the same as that of a square whose sides are each 103.33 inches long.

The Great Pyramid sat for centuries without revealing any of its secrets to mankind, and no one was able to locate an entrance to the interior of the structure. Then, around 813 AD, the Arab Caliph, Al Malmoun decided to burrow into the north side of the pyramid to see if he could locate any inner chambers that might contain hidden treasure. Al Malmoun and his men had a difficult time trying to chisel through the hard rock of the pyramid, but soon discovered that they could use fire to heat the stone, and then throw water on it, causing it to shatter. Using this method, Malmoun and his men were successfully able to tunnel about 150 feet into the north side of the pyramid, where they suddenly came upon a hidden interior shaft. This shaft then led them to a hidden staircase leading up into two secret chambers located deep within the structure. The uppermost of these two chambers contained a stone sarcophagus that today has been found to contain no trace of human remains. This upper chamber was later dubbed the "King's Chamber" by European archeologists.

The original 330-foot long passageway discovered by Al Malmoun and his men, led down at an angle from the exterior of the pyramid and ended in a rough-hewn chamber located approximately 100 feet below the pyramid's base. A second passageway broke off from this passage at a point about 100 feet down, and led up into the pyramid's two internal chambers. This passage then widened abruptly at a certain point into a much larger hallway now known as the "Grand Gallery," before finally arriving at the entrance to the King's Chamber. Due to the design of the entrance to the King's Chamber, one had to bow down before entering that room.

Later investigations would lead to the discovery of a relationship between the length of these passageways and the chronology of the history of civilized society. It was discovered that, by using the equation of one inch per year, it was possible to trace the history of mankind down through the ages. Beginning at a point where the original shaft led in from the exterior of the pyramid, and assigning that point a value of 4000 BC, the second shaft broke off at the 1470 BC point, or the date of the biblical Exodus. This second shaft then expanded abruptly at the date of Jesus' birth, accurately recording his 33-year life here on Earth.

This passageway ended at the King's Chamber, representing roughly the 2000 AD point in the chronology of man's history. Archeologists surmised that these passageways traced the history of human civilization from its roots in ancient Sumeria in 4000 BC, to its ultimate end around the year 2000 AD. Many key events in the history of man did indeed seem to be marked on the inner walls of these passageways. Did all this mean that man would realize his final destiny around the year 2000? This theory was just too much for the scientific community to accept, and many archeologists supporting the theory were publicly ridiculed for their views.

The Great Pyramid still remains a source of great controversy in the scientific world today. It stands in silent testimony to the existence of a past civilization far in advance of our own. The ancient Jewish historian Josephus recorded for us that the Great Pyramid was built by the children of Seth before the Flood for the purpose of preserving all knowledge. Josephus also related that the knowledge of the patriarchs was recorded in the Tower of Babel as well, but that God had destroyed the Tower of Babel long before Josephus' time.

Could it be possible that the Great Pyramid really is proof of the existence of the biblical patriarchs, who lived for hundreds of years and attained great knowledge? Are we merely a garden colony placed on this planet by a superior race who is farming us for some as yet unknown purpose? There is just no explaining the strange enigma of the Great Pyramid of Giza, and scientists are still struggling to attempt to explain its existence. The Great Pyramid still stands today as the most amazing structure on Earth and no one has yet been able to satisfactorily explain its haunting mysteries.

CHAPTER 5

LOUIS PASTEUR

"The more I study nature, the more I am amazed at the work of the Creator."

Louis Pasteur

The prophet Nostradamus is said to have recorded many prophecies for us concerning future events. One of his most famous prophecies describes the accomplishments of the great microbiologist Louis Pasteur. Pasteur's famous discovery of the microbe was one of the most important events in all of scientific history.

Nostradamus recorded his prophecies in the form of four-line French poems known as quatrains. In Chapter 1, Quatrain #25 of his famous book, the *Centuries*, Nostradamus not only included Pasteur's name in the prophecy, but told of the great scientist's revelation of the microbe, and also described the persecution and ridicule Pasteur suffered at the hands of his jealous peers in the European medical community. What is so incredible about this famous prophecy is that it was recorded by Nostradamus over 200 years before Pasteur was born.

Not many people are familiar with the predictions of the 16th century Hebrew prophet Nostradamus. Nostradamus was a physician and prophet who claimed to have received numerous visions of future events. He recorded his visions in the form of four-line poems written in the Old French language, published in a book he called the *Centuries*. The first edition of his book contained seven chapters of 100 quatrains each. Unfortunately, this seven chapter edition suffered severe damage to its last pages, and only 42 of the quatrains from Chapter 7 still exist today. Later editions of the quatrains added three more chapters, then two additional chapters. Of the original 1200 or so quatrains, only about 962 are still in existence today.

Dating Nostradamus' quatrains can be very difficult, since he uses a combination of actual calendar dates, astrological dates, and other complex dating systems in order to confound those attempting to interpret his prophecies before their time. Nostradamus also made use of anagrams and other word games in order to further confuse later would be interpreters of his quatrains.

The prophecies of Nostradamus have generated enormous controversy over the centuries, concerning his alleged ability to see through time. The world's foremost scientists and astrophysicists all agree that it is impossible for man to pierce the bonds of time to foretell future events, thus placing scientific theory in direct opposition to the writings of the Hebrew prophets of the Bible whose prophecies have been accurately predicting the course of human events for untold centuries.

Nostradamus' famous prophecy on Louis Pasteur however, seems to defy that popularly held belief. The following is an English translation of Nostradamus' famous poem about Louis Pasteur. The poem can be found in Chapter 1, Quatrain #25 of the *Centuries*, and does in fact seem to accurately describe the life of the great scientist, even going so far as to spell his name correctly, and giving an exact date for his accomplishments. The following is a rough English translation of the poem that appears in many earlier Nostradamus books.

Chapter 1, Quatrain 25 (English translation)

The unseen is revealed, hidden for such a long time.
Pasteur is honored as a demi-God.
This is when the Moon completes her great cycle (1880's).
But through slander by others, he will be dishonored.

Louis Pasteur was born in Dole, Jura, France in the year 1822, the son of a tanner. His family moved to Arbois, France when he was only two months old. Pasteur received his education at the College Communal at Arbois, but his main interests always seemed to center around science. He went on to study at Besancon, and eventually entered the Ecole school in Paris. In 1847 he graduated with a degree in Physical Science.

In 1848, Pasteur's discoveries on the refraction of light (spectroscopy) through various chemical substances won him a teaching position at the University of Strasburg as a laboratory chemist. He went on to other professorships at various universities, and in 1859 performed his famous research on the scientific aspects of the fermentation process as it related to the wine industry of France.

It was the 19th century, and science was rapidly emerging as the preferred method of explaining the many mysteries of God's universe. In the 19th century, the fermentation process was originally thought to occur as the result of the "spontaneous generation" of certain molds or fungi. This somewhat religious viewpoint on the cause of fermentation developed as a result of unexplained events often being attributed to the intervention of God. Any process that could not be completely understood or explained was usually attributed to an Act of God.

The process of "spontaneous generation" might be compared to the "spontaneous creation" theory of man's origins, as described in the book of Genesis. The scientific community had always sought more reasonable explanations for such unexplained phenomena. There was therefore a controversy developing between the scientific and religious communities over such issues. Some people held the religious viewpoint that such processes occurred through "spontaneous generation," while others preferred the scientific explanation. This ongoing battle between science and religion began many centuries earlier, as science became a more reasonable way of explaining the many mysteries of God's universe.

The hierarchy of the Roman Catholic Church had always viewed science as a threat to its religious authority. In fact, the Pope himself had at one point placed the great astronomer Galileo under house arrest when he had the audacity to suggest that the sun, rather than the Earth, was the center of the known universe. The Catholic Church had always taught that the Earth was the center of the universe, and that the sun revolved around it.

The idea that the Earth might actually revolve around the sun was not a new concept. Aristarchus of Samos had expounded this controversial theory as early as 250 BC. The theory was long held as a fact by ancient Greek philosophers like Pythagoras and Solon, who had studied at the great universities in Alexandria, Egypt. This heliocentric theory for the construction of the planetary universe was later confirmed by many famous astronomers, including Nicholas Copernicus, and Johannes Kepler. The Catholic Church however, held supreme authority in Europe, and would not hesitate to execute anyone daring to disagree with its opinions. The Church in fact, did not admit to its error in this incident involving Galileo until the year 1992, when Pope John Paul II finally issued a formal apology to the scientific community for the Church's unfortunate error.

When the microscope was first invented around the year 1600, it began to reveal a previously unseen world of microscopic life forms. In the 1700's, an Englishman named Needham suddenly announced that he had "spontaneously generated" some worms (or "eels," as he called them) in a sealed jar containing putrefied animal matter.

When the French philosopher Voltaire heard of Needham's miraculous "creation" he remarked "It is very strange indeed that men should deny a Creator, and yet attribute to themselves, the power to create eels."

This religious view on the "spontaneous creation" of life was eventually challenged in many different fields of endeavor. Pasteur was able to scientifically demonstrate that the process of fermentation was actually caused by tiny living organisms too small to be seen by the naked eye. Pasteur was both fascinated and frustrated by the hypocrisy of the great men of his time who refused to believe in what they could not see, even though they all professed to believe in an invisible God.

The invention of the microscope revolutionized the field of science, and revealed many previously unknown secrets about the long-hidden world of the microbe. Pasteur demonstrated that the organisms responsible for the fermentation process existed in this unseen world, but were nevertheless subject to many of the same laws and rules that governed the existence of larger, and more visible, organisms. He also demonstrated that these tiny organisms could be killed off through the use of heat and exposure to certain chemicals.

The wine industry of France had always been plagued by wine that soured during the fermentation process. Pasteur was able to demonstrate that this problem was due to undesirable bacteria becoming involved in the fermentation process. He was able to kill off these unwanted bacteria by exposing them to high heat through a boiling process (pasteurization), and as a result, was able to save the wine industry of France from economic ruin.

When France's silk industry experienced an epidemic of disease in its silkworm population, Pasteur was called upon to investigate the problem. Pasteur soon discovered that only some of the silkworms carried this disease. When silkworm production was modified to separate the eggs of diseased silkworms from those of healthy silkworms, the disease was successfully controlled and eliminated.

Around the year 1880, Pasteur further extended his studies into the world of medicine. Pasteur's work was not so eagerly accepted by the leaders of the European medical community because his views went against many popularly held beliefs of that era. His work was both rejected and ridiculed by many of Europe's top medical professionals, because he dared to challenge their long held opinions.

Pasteur was not welcomed in many of Europe's hospitals because his views were seen to conflict with "spontaneous generation" and many other theories held by the senior members of the medical community. Pasteur however, had made many friends in the business community, and was ultimately able to fund the creation of his own medical institution known as the Pasteur Institute. Pasteur was responsible for many revolutionary new discoveries in the field of medicine. He demonstrated that microbes were able to travel through the air as tiny particles, and thus transfer themselves to other hosts. He also discovered that these microbes were subject to the negative effects of heat, light and many chemicals.

Pasteur's work in the sphere of medicine completely revolutionized that field. He demonstrated that the human body contained microbes of its own that could defend it against invasion by foreign organisms. Pasteur also showed that the disease-causing effects of certain microbes could be weakened through outside manipulation. These weakened microbes could then be introduced into the human body, thereby strengthening the body's resistance to diseases. This process of "vaccination" had been used for many centuries by the people of the Caucuses Mountains in southern Russia to immunize their people against communicable diseases. Pasteur was able to finally explain this process, and utilize it to develop powerful vaccines to protect both humans and animals from many common diseases. Pasteur produced highly effective vaccines against cholera, rabies, and anthrax.

In one famous experiment involving a herd of 50 sheep, Pasteur inoculated 25 of the sheep with an anthrax vaccine. He then introduced anthrax to the entire herd. The 25 sheep that had not received the vaccine all died; the 25 that had received the vaccine all survived. Pasteur performed similarly successful experiments with a rabies vaccine for dogs. Pasteur's experiments were always performed under precise laboratory conditions of exactness and efficiency. In the year 1887, Pasteur began his work on the identification of the three most common human microbes, staphylococcus, streptococcus and pneumococcus, exactly as Nostradamus had predicted in his famous prophecy on Pasteur, written centuries earlier.

There can be no doubt that Pasteur's discoveries represented the most revolutionary advances ever experienced in the field of medicine. Pasteur's discovery of the microbe eventually led to the pasteurization of milk, the sterilization of medical instruments, and widespread use of antibiotics and antiseptics. Pasteur's contributions to the surgical profession were nothing short of amazing. Surgical survival rates went up from less than 50 percent to more than 95 percent through improved sanitation and the introduction of sterilization techniques. Prior to the introduction of these changes, more soldiers were killed by army surgeons, than by the enemy. In spite of all these modern miracles however, it seems that men still failed to comprehend the nature of disease itself.

Our many successes in the field of medicine have not produced a disease-free world. In fact, quite the opposite is true. While medicine has succeeded in reducing the incidence of child mortality worldwide, the incidence of human disease in the adult population has mushroomed to incredible proportions. Today, almost everyone you meet subscribes to a long list of drugs and medicines that they must take daily in order to survive, and genetic illnesses are now appearing as a new threat to public health. Medical costs have also risen to unprecedented levels. The average life span for modern Americans has supposedly improved dramatically in the last two centuries, but a closer examination of this data reveals that this statistic is actually due to a sharp drop in the child mortality rate being factored into the equation. In the early years of our nation, infant mortality was very high. Even Thomas Jefferson lost three of his children to smallpox before the widespread use of the smallpox vaccine.

In today's world where God has been successfully excised from our nation's classrooms, people in the academic community are now hailing Pasteur as the great scientist who discredited the old religious theory of "spontaneous generation."

Discrediting religious theory was never Pasteur's intent. Pasteur was a deeply religious man, who sought only to further explain life's many mysteries through scientific investigation. He never sought to diminish God in any way, but merely desired to explain what was not previously understood. Pasteur did not view science as being in conflict with religion. He wondered at the many mysteries of God's universe, and merely wished to promote a better understanding of them. Pasteur passed away near Sevres, France, on the 27th of September, 1895.

The prophet Nostradamus was also a great physician in his time, and, having foreseen Pasteur's discovery of the microbe, was able to employ sanitary procedures to cure many diseases long before Pasteur. Unfortunately however, Nostradamus' first wife, Adriete de Loubejac of Agen, and his two children, contracted the deadly pneumonic (mouse) form of the black plague, which many times cannot be cured even by modern antibiotics. Nostradamus therefore was unable to save his own wife and children.

The prophecies of Nostradamus have generated tremendous controversy in the world of science, as scientists still refuse to believe in what they cannot explain. The long-standing dispute between science and religion therefore, still rages on.

Science has always been based upon demonstrable fact, and modern scientists refuse to accept anything that cannot be scientifically proven. The fields of religion and prophecy however, are based upon faith, not scientific experimentation.

Scientists might therefore take note of the fact that the following quatrain concerning Louis Pasteur, was taken from a book published more than two centuries before Pasteur was born. For your convenience I've included a glossary of the Old French and Latin terms.

Chapter 1, Quatrain 25 (Old French)

> **The unseen is revealed, hidden for such a long time.**
> *Perdu trouve, cache de si long siecle.*
> **He will, Pasteur, as a demi-God be honored.**
> *Sera Pasteur, demi Dieu honore.*
> **This is when the Moon completes her great cycle (Roussat - 1888).**
> *Ains que la lune acheve son grand siecle,*
> **But through others' slanders, he will be dishonored.**
> *Par autres vents, sera dishonore.*

OLD FRENCH (O.F.) AND LATIN (L.) DEFINITIONS:
    Acheve - (O.F.) achieves, finishes, completes
    Ains – (L.) this is, it is
    Autres – (F.) others
    Cache – (F.) hidden
    Demi Deiu – (O.F.) demi-god
    Dis-honore – (O.F.) dishonored
    Grand – (F.) grand, great
    Honore – (O.F.) honored
    Long – (F.) long
    Lune – (F.) Moon
    Par – (F.) but, for, through, by
    Perdu – (F.) lost, hidden
    Que – (F.) when
    Sera – (O.F.) *he* will be
    Si – (F.) so, such

Siecle – (O.F.) cycle, time

Son – (F.) her, its

Trouve – (F.) found, revealed

Vents – (O.F.) idle talk, slander

Louis Pasteur's work has resulted in many modern miracles in the world of science and medicine. His name is still recognized today the world over. This prophecy on Louis Pasteur is therefore one of the most famous of all the prophecies in Nostradamus' vast collection. It would therefore be difficult for us to deny the accuracy of this prophecy, since Nostradamus actually includes Pasteur's name, and accurately describes his work, even going so far as to include the date of the accomplishment at the end of the great Roussat Moon cycle in 1888.

Prophecies such as this one have caused people all over the world to sit up and take notice of the works of this amazing Hebrew prophet. His prophecies are also interesting because they were written a mere 450 years ago, and are therefore not as difficult to translate as Bible prophecies. They also seem to agree with Bible prophecies, and in many cases, help to further explain them.

Nostradamus' prophecies were written in a relatively modern language that is not so difficult to translate as the ancient Bible languages, whose limited vocabularies allow for a wide variety of interpretations. They were also not subject to multiple inter-language transcriptions throughout the centuries as is the case with Bible prophecy.

For these reasons and many others, the prophecies of Nostradamus have captured the attention of the entire world, and are still a focus of international attention every time a major world event occurs.

CHAPTER 6

THE ANTICHRIST

And they had a King over them, which is the angel of the bottomless pit, whose name in the Hebrew tongue is Abaddon, but in the Greek tongue hath his name Apollyon.

Rev. 9:11

The history of the United States has been blessed many times by good fortune, but there has also been an evil influence lurking as well. It behooves us therefore to also take a look at the influence this evil has had upon our past and present.

If you wake up early on a Sunday morning and turn on the radio, TV, or computer, you'll often be treated to a sermon on the coming of the antichrist. Bible evangelists have been preaching about the coming of this evil figure for many decades, intimidating their listeners with stories about this frightening entity that is supposedly coming to take over the world.

Since the coming of the antichrist is a purely religious subject, we should probably look to the Bible to see what it has to say about this controversial figure; and it might be appropriate for us to search at the very beginning of the Bible, in the book of Genesis.

The book of Genesis tells us that approximately 6000 years ago, a young woman named Eve succumbed to the sweet whisperings of the Serpent, and stole knowledge she was forbidden to possess. The Serpent promised Eve that her stolen prize would endow her with god-like powers, enabling her to determine her own destiny. Eve, not wishing to be alone in her sin, then seduced her husband Adam into also partaking of the forbidden Tree of Knowledge.

Ever since this ancient Bible event, so aptly described in the book of Genesis, mankind has been on an eternal quest to use this stolen knowledge to create the perfect human society, a society free from all strife and suffering, a society of man governing man, instead of God governing man.

This Genesis story actually describes the beginning of man's 6000-year journey along the path to his own ultimate destiny. The Bible carefully chronicles this story of mankind's 6000-year quest to create the perfect human society. Many great societies have appeared on Earth over the centuries, each hoping it would be the one to finally fulfill the greatest hopes and dreams of mankind, but it seems none of them succeeded.

If we look at the very end of the Bible, in the book of Revelation Chapter 17, Verse 10, an angel tells us about a series of seven kingdoms that will be created by men in vain attempts to achieve this perfect human society. The Bible refers to these kingdoms as "beasts," because they were all destined to fail and turn on their creators, martyring millions of God's people in the process.

The exact identity, and chronology, of these seven kingdoms is therefore crucial in determining where we now stand along the path to our own ultimate destiny. The identity of these seven kingdoms, or world empires, has been a source of great controversy in the religious world for many decades. There has also been much confusion over the identity of the serpent himself, who is often identified as the beast of Revelation, or the biblical antichrist.

The question is, exactly who is this antichrist, and when will he arrive? Many great minds have pondered this question down through history, and volumes of information have been written on the subject. The truth of the ancient prophecies however, was long ago sealed up from the eyes of man (Dan. 12:9), and therefore unavailable to us until the Last Days.

In the Christian Bible, you will see many different words used to describe these beasts, or antichrist entities. Generally a beast, in prophecy, is defined as a world-conquering empire that oppresses God's people. There have been many world-conquering empires down through history, but the Bible concerns itself only with those that oppressed God's people.

Words like beast, antichrist, king, kingdom, horn and crown are often used interchangeably in the Bible. The reason we must deal with so many overlapping definitions is that most ancient languages contained vocabularies of only about 5000 words. Modern languages, by comparison, often contain vocabularies of 50,000 words or more.

What this means for us, is that there may have been only one word in a particular dialect that meant nation for instance, whereas in a modern language, there might be ten times as many words available to further define that nation, such as kingdom, republic, empire, country ….well you get the idea. When early Bible writers were interpreting the Holy Scriptures, they might have used any of these words to translate that original word. Their word usage however, was generally applied with some degree of logic.

A horn for instance, is defined in prophecy as a military leader, or army general. A horn and a beast might be one and the same, if the horn was the leader of his empire and also the supreme commander of its armies. This was especially true if when this leader died, his empire died along with him. In that case he and his empire were considered to be one and the same entity. This was the case for instance with Adolph Hitler. Adolph Hitler was not only the supreme leader of the Nazi Empire, but was also supreme commander of its armies, so when he died, his empire died with him.

In Bible prophecy, words like beast, king, kingdom, antichrist, horn, and crown, can sometimes all have the same meaning. These subtleties must be kept in mind when attempting to accurately interpret biblical prophecy.

The Bible provides us with many different descriptions of these numerous beasts, or antichrists, some of which are extremely detailed. These descriptions are repeated multiple times in many different chapters and books of the Bible. This was done on purpose in order to provide multiple sources to protect and verify the truth of the Scriptures.

In the book of Revelation Chapter 17, Verses 10 and 11, an angel tells John that there will be a total of seven kings, or kingdoms, appearing on Earth to oppress God's people throughout history. This angel then says that five of these kingdoms, or empires, have already fallen, and that a sixth empire is just coming into existence at the time this prophecy was given, which was around the second century AD.

The angel then tells us that a seventh empire will eventually appear sometime in the future, but the angel does not provide the identity of this seventh empire. History tells us that the seven great empires of the western world were all part of an unbroken chain, each empire conquering the one before it. The first five beasts, or empires, to oppress God's Hebrews are well known. They are the five great empires of history, the Egyptian, Babylonian, Persian, Greek, and Roman empires. The Bible carefully chronicles the journey of the ancient Hebrews out of their oppression in Egypt, and through further oppressions under the Babylonian, Persian, Greek, and Roman empires.

The prophecies of Daniel provide us with even more details about this succession of beasts, starting with Babylon, and following the trail one step further to include a sixth empire. Daniel Chapter 2 tells us about King Nebuchadnezzar's dream of a statue with a golden head, silver breast, brass belly, iron legs, and ten toes of iron and clay that will not mix together. Daniel explains to the king that this statue represents his great Babylonian Empire and the four empires that will follow it, which are in turn, the Persian, Greek, Roman, and Holy Roman empires.

Later, in Daniel Chapter 7, we learn about a dream that Daniel has concerning four beasts. In Daniel's dream, the first beast is a winged lion, the second beast is a bear raised up on one side, and the third beast is a leopard with four heads

A fourth beast in Daniel's dream is described as a terrible creature with great iron teeth that devours everything before it. This fourth beast eventually breaks up into ten pieces, and gives rise to a "little horn" with the eyes of a man, who plucks up three of the ten horns, or kingdoms, before him. This "little horn," or little military leader, is the first of two coming male antichrists

The winged lion of course, is the great symbol of Babylon. As you passed through the main gate of the ancient city, 120 of these great winged lions, each about 8-feet long, stared down at you from the magnificent blue-tiled walls of Babylon's great Processional Way.

The bear raised up on one side was the symbol of the Persian Empire that consisted of both the Median, and the stronger Persian, nations.

The four-headed leopard was the symbol of Greece, divided up into four parts by the four generals of Alexander the Great, and finally, as the Iron Age arrives, we have the Iron Age kingdom of Rome that eventually breaks up into ten pieces on the old Roman (Italian) peninsula.

Daniel Chapter 8 tells us about another vision that Daniel has, involving a two-horned ram that is overcome by a rough goat. This he-goat then divides into four smaller kingdoms. One of these kingdoms in the latter days gives rise to a "little horn," or military leader. The angel Gabriel explains the meaning of this vision to Daniel, telling him that the ram represents the kingdom of Media-Persia, and that the he-goat represents the kingdom of Greece.

We should also note that the ram with one horn higher than the other denotes the fact that the Persian Empire came up after the Median Empire, but grew to be stronger of the two. Both these empires came together under the emperor Cyrus, who inherited one of them from his father, Cambyses, and won the other from his maternal grandfather Astyages.

The angel Gabriel also tells Daniel that the he-goat with four horns represents the kingdom of Greece, whose four generals divided up the Greek Empire amongst themselves after the untimely death of Alexander the Great at the age of only 32. This vision provides us with an interesting detail about the "little horn," or antichrist, It tells us that this antichrist will rise out of one of the four parts of the old Greek Empire.

The sixth empire, or "Holy" Roman Empire, rose up after the Roman Empire and flowered in the 16th century with the Renaissance (rebirth) of Rome. This sixth empire came into existence as a result of the takeover of the old Roman Empire from within, by the forces of Christianity. This sixth empire eventually split the Roman peninsula, by then called Italy, into ten pieces; five existing as strong independent Roman kingdoms, and five existing as provinces of the Catholic

Church, thus forming the ten toes of King Nebuchadnezzar's dream, five strong, and five weak, that would not mix together.

The identity of the seventh, and also an eighth, beast of Revelation is revealed only in the Last Days. The seventh and eighth beasts are described in greater detail in Revelation Chapter 13. In Revelation Chapter 13, we can read about these two beasts, or two antichrists, and receive some valuable information about them. But before we review this information, we should first review our list of world empires.

THE MAJOR EMPIRES OF HISTORY

1.	Egyptian Empire	3400 BC
2.	Babylonian Empire	650 BC
3.	Medo-Persian Empire	550 BC
4.	Grecian Empire	330 BC
5.	Roman Empire	170 BC
6.	Holy Roman Empire	313 AD
7.	unknown	
8.	unknown	

As we mentioned previously, a beast is an empire, or antichrist, that oppresses God's people. We should also note that the beast's heads represent the nations making up that empire. In other words, if the beast has seven heads, the empire is made up of seven nations. Crowns, also sometimes called kings, represent the political leaders of those nations.

The vision described for us in Revelation Chapter 13 is of two beasts (antichrists), and is given to us by John, who at the time is being held prisoner on the Greek island of Patmos. As John gazes out west across the great Mediterranean Sea, he sees the first beast, or first antichrist, rising up out of that sea. John tells us that this first antichrist has seven heads, which means that his empire is made up of seven nations. This beast also has ten horns, or crowns, which means that three extra kings sit upon the thrones of his seven-nation empire. This is another very unusual fact that may help us to identify this mysterious first antichrist.

John then tells us that this first beast looks like a leopard, which backs up what the angel Gabriel told us about his Greek origins. This leopard has the feet of a bear, which means that his armies move swiftly, like the ancient Persian armies, living off the food of the lands they conquer, like locusts. This leopard also has the mouth of a lion, which means he speaks the Babylonian philosophy that he, the emperor, is God. We then read that one of his seven heads, or nations, is put down in total military defeat, but somehow miraculously recovers.

The next four verses of the prophecy tell us that this first antichrist is given the power to blaspheme God and to overcome the Church and its saints for a period of 42 months. We are also told that the people of the world will worship this antichrist as a great figure in history because of his great military skills and accomplishments, and that only the people of God will learn of his true identity.

In Revelation Chapter 13, Verse 10, we encounter a rather unique sentence that neatly divides the descriptions of these last two beasts (antichrists). What this sentence does, is to describe the ultimate fate of each of these two antichrists. The first half of the sentence tells us that the first beast, or first antichrist, causes God's people to be led into captivity, and that for this sin it is his fate to similarly die in captivity. We can skip the second half of this sentence, because it concerns only the second antichrist (the mysterious eighth beast).

We should now assemble all the information we've learned about this first antichrist, or seventh beast, into a list for review.

1. We know that this first antichrist comes out of one of the ten pieces of the old Roman Empire, and also out of one of the four pieces of the ancient Greek Empire.

2. We know that he plucks up three of the ten pieces of the old Roman Empire, and takes them into his new empire.

3. We learn that his empire teaches the sinful ideas and laws of men, thus blaspheming the laws of God.

4. We know that he rises out of the sea.

5. We know that his empire consists of 7 nations, including 3 of the 10 nations that remain of the old Roman Empire on the Italian peninsula.

6. We also know that he appoints three extra kings to rule over his 7-nation realm.

7. We are told that he looks like a leopard, or Greek.

8. We know that his armies move swiftly like the ancient Persian armies, living off the food of the lands they conquer, like locusts.

9. We know he speaks the Babylonian philosophy that he, the emperor, is a God.

10. We learn that the army of one of his seven nations is completely destroyed, but then miraculously recovers.

11. We know that he is given the power to blaspheme God and hold the Church and its saints captive for a period of 42 months.

12. We are told that the people of the world won't view him as an antichrist, but will instead worship his great military skills.

13. We learn that his ultimate destiny is to die in captivity.

Now, armed with all this information, it should not be too difficult for us to identify this first beast, or first antichrist, of Revelation Chapter 13. One detail is still missing though. We need some sort of timetable for his arrival.

Since in Revelation Chapter 17 we learned that his empire was part of an unbroken chain of empires, we might simply look to the end of the sixth empire for his appearance. In order to do this however, we must first take a closer look at the history of that sixth empire.

The sixth empire, or Holy Roman Empire, came into existence as the result of the old Roman Empire being taken over from within by the forces of Christianity. History tells us that the teachings of Jesus Christ had spread throughout most of the Roman Empire by AD 100.

The pagan sun-worshippers of Rome desperately tried to prevent this internal takeover by declaring war on Christianity; but the more cruelty the Romans inflicted upon their Christian masses, the more their subjects turned toward the kindness and mercy of the Christians.

After engaging in this futile struggle with the Christians for many years, the Roman government under the emperor Constantine finally gave in and agreed to form a union with the Christian Church in order to create a new empire. This new empire, now known as the "Holy" Roman Empire, was part Roman and part Christian, and governed by both a Roman Emperor and a Christian Pope. This strange marriage was destined to last for over one and a half millennia.

By the year 1800, the old Roman (now Italian) peninsula had been broken up into ten kingdoms. Five existed as independent secular civil controlled kingdoms, and five fell under church control, thus forming the ten toes of King Nebuchadnezzar's statue, five strong and five weak, that would not mix together.

The Holy Roman Empire finally came to an end when the last Holy Roman Emperor, Francis II of Austria, gave up his empire around the year 1806. The person that Francis II surrendered his empire to (and I hope you're referring to your previous list) was:

1.   Born and raised on the Mediterranean island of Corsica, which is a part of the Republic of Genoa,

one of the 10 pieces of the old Roman Empire, and also once a portion of one of the 4 pieces of the ancient Greek Empire.

2.   He was also the man who plucked up three kingdoms on the old Roman peninsula, and took them into his new empire. The three kingdoms he usurped were the Kingdom of Naples, the Illyrian Provinces, and the Kingdom of Venice.

3.   He imposed a new code of law, and a new system of weights and measures (the Metric System) upon the world, and promoted secular humanist philosophies, thus blaspheming the laws of God.

4.   He rose up out of the Mediterranean Sea from the island of Corsica.

5.   He led a 7-nation empire that included 3 of the 10 provinces of the old Roman Empire on the Italian peninsula.

6.   He ultimately appointed three extra kings to watch over his "seven realms." They were his three brothers, Jerome, King of Westphalia, Louis, King of Holland, and Joseph, King of Spain.

7.   He was a "little man" who stood only 5 feet 2 inches tall, and had the black hair and olive complexion of his Greek ancestors.

8.   His army was described by Tsar Alexander I of Russia, as an "army of locusts," because it lived off the food of the lands it conquered, like the ancient Persian armies.

9.   He was able to seize complete military and religious control of the world, and crown himself emperor of it all.

10. The army of one of his nations, France, was completely destroyed, and its emperor sent into exile, but the French army miraculously recovered when its emperor returned from exile to raise a new army.

11. He held the pope of Rome captive for 42 months, placing the pope's crown on his own head, and declaring himself religious head of the world.

12. He is still admired by the New World Order today as a great military leader, and champion of the Enlightenment.

13. In 1821, after being held as a prisoner in exile on the island of St. Helena, he died a miserable death in captivity.

Tsar Alexander I of Russia was in fact the first person to successfully identify Napoleon Bonaparte as the first antichrist (seventh beast) of the book of Revelation Chapter 13. Napoleon was indeed the man who ended the reign of the Holy Roman Empire when the last Holy Roman Emperor, Francis II of Austria, surrendered his empire, and his daughter (in marriage) to Napoleon in the year 1806. As leader of the seventh empire to control the western world, Napoleon fulfilled all Bible prophecies concerning the first antichrist of Revelation Chapter 13, even adding his bloodline to that of the Holy Roman Empire, when he married Francis II's daughter and produced an heir to the throne.

When Napoleon decided to invade Russia in 1812 however, he came to the attention of Tsar Alexander I, a devoted student of the Bible. Alexander quickly identified Napoleon as the first antichrist through three famous Bible references to him. The first reference was in Revelation Chapter 9, Verse 11, where he is identified as "Apollyon," leader of the army of locusts. Napoleon was known to sign his name using only the letter "N." When that letter was placed before his biblical name, "Apollyon," it yielded his true (Greek) identity of "Napollyon," the Destroyer.

The second biblical reference to Napoleon was in Daniel Chapter 7, Verse 8, where he is referred to as the "little horn." The emperor, because of his short stature and cockiness, was often referred to as the "little corporal" or "little general." In Daniel 7, Verse 8, he is identified as the "little horn" who plucks up three of the pieces of the fallen Roman Empire. Napoleon did in fact conquer three provinces on the old Roman peninsula and take them into his empire.

Alexander also read in Daniel 7, Verse 25, that Napoleon would attempt to institute new standards of "times and laws" upon the world, and noted Napoleon's attempts to also institute the new International Metric System of times, weights and measures, and impose his Napoleonic Code of law upon Europe.

When Napoleon launched his invasion of Russia in 1812, Alexander vowed never to allow Napoleon and his "army of locusts" to invade the Russian motherland. Alexander followed Bible instructions on how to defeat this biblical antichrist and his locust army. Alexander had read in the Bible that Napoleon's troops fed off the food of the lands they conquered, like locusts, and were thus dependent upon that food to successfully complete their next flight.

Having identified this vulnerability, Alexander decided to use locust destroying tactics to stop Napoleon. Alexander immediately ordered all the towns in Napoleon's path to be stripped of food, and burned to the ground. When Napoleon's troops arrived in each town, they found the towns totally devoid of all food and supplies. There was not even hay for their horses to eat. The horses began to eat the thatch from house roofs, and quickly bloated and died.

Napoleon began his campaign against Russia with one of the largest armies ever assembled in all of history. He left Paris with almost 600,000 troops and 10,000 horses. Napoleon's troops however were soon faced with the problem of no food to eat, and gradually began to succumb to the effects of slow starvation. The Emperor would not admit defeat however, and stubbornly drove his army on to Russia. When Napoleon crossed into Russia from Poland, an official census shows that he still had over 422,000 troops under his command.

The Russian army did not even bother to stop and do battle with the French, but simply stayed out in front of them, burning everything in their path. When Napoleon finally arrived at the gates of Moscow, his army had now dwindled from 422,000 men to only 150,000 men, the same size as the Russian army. Alexander's locust-eradication tactics had been incredibly effective against Napoleon's onslaught.

The Russians met Napoleon in battle outside Moscow, but then retreated, allowing the French to enter the city. When

Napoleon entered Moscow, he found that it too had been stripped of all food and supplies. When winter finally came, Tsar Alexander ordered the city of Moscow to be burned as well.

Napoleon and his generals were nearly killed trying to escape the great fire of Moscow, and attempted to beat a hasty retreat back to France, but things did not go well for them. Russian Cossack troops proceeded to cut the remains of the French army to pieces, and the Emperor was nearly captured. Temperatures were now hovering at 30 below zero, and Napoleon's troops were dropping by the side of the road and freezing to death. When the tattered remains of Napoleon's army finally crossed the Neiman River back into Poland, an official census records their number at only 10,000 men.

To save their Emperor's life, the French decided to send Napoleon on ahead in a carriage in disguise. The Emperor did finally arrive safely back in Paris, but he was completely alone and defeated. His entire army had been totally destroyed by Russia's Tsar Alexander. Napoleon needed to raise a new army quickly in order to protect himself from his enemies who were now on their way to dethrone him.

Forty-two months earlier, Napoleon had taken Pope Pius XII prisoner. For three and one half years, from July 1809 to January 1813, Napoleon had held the Pope in confinement at Verona, and then at Fontainebleau. The Pope had not yet heard about Napoleon's disastrous Russian defeat, and when the Emperor approached him with a contract granting him his freedom in exchange for the right to raise a new army from the ranks of the Catholics of Germany, the Pope gladly signed the agreement.

The following week, when the pontiff found out that he'd been tricked, he quickly tried to back out of the agreement by announcing that he'd made a mistake. When Napoleon heard of the Pope's announcement, he quipped with a sly smile, "His Holiness, being infallible, could not possibly have made a mistake."

Tsar Alexander's tactics had worked perfectly. He'd completely destroyed Napoleon's entire army of over half a million men, by using simple locust eradication tactics. Napoleon's new army was unable to defend its Emperor for very long, and Alexander ultimately marched into Paris and deposed Napoleon from the throne of France. The Emperor was sent into exile on the island of Elba, and it was rumored that Tsar Alexander even became involved in an affair with Napoleon's empress, Josephine, who died in Alexander's arms in 1814.

Alexander had originally revealed Napoleon's identity through his name, which in the Greek language meant "The Destroyer". Alexander however, failed to take notice of the name of the island on which he'd exiled the Emperor, for the name "Elba" means "place of returning," and it was Napoleon's destiny to eventually return from Elba. Napoleon's return from exile however, was brief, and the second time the Emperor was imprisoned, it was upon the island of Helena, which in the Greek language means "Hell." Napoleon did not escape Helena alive.

Napoleon was indeed the little man who successfully ended the reign of the Holy Roman Empire. He was also emperor of the seventh empire to rule the world. We are told that Napoleon was defeated by the British at the Battle of Waterloo, but that is an inflated version of the truth. Compared to the Siege of Moscow, Waterloo was a mere skirmish as battles with Napoleon went. Napoleon's defeat occurred long before Waterloo. On his march to Moscow, Napoleon lost over a half million men to Tsar Alexander I of Russia. It was Alexander and God who actually ended the reign of Napoleon, but not before the Emperor had made many changes to the world as we know it.

Tsar Alexander was the grandson of Catherine the Great, Queen of all Russia. Catherine was of the German royal bloodlines and born in Poland. She was cousin to the Queen of England, and therefore part of the royal House of David seated upon the thrones of Europe at the time. She passed on her royal heritage to her grandson Alexander. It was therefore Alexander's prophetic destiny to defeat the antichrist Napoleon.

Alexander did everything in his power to save the thrones of Europe from the onslaught of the Enlightenment, but his efforts were in vain. It seems that men still wished to pursue their dream of the perfect human society.

Tsar Alexander later attempted to establish religious-based agrarian societies in Russia, similar to those of the Amish people in America. These communities functioned as religious-based farming communes. But they unfortunately were later replaced by atheistic socialist communes under the reign of communist revolutionaries following the liberal socialist doctrines of men like Karl Marx and Leon Trotsky. These godless social parasites had their own ideas on how human society should be run.

Tsar Alexander was supposed to have died on November 19, 1826. But a few weeks later, a mysterious bearded hermit named Fedor Kuzmich turned up in the eastern Russian city of Tomsk, and it was rumored that Kuzmich was actually Tsar Alexander.

When socialist revolutionaries opened Alexander's tomb in 1926 in order to desecrate it, they found that the tomb was indeed empty. You see, Alexander knew that a second antichrist, or eighth beast, was yet to come, and he wanted to make arrangements for the demise of this final beast as well. It was rumored throughout Russia that Alexander had gone into the service of the Russian Orthodox Church and had become a hermetic monk living in eastern Russia. The hermit Fedor Kuzmich died in 1864 and was heard to remark on his deathbed that only God knew his true identity.

But exactly who was this eighth beast that Tsar Alexander was so concerned about? You may find the answer to that question in another chapter of this book.

CHAPTER 7

THE FLOOD

And God saw that the wickedness of man was great in the earth, and that every imagination of the thoughts of his heart was only evil continually. And it repented the Lord that he had made man on the earth, and it grieved him at his heart. And the Lord said, I will destroy man, whom I have created, from the face of the earth….

Gen. 6:5-7

One of the best known of all the Old Testament stories is the story of Noah and the Great Flood. This narration is found in the Bible book of Genesis, Chapters 6 through 8. Most of us are thoroughly familiar with this story of how Noah and his family, and a great host of animals, were saved from the devastation caused by this huge catastrophe. Many of these early Bible stories have been viewed as being figurative in nature, serving only to prove a point, and not many biblical scholars consider them to be literal happenings.

The writings in the Old Testament represent the best efforts of early Bible writers to translate these ancient stories into modern languages. These stories however, leave much to be desired when it comes to exact literal interpretation. Assuming that there is some underlying truth to the story of the Flood, it still remains for us to determine through scientific means, whether or not this event could have actually taken place.

The story of the biblical Exodus was once viewed in the same perspective as the Flood. Recently however, it has been established through scientific means that the timing of the biblical Exodus exactly coincided with the explosion and sinking of the great volcanic island of Stronghyli (Santorini) in the eastern Aegean Sea. It is therefore a scientific reality that the tidal wave created by the collapse of this huge island would have most certainly caused the Red Sea Canal to be completely emptied of seawater in advance of the arrival of a great tidal wave. The only scientific question that remains for us to answer is how Moses was able to time the event so well.

The biblical Flood on the other hand, is a catastrophe on a much greater scale than that of the parting of the Red Sea, and would therefore require a much greater natural cataclysm in order to explain it. We do know for instance, that there is not enough water available on our planet to completely cover the "face of the whole earth". So how could the biblical Flood have possibly taken place, and is there any scientific evidence to support such a flood?

One very famous archeological discovery that does seem to lend some credence to the Flood theory, was a discovery made in 1929 by a British archeologist named Sir Charles Leonard Woolley. Woolley was excavating in the ancient ruins of the Mesopotamian city of Ur, when he made one of the most amazing archeological finds of all time. He and his workmen were digging a 5-foot square vertical shaft in a cemetery near the ancient city of Ur, when they suddenly came upon a layer of water-laid mud that contained absolutely no archeological ruins.

Woolley's diggers assumed they had finally struck virgin soil, and ceased to dig any deeper into the shaft. Woolley however, was bothered by the fact that the archeological rubble had ended so soon. He therefore ordered his diggers to keep on digging. The diggers begrudgingly complied with Woolley's request, and after removing another 8 to 10 feet of this mud, suddenly came upon more archeological ruins. Strangely, these earlier ruins recorded the reigns of Sumerian kings that lasted for incredibly long periods of time.

Puzzled by the presence of this incredibly thick layer of water laid clay, Woolley revisited the excavation the next day with his wife, who walked away remarking that this must of course be the Great Flood. The mud after all, was located at the 2500 BC level of the excavation.

Woolley was absolutely floored by the prospect that this layer of water-laid clay might actually be physical evidence of the great Deluge, but what other explanation was there? After all, he had just excavated almost 4500 years of continuous human existence at this location, and there was no other plausible theory for this unexplained layer of water-laid clay. Could it be that the biblical Flood actually did take place?

As with many other religious questions, it would probably be best for us to look to the Bible for an answer to this question. As we read through the book of Genesis, we may notice a few unusual things about its early chronicles. For instance, when Cain, the son of Adam, slew his brother Abel, and was banished by God to the land of Nod. Cain begged the Lord not to send him to Nod because he feared that everyone who found him there would slay him. The question then logically arises as to exactly who "everyone" was, since the Bible tells us of only three people living on Earth at this time. So who were these people who were going to slay him? Is it possible that there were other people living on Earth at the same time as Adam, Eve, and Cain?

This same question comes up once again in Genesis Chapter 12. In this narration, describing the famous dissemination of the sons of Noah and their families throughout the area around Iraq, Abram decides to leave the land of his kin in Ur and sojourn southward into the land of Egypt in order to avoid a famine that has struck his land. So he sojourns south into the land of the Egyptians. The question again arises as to exactly where these Egyptians came from, since they are not accounted for in any of the descendants of God's people.

There are also many other scientific facts that do not seem to be compatible with a worldwide flood theory. Archeologists have for instance uncovered indisputable evidence of the continuous existence for over 10,000 years, of people of the black race on the continent of Africa, and people of the oriental race on the continent of Asia. These archeological records include colored drawings of these people of various races on cave walls and on pieces of pottery. If these races were totally destroyed in the Flood in 2500 BC, how do we explain the fact that these exact same races managed to reappear later in these exact same locations after the flood?

Those supporting the worldwide flood theory, base much of their theory on the fact that the Bible describes the flood waters as covering the "face of the whole earth" (Gen.8:9). But this same phrase is also used in the book of Exodus to describe the plague of locusts in Egypt. It says in the book of Exodus that the locusts covered "the face of the whole earth" (Ex. 10:15). We know that in this case the writer was only referring to the area around Egypt. The Hebrew word "earth" may also be translated as meaning "land", which would lend a much more acceptable meaning to these phrases.

These specific Bible references, and many others as well, raise the possibility that perhaps the great Deluge was confined to only one specific area of our planet. God, after all, was only trying to cleanse the land of the Patriarchs, not the entire Earth. This theory would make a lot more sense from a scientific viewpoint. If this theory is in fact correct, the question then arises as to what sort of an occurrence could have accounted for a catastrophe on such a scale?

There is one possible scenario that might explain this sort of a disaster. We do know for instance, that the motion of the ocean tides on Earth is caused by the gravitational attraction of the Moon drawing up the oceans onto one side of the planet, resulting in the daily rising and falling of the ocean tides. This gravitational force is so strong that in some areas of the Bay of Fundy, the ocean tide rises and falls as much as 46 feet in a single day.

It might therefore be possible to draw the world's oceans up onto one side of the Earth and produce conditions similar to those of the Flood, if a strong enough gravitational force could be generated on one side of the planet. This situation could have occurred if a large astronomical object passed by very close to our planet. These conditions may have been even more pronounced if this object had passed by on the same side of the Earth as the moon was positioned in at the time.

These circumstances could most certainly have produced a high tide on one side of the Earth capable of submerging a very large portion of the globe. The meteorological disturbances created by such a planetary near-miss would have most certainly lasted for many weeks. The Biblical story of the Flood recounts a rainstorm lasting for 40 days, but an earlier account of the Flood, known as the Gilgamesh Epic, records the fact that the rain and flooding itself lasted for only seven days.

The Gilgamesh Epic tells us essentially the same story as the Bible Flood, but without as many embellishments. This account was written by Gilgamesh, whose tale was found recorded on clay tablets found in the ancient ruins of the city of Nippur. This story tells about Zuisusha (the Sumerian Noah) who stands by a holy wall and receives a message from the assembly of the gods that the seed of mankind will soon be destroyed by a great flood.

Zuisusha builds a giant boat and witnesses a storm approaching from the south that is bringing the ocean inland. After 7 days the storm begins to subside and Zuisusha opens the window of the Ark to release a bird, but the bird immediately returns to the boat. A few days later he releases the bird again and this time it does not return, signaling that it is finally safe to leave the Ark. One eerie statement made in both tales, is a description of the appearance of the landscape when the door of the Ark is finally opened. Both stories describe the earth as "a vast sea of clay, as flat as a roof, where once there had been civilization".

If in 2500 BC, a large unidentified object from space did pass by very close to Earth, then the Great Flood may have indeed occurred exactly as the Holy Scriptures describe. This massive astronomical mass might have been a comet, an asteroid, or even an undiscovered planet within our own solar system. This large object may possess a widely eccentric orbit that brings around our sun only once every few hundred years. As such, it might not have been noticed by early astronomers here on Earth. This theory would fulfill all the scientific requirements of the physical conditions necessary to produce the massive flooding described in the book of Genesis.

It is much too early for scientists to subscribe to any such theory, but you never know, someday this object may decide to come around again and take another swipe at us

CHAPTER 8

THE METRIC SYSTEM

Thus pounds and feet and inches
Were very soon replaced
By kilograms and meters
To suit the Devil's taste.

Have you ever wondered why we presently have two measuring systems in America? The introduction of the Metric System into the U.S. has gone mostly unnoticed by the general public, but it may be important for us to take a closer look at the Metric System before simply accepting it as a replacement for our original system of weights and measures.

If you'll take a brief moment to glance at your automobile speedometer, you may notice that it is graduated in both miles per hour, and kilometers per hour. It wasn't until recently that this kilometers per hour addition was made beneath the miles per hour portion of the gauge. Most Americans regarded this change as a minor inconvenience, and really weren't very concerned about it. But nothing happens without a plan or a reason, and the plan behind the introduction of the Metric System into America needs to be more closely examined.

Up until the middle of the 20th century, the Metric System was practically unheard of in the United States. Then in the late 1960's, foreign automobiles began to appear on America's highways in significant numbers, as America's liberal elite began focusing their attention upon the European lifestyle. In order to repair these little foreign cars, it was necessary for

American automobile mechanics to use wrenches based on metric sizing. By the mid-1970's, road signs on America's highways listing distance in miles were suddenly removed from America's highways, and replaced by road signs listing distances in kilometers. Soon, metric weights and measures were printed on goods purchased in America's stores. In 1975, President Gerald R. Ford had officially signed the Metric Conversion Act, setting off a full-fledged invasion of the United States by the Metric System.

Most Americans had never dealt with the Metric System before, and were reluctant to have to buy a new set of wrenches just to change the carburetor on their teenager's foreign car. In fact most people in the U.S. had no use for the Metric System, but it appeared as if they were stuck with it whether they wanted it or not. The thought that there might be any prophetic significance to the appearance of the Metric System in the U.S. has probably never crossed the minds of most people, but the Bible has much to say about the Metric System, and also about the person who first proposed its widespread use.

In order for us to better understand the reasons behind the introduction of the Metric System into America, it will first be necessary for us to examine the roots of our own American system of weights and measures. To do this, we must go all the way back to the time of Abraham, the biblical progenitor of the Hebrew people.

In the time of Abraham, God had provided a set of laws and standards for His people to live by. Included in this set of standards was a system of weights and measures that was based upon a unit of measure known as the cubit. The cubit's length was in turn based upon the physical size of the Earth. The "sacred cubit," as it was called, was a unit of measure equal to one 10,000,000[th] part of the distance between the North Pole and the center of the Earth. It was also a length equal to 25 English inches, or 7 "hands". If you do the math on this, it turns out that in the time of the book of Genesis, the Earth measured exactly half a billion inches tall from the North Pole to the South Pole. This dimension has lengthened just slightly over the millennia due to a process that scientists refer to as Post-Glacial Rebound. This process resulted in a gradual lengthening of the distance between the Earth's poles over time, due to a loss of polar mass from the melting of the Earth's polar ice caps.

Most Americans are still accustomed to using inches and feet to measure distance, and the ancient "hand" measure is still used today by those who raise horses. The height of a horse is still given in "hands" measure. The "hand" is a length of just under 4 inches (originally 3.571 inches to be exact), and was equal to the width of a man's hand, not including the thumb. Seven of these hand measures equaled one Sacred Cubit of 25 English inches.

The ancient Hebrews used God's measuring system exclusively, and God intended for His people to use this measuring system for all time. When the ancient Hebrews scattered over the globe, they carried their cubit-based measuring system along with them. The system was eventually adopted by many of the world's greatest nations, and centuries later, the people of Great Britain established the system all around the world in their many trading colonies. The British system of weights and measures eventually found its way into the United States through the English-speaking people (Joseph – Ephraim) who first founded our nation.

Our measuring system in America is still based upon this original Sacred Cubit measurement of 25 English inches. Since the Sacred Cubit was an Earth-based measure, it was also used to parcel out land. The U.S. acre is in fact a land area equal to 100 cubits square. Since a cubit equals 25 English inches, the U.S. acre is actually a square of land whose sides are each, 2500 inches long. This U.S. acre of 2500 inches per side is still used today on practically every land deed in America, and varies only slightly from its original dimension.

Over the centuries, this Sacred Cubit measure was corrupted in the marketplace by unscrupulous merchants, who would often try to cheat their uneducated customers. The original Sacred Cubit measure of 7 hands was eventually corrupted down to a lesser cubit of 6 hands, or 21.43 inches. This lesser cubit is still used today in some parts of Ethiopia and Somalia. This 6-handed cubit was then further corrupted down to a 5-hand cubit of only 17.86 inches that was adopted by most other nations using the cubit measure.

The original "people of God" were stone masons by trade, and were often employed by other civilizations as architects and engineers whenever large stone monuments or buildings needed to be erected. These ancient Hebrew masons were experts in mathematics and geometry, and used their cubit-based measuring system when constructing these monuments and buildings. Thus, the ancient cubit measure is preserved for all eternity in the dimensions of many of these ancient stone structures.

The King James edition of the English Bible tells us in the book of Isaiah, Chapter 19, Verse 19, that in the last days, one of these stone monuments would still be standing in the midst of Egypt as a testament to the Lord. And indeed, the Great Pyramid of Giza (pronounced Jeezah), the most massive stone structure ever built by man, still stands today, preserving this Sacred Cubit measure. The Great Pyramid was designed and built by the children of Seth over 4000 years ago, and is truly a magnificent monument, containing a great wealth of information about God's universe and the history of man. The Great Pyramid was specifically designed to preserve this ancient knowledge.

The Great Pyramid is a four-sided geometric structure whose height is in proportion to the distance around its base, in the same proportions as the radius of a circle holds to the circumference of a circle. The pyramid thus records for us the value of pi, and also preserves the unique geometric relationship between a circle and a square. Each side of the Great Pyramid's base is exactly 365.242 Sacred Cubits in length, thus recording the exact length of Earth's solar year. Scientists have been studying this last of the Seven Wonders of the World for many centuries, and men like Sir Charles Piazzi Smyth, Royal Astronomer of Scotland, have been able to reveal many of its secrets.

Most people in the United States don't give much thought to what measuring system they use each day. Our Saxon forefathers brought this measuring system along with them when they first arrived on America's shores from England (Angle-land) seeking refuge from the religious oppression of the Holy Roman Church of Europe.

The idea that the appearance of the Metric System in our nation might have any biblical significance, has probably never occurred to most people. But the Bible contains a warning for us about this new measuring system that is now being proposed as a replacement for God's original cubit-based measuring system.

Since many of our goods and services now come to us from foreign lands, we find ourselves having to deal with the Metric System more and more each day. There are some people who think that it is now time for us to give up our American system of weights and measures and convert to the French Metric System. These people tell us that it would be in our "best interests" to join in with a new One World economic and social order.

This One World movement in America had its roots in the early 1960's on college campuses across our nation, where the idea of a socially and morally unrestricted world was growing very popular. By the mid 1960's, liberal ideas and attitudes were popularly supported by many of America's university students, who drove around in little foreign cars shaped like lady bugs. Most people are totally unaware that these little cars were actually the brainchild of Adolph Hitler, who wanted his "people's car" to serve as the perfect commuter vehicle for the members of his new superior Aryan society. Hitler even drew the shape of his beetle shaped car on a piece of paper and gave it to Mr. Porsche to build for him. The antichrist's New World Order followers would love and drive his car for many decades to come. It was Hitler's intention to also establish his new One World Order that would finally achieve the perfect human society. The new messiah, Adolf Hitler, promised to lead his promised people into a perfect human society, lasting for 1000 years.

Many liberal-thinking Americans also subscribed to this new One World Order theory that would eventually lead us into a more "enlightened" society. Our original Christian society, based upon strict Bible principles, was about to undergo a massive reformation involving the more "enlightened" New Age concepts and moral standards of Europe. As part of this reformation, it would also be necessary for us to convert our American system of weights and measures to conform to the International Metric System of Europe.

It is interesting to note that among the many Bible warnings we receive about the coming of the antichrist, is one concerning this antichrist's mission to change what early Bible writers referred to as our "times and laws." Many Bible scholars now insist that this phrase should have more accurately been interpreted "weights and measures", for it was indeed the Emperor Napoleon, the man identified by Tsar Alexander I of Russia as the first biblical antichrist, who introduced us to the Metric System.

In the year 1790, Napoleon's good friend and associate, the Catholic bishop Charles Talleyrand, was sent on a mission to Paris by the Catholic Church in order to form a special committee of the Paris Academy of Sciences, to establish a new One World unified system of times, weights and measures. The purpose of this new system would be to replace, and totally eliminate, the English cubit-based measuring system from the face of the Earth.

Since the cubit's length was equal to one 10,000,000[th] part of the distance from the North Pole to the center of the Earth, Napoleon's new measuring unit, known as the meter, was designed to be equal to one 10,000,000[th] part of the distance from the North Pole to the Equator.

Cubit = 1/10,000,000[th] part N. Pole to Earth's Center
Meter = 1/10,000,000[th] part N. Pole to Earth's Equator

Napoleon wanted the new base distance for his meter to be measured along the Paris meridian that ran through his private estate in France known as Mal-maison (Evil-house). He also wanted all world standards for time, date, and measure to be established along the Paris, France meridian, instead of the Greenwich, England meridian. He even introduced a new calendar based on the birth of the French Revolution, instead of the birth of Jesus Christ. The English however, were not about to give the French emperor that pleasure.

Since the meter's base distance was taken over the imperfect surface of the globe, the meter still remains a flawed measure today. Napoleon's new measuring unit was named from the Greek (Hellas) word "metron," meaning "measure." The Emperor set his new Metric System into law on the 10th of December 1799, and immediately launched a program to establish this New Age measuring system all around the globe. He standardized his Metric System throughout his entire empire, which at the time included most of Europe.

It was Napoleon's intention that this new measuring system would eventually eliminate God's cubit-based measuring system from the face of the Earth. Napoleon's new Metric System however, was not so readily accepted by the English-speaking people of Britain and the United States. Napoleon had easily deceived the left-wing Jacobins, who overthrew their monarchy in the name of the Enlightenment. He then led them down the path to Hecatomb, marching his armies across Europe in a campaign of death and destruction unmatched in all of human history.

Napoleon's plans for world conquest however, were soon ended by Tsar Alexander I of Russia, a devoted student of the Bible. Alexander identified Napoleon as the first antichrist of Revelation Chapter 13, citing a prophecy found in Daniel Chapter 7, Verse 25, indicating that this antichrist would seek to change "times". Alexander observed that Napoleon's "meter" was based upon the length of a pendulum with a "timed" half-arc of one second. Alexander also noted that in Daniel Chapter 7, Verse 25, this antichrist "Napollyon" would attempt to institute new standards of "laws" upon the world, and Napoleon was indeed attempting to institute his Napoleonic Code of law upon the world.

When Napoleon attacked Russia in 1812, Tsar Alexander was ready for him. Alexander ordered everything in Napoleon's path burned to the ground. Napollyon was the biblical leader of the army of locusts, and by using locust defense tactics, Alexander was able to completely destroy Napoleon's grand army of more than 500,000 troops. When Alexander ordered the burning of Moscow as well, Napoleon's troops fled the city in terror, but were cut to pieces by Russian troops. Napoleon's locust army was completely destroyed by Tsar Alexander.

Alexander had defeated Napoleon, but the Emperor's Metric System managed to survive the collapse of his empire, and lived on in the European marketplace. The same liberal academics who originally supported the system, still found it appealing, and did their best to carry on Napoleon's dream of a new One World social and economic order. They worked to legislate the Metric System into the laws of every nation on Earth. Even the United States government in 1975, under the administration of President Gerald R. Ford, foolishly signed on to the Metric Conversion Act, moving America one step closer to the total elimination of God's sacred cubit-based measuring system.

The long-range plan of the supporters of the One World Order, now known as the New World Order (George Bush speech 1990) is to establish a single unified system of commerce and government all around the globe. In order to accomplish this task, it will first be necessary for them to create a unified One World economic, monetary, and social order, with a unified system of weights and measures. To this end, the supporters of the One World Order have incorporated their deceptive plan into the curriculum of America's schools, and are now educating the schoolchildren of America on the many advantages of this new One World measuring system. Many Christians in America however, have not taken kindly to the Metric System, in spite of the barrage of government propaganda in its favor. Most Americans don't particularly care for the Metric System, and have in fact refused to accept it as their national system of weights and measures.

The prophets tell us that God's holy remnant in America will never accept the measuring system of the Serpent, in spite of the fact that it is being taught in their schools, and supported in their courts. The founders of our nation came here seeking freedom and independence from the moral corruption of the Roman Church in Europe, which had strayed from God's laws and condemned Europeans to the reigns of evil dictators like Napoleon and Hitler. They understood the methods of the children of The Great Deceiver, who were constantly deceiving men into committing acts that would offend God.

Our founding fathers established the United States of America as a sovereign Republic, operating "under God.," The United States is the only nation on Earth where every individual is guaranteed God-given freedoms against the tyranny of government. Our founding fathers were Protestants who rejected the failures of the Roman Church and Europe's antichrists.

The founders established America as a "free society," where the ultimate powers would be vested in the people themselves, and not in the government or a political despot. They included the words "Creator" and "God" in the original charter used to found this nation on July 4th, 1776, and defined the God-given rights that all free individuals would forever hold against the forces of both church and state in our nation's "Bill of Rights."

Now that we've successfully entered the Seventh Millennium of man's civilized existence here on Earth, there is a sudden renewed interest in Bible prophecy. Christians everywhere are beginning to re-examine the basic truths underlying the changes now taking place in the world around them. These truths have always been there for everyone to plainly read within the pages of the Holy Scriptures.

It is important for all Americans to understand the subtle forces behind the social changes that are now being urged in our society. It is also necessary for all Americans to closely examine the motives of those who tell us that they have only our "best interests" in mind.

The founding fathers believed that a society based upon the plans and desires of sinful men was a society doomed to failure, and that if men wished to establish a better society here on Earth, it would need to be a society based upon the supreme laws of the Creator.

CHAPTER 9

THE YEAR WITHOUT A SUMMER

"I believe in one God, Creator of the universe. That He governs it by His providence. That He ought to be worshipped. That the most acceptable service we render Him is doing good to His other children. That the soul of man is immortal and will be treated with justice in another life, respecting its conduct in this."

Benjamin Franklin

Are weather events actually Acts of God? In this modern scientific world, we don't often consider weather events to be true Acts of God, even though we still sometimes refer to them as such. Many years ago however, all weather events were thought to be Acts of God. The early American colonists were firm Bible believers who attributed all natural events to the will of God. The Bible tells us that in the Last Days, people would worship a God of their own making, denying His power to act through such things as weather (II Tim 3:5).

The following story recounts an extremely unusual weather event that took place in early American history. Could this weather event have actually been an Act of God? You decide.

It happened two centuries ago, and still stands today as one of the strangest events in all of history. It has long since been forgotten by most New Englanders, but nevertheless constitutes an important event in the early history of our nation. Its occurrence needs to be examined more closely if we are to determine its prophetic significance, if any.

It is difficult for modern Americans to think of weather events as being prophetic, but sometimes, as in the case of the biblical Flood, they can be. When the early settlers of this nation arrived on America's shores, they entered into a much harsher climate than the one they had left behind in Europe. Temperatures in the New World could rise as high as 110 degrees Fahrenheit in the summer, and dip to as low as 40 below zero in the winter. These European adventurers found the harsh New England climate very difficult to deal with. European weather was somewhat similar to that of the New World, in that the four seasons of the year were well defined, but in Europe the warm breezes off the Atlantic Ocean tended to keep Europe's summers and winters much milder than those of America.

Since in those days people lived closer to, and thus were more dependent upon, the weather for their survival, the weather in any given year was of paramount importance to every New Englander. The survival of their summer crops was vital to their year's food supply, and even a sudden unexpected thunderstorm could damage crops or food storage facilities. Weather events were therefore viewed with much more concern than they are today.

In today's world, we do not tend to view the cycles of the seasons with as much trepidation as the early New Englanders did, but occasionally we do experience a hurricane or other natural disaster that can threaten our homes or property.

The early Christians of New England on the other hand, saw God as an integral part of their lives, and drew a direct connection between God and all natural events, including the weather. So-called "natural" disasters, such as earthquakes, hurricanes, and floods, were thought to be Acts of God brought down upon mankind as vengeance for sins that men had knowingly, or unknowingly, committed. Early in the 19th century, a natural event occurred that was so unusual as to stand out as just such an occurrence. It happened in the year 1816, and is remembered today as the most unusual weather event in history. The year 1816 is recorded in American folklore as "The Year Without a Summer."

As with many natural disasters, the possibility that this event may have had any prophetic significance was never even considered by those who later recorded it. But its story must be told, if we are to understand the role this event may have played in the overall order of our nation's prophetic destiny.

The winter of 1815-1816 came in like an angry lion. It started off with the largest hurricane to strike New England in over a century. The hurricane uprooted hundreds of thousands of trees, and destroyed many houses and barns all across New England. Then, just when New Englanders had finally finished repairing and rebuilding all the damage caused by this monster storm, a terrible plague descended upon New England.

The excessive rains had produced an overabundance of grains and seeds, followed by a massive overpopulation of mice and other rodents. Nature then sent a plague upon the rodents to reduce their population, but the "Spotted Fever" would cross over into the human population and kill many people in the northeastern United States. All this was then followed by an extremely harsh New England winter.

By the spring of 1816, many exhausted New Englanders were anxiously waiting for winter to loosen its harsh grip on their land. But spring that year was unusually late, and for some unknown reason, the winter cold just refused to release its grip on the New England landscape. Deep winter snows in the Appalachian Mountains were not melting normally, and winter temperatures were not moderating as spring approached. Many people had also noticed that there was an eerie corona around the moon every night, and there was a constant haze in the heavens that just wouldn't go away. On most normal evenings New Englanders could gaze up into the sky and admire the thousands of stars that dotted the heavens, but now, not even a single star was visible in the evening sky.

Everyone was anxiously waiting for the sun to start warming the ground, signaling the start of summer, but somehow that warmth seemed to be avoiding New England this year.

As the summer grew closer, many people were becoming concerned that something was very wrong. It wasn't that the days weren't warm, in fact some days it was downright hot. The problem was that each night the temperature would drop sharply, and by morning there would be a frost on the ground. Many New England farmers were hesitant to plant their crops, only to have the frost kill the young plants, but spring was rapidly waning, and planting had to be undertaken soon, or there would be no crops at all. There were only so many weeks to the growing season in New England, and in northern New England particularly, it was necessary to take advantage of every one of them. By June 1st, most farmers had already sown their fields, and by June 5th, daytime temperatures were hovering in the 80's. It appeared as if spring had finally arrived.

Then, on June 6th, a strange thing happened, it began to snow! It started slowly at first, but by the following morning it was snowing much harder, and by that evening, all of New England was in the grip of a full-blown blizzard! Four days later New Englanders opened their doors to snow drifts over two feet high in many places. All the way up and down the Appalachian mountain chain from Canada to Pennsylvania, it seems the U.S. had suffered a major snow and ice storm!

No one in the Northeast could remember anything like this ever happening before in the month of June. Even Native Americans, who had lived in the New World for thousands of years, had no recollection of a similar event ever occurring. Most New Englanders were very concerned and frightened by all this strange weather, and thousands of them crowded into their local churches seeking answers from their religious leaders. They wanted to know why God was visiting all these terrible punishments upon them. What had they done to provoke His wrath? But church leaders had no answers for them. They too, were helpless to explain this act of God's vengeance.

The unusual weather had given rise to all sorts of strange events. Birds that had flown north to enjoy the warm New England summer, now suddenly found themselves in conditions for which they were totally unprepared. They desperately began to seek the shelter and warmth of people's homes and barns. If anyone were careless enough to leave a window open, a bird would immediately fly in. There was soon not enough room in the barns or houses of New England to fit in one more bird.

All over the Northeast, the carcasses of hundreds of thousands of birds that had died from cold and lack of food, lay strewn everywhere across the New England landscape. The same fate was also visited upon insects. Millions of them, brought out of their winter sleep by the brief warm spell, now lay dead or dying on the pure white blanket of snow.

It was a hellish scene to behold, and many people thought it was the first sign of the dreaded Judgment Day. There were prophecies in the Bible about the stars disappearing from the sky, and dark days occurring just prior to the Day of Judgment. Churches all over New England were suddenly packed with Christians praying for forgiveness for whatever it was they had done to offend God. There was widespread fear of starvation as farmers stared out their windows at the ruined crops in their fields.

Many new spring lambs were unable to survive the bitter cold, and quickly succumbed to the severe winter-like temperatures. Adult sheep, having just been freshly shorn, could not now defend themselves from the lethal cold, even though they sought the shelter of barns. All over the Northeast, thousands of farm animals lay dead or dying in the fields. The high temperature on many days hovered at only 30 to 40 degrees Fahrenheit.

By June 10th, ponds that had completely thawed out were once again frozen over by ice up to an inch thick. Water troughs were capped with ice every morning, and had to be emptied and refilled daily so farm animals could drink. It was June, but most people were still walking around in their winter attire.

Many families willingly sacrificed their farm animals in order to provide meat for their families and neighbors. There would be little or no hay or grain with which to feed the animals anyway. Most smokehouses were working overtime trying to preserve as much meat as possible, just in case the winter-like temperatures continued. Neighbor would help neighbor. It was the Christian thing to do.

Another strange phenomenon was also noted. In larger river valleys, a thick fog would form each night due to the reaction of the cold air and warmer river water. Some farmers noticed that crops planted near these larger rivers were protected from the frost by this heavy warm mist. This phenomenon was well known to the ancient mountain dwelling Indian tribes of Aztecs and Incas, who purposely dug such water canals through their fields in order to generate these same protective mists. Farmers whose fields were located near these larger rivers would at least be able to provide some grain for their less fortunate neighbors.

After the first snowfall in June, the weather began to improve a bit, and it soon appeared as if things were changing for the better. People began joking about all the talk of impending doom the unusual weather had generated. Warm weather just before the cold had brought out all the insects, and most of them had been killed off by the frost. For the following few weeks the weather had grown much warmer, and now, with no insects to attack their crops, it appeared as if the growing season would be the best one New England had ever seen.

Then, just when it seemed that all the danger had passed, the weather again turned sour. By the 4th of July, men could be seen working outside in their overcoats, at noontime, in full sunshine! It seemed as if winter had once again returned. Killing frosts were recorded on June 10th, July 9th, August 13th, and all through the summer. Snow fell again in July, and on the tops of many mountains, the trees were reverting back to fall colors.

On the tops of most New England mountains, green leaves were now turning bright autumn colors and falling to the ground. Many mountaintops were totally devoid of foliage. The whole scene looked like an eerie winter landscape. Never in the history of New England had there been a summer like this one.

Women were soon forced to venture out into the forest to dig for roots, and children were sent to pick what wild berries were to be had, either for canning, or to be used immediately as food. Milk from cows and sheep, which fed on grass, soon became a major food source for both children and adults. What extra milk there was, could be turned into cheese and stored for later use. Farmers desperately hunted squirrels, rabbits, deer, and just about any other creature that could be eaten. Freshwater fish from ponds and rivers were also used to supplement the meager food supplies.

As summer advanced, food grew even more scarce, and food rationing became a normal part of life for most New Englanders. Corn, which comprised the major food crop, was over 90 percent destroyed by the weather. What corn was for sale in the marketplace sold for ten times normal price, and was mostly unfit for human consumption. Only the hardiest and coarsest grains could be purchased in stores, and at vastly inflated prices. There was no decent food to be had anywhere, for any price, and rich and poor alike suffered from the starvation rations. People soon began to call 1816 "The Poverty Year" and "Eighteen Hundred Froze to Death."

Decades earlier, America's great scientific genius, Benjamin Franklin, had performed studies on this kind of natural phenomena. Franklin wrote that this weather was often caused by layers of ash in Earth's upper atmosphere that prevented sunlight from reaching the ground. It was Franklin's opinion that such phenomena often resulted from volcanic activity elsewhere on the globe.

Franklin also noted that abnormal sunspot activity sometimes contributed to the process. Franklin taught that it was often a combination of reduced sunspot activity and volcanic dust in the upper atmosphere that resulted in reduced solar radiation here on Earth. Franklin demonstrated that a magnifying glass could not even set a piece of paper on fire under such circumstances.

Most New Englanders were totally unaware that on April 11th of the previous year, a giant volcano had indeed erupted on a remote island in the Dutch East Indies. This huge volcanic explosion sent a giant cloud of volcanic ash high up into Earth's atmosphere, much higher than normal rain clouds could reach; for it was rain that normally brought such ash back down to Earth.

Volcanoes sometimes erupt slowly, but at other times they can erupt in one gigantic explosion. The modern Mount St. Helens volcano erupted in just such an explosion, but it luckily exploded sideways instead of straight upward, thereby depositing very little ash into the upper atmosphere. The giant East Indies volcano called Mt. Tambora however, had exploded straight upward, depositing enormous quantities of volcanic dust into Earth's upper stratosphere.

In 1815, Tambora's volcanic cloud had created winter-like conditions in southern Europe, ruining food crops and leading to widespread starvation and food riots in France. The cloud undermined the emperor Napoleon's attempts to return from exile, and left him with no food with which to feed his troops. The cloud had completely collapsed the already ruined economy of France. Was this God's punishment upon the emperor Napoleon? As champion of the Enlightenment, Napoleon had left a massive trail of death and destruction across Europe in his effort to establish his new One World Order, and it seems that the fledgling United States had unwittingly supported Napoleon in these efforts.

Napoleon had fought more battles, conquered more land, and killed more people than any previous world conqueror, and he did much of this with money from the United States. When

Napoleon needed funds to finance his attempt at world conquest, he worked out a deal with the U.S. government for the purchase of the French-owned Louisiana Territories. Napoleon's personal emissary, the Catholic bishop Charles Talleyrand, was sent to work out a deal with America's politicians. Talleyrand used the money from the land sale to support Napoleon's war efforts in Europe. It was therefore America's money that financed more death and destruction than the world had ever before seen.

American politicians however, were unconcerned with the human slaughter their money was funding in Europe. They were too busy celebrating all the newfound wealth suddenly made available to them through their new Louisiana Purchase. Mount Tambora's cloud of volcanic ash, after aiding in Napoleon's downfall, had completely circled the globe, and was now visiting its wrath upon the people of the United States.

If the church masters of New England had been more watchful over the affairs of their own government, they might have been able to better answer the questions being posed to them by their Christian congregations.

Luckily, Tsar Alexander I of Russia had done a better job of studying his Bible, for it was Tsar Alexander who successfully identified the emperor Napoleon as the first antichrist, and thus prevented his takeover of the world. Alexander identified Napoleon by his Greek name "Napollyon," leader of the army of locusts, and followed Bible instructions to use locust eradication tactics to defeat Napoleon's army. If not for Tsar Alexander, the world would be a much different place today.

In Matthew Chapter 24, Verse 24, Jesus warned us about the coming of many false Christs, or antichrists. Napoleon Bonaparte was identified by Tsar Alexander as the first of these antichrists. America's rich businessmen and politicians however, identified Napoleon only as a friend.

For many years in their war against the English, the Americans had allied themselves with the French. The French however, were not so pro-American as they were anti-English. The French had been easily deceived by the antichrist Napoleon, and followed him down the road to ruin.

If Napoleon had succeeded in his world conquest, there would be a global government in place today that would make the Roman Empire seem docile by comparison. American politicians, in their greedy quest for power and money, had been more than willing to deal with the devil.

There were some American church leaders who did object to America's purchase of the Louisiana Territories, because they knew the money would be used fund massive death and destruction in Europe. But their voices went unheeded in the mad rush for land and profit in America. All in all, the year 1816 was a time of terrible suffering for America's poor settlers.

The following year marked the greatest exodus of Americans southward and westward in New England history. Many settlers, particularly those in northern sections of New England and Canada, immediately pulled up stakes and headed for warmer places. No one wanted to experience a year like this one ever again.

In retrospect, we may never know if the weather during the year 1816 was truly an Act of God or not, but it certainly was an event that changed the course of American history, and resulted in terrible suffering for the American people.

CHAPTER 10

REVEREND MILLER'S RAPTURE

The End in 2300 years,
The prophecy had said.
If not for Miller's Rapture,
They all would soon be dead!

The following story concerns one man's attempt to interpret Bible prophecy. That attempt caused quite a stir in the church world of early America. The story you are about to read took place over 150 years ago, but even today this man's work is still the subject of much discussion in church circles. His name is Reverend William Miller, and his work still forms the basis for most modern interpretations of the book of Daniel.

In the annals of New England church history, there is no story told with more amusement than the story of Reverend William Miller. Reverend Miller was one of the first persons to seriously preach the doctrine of the pre-millennium Rapture (see also Pretribulationalism – John Darby). The Rapture theory is still a source of great controversy in the modern church world today.

For those of you unacquainted with this doctrine, I should explain that it stems from a prophecy quoted in Matthew Chapter 24, Verses 40 and 41, and in Luke Chapter 17, Verses 34 through 36, where Jesus tells his disciples about an event that will occur in the last days. Jesus tells his disciples that in the last days, two men would be working in the field, and that one would be taken and the other remain, and that two women would be grinding at the mill, and one would be taken and the other left.

This prophecy was the subject of much anxious discussion in church groups that assembled every Sunday in many New England towns and villages in the early 1800's. The prophecy was interpreted by many people to mean that the Lord Jesus himself would lift his followers up into the sky to meet him in a great heavenly Rapture, thus saving them from the terrible tribulations of the Judgment Day. In those days there were many Christians who believed that this great Day of Judgment was just around the corner. The early New England colonists took great interest in the Bible and all of its prophecies. Most had come to America seeking religious freedom from the oppression of the Roman Catholic Church of Europe, and lived their lives according to strict Bible principles.

The Bible in Europe was for many centuries the exclusive domain of the rich and privileged upper classes, who could read it in its original Greek and Latin texts. The clergy of the Holy Roman Church discouraged its parishioners from reading directly from the Holy Scriptures. It was instead accepted practice for all interpretation of the Bible to be taken from official church doctrine. There were a few of the liberal elite, educated in the classical languages, who could read the Scriptures for themselves, but in general it was not permitted for Catholics to read directly from the Bible.

The Holy Roman Church held absolute power over all of Europe for more than 1500 years, and totally controlled the affairs of both church and state on the European continent. Around the year 1500 however, the Church fell into a state of decay, and even resorted to selling tickets for free passage into heaven, signed by the Pope himself, to anyone with enough money to purchase them. These passes into heaven, called

Indulgences, guaranteed the bearer free passage into the hereafter, and forgiveness for all sins.

A German Saxon priest by the name of Martin Luther rebelled against the sinful authorities running the church at the time, and decided it was time for the common man to be able to read the truth of the Holy Scriptures for himself. Luther therefore decided to print the Bible in the common German language, so anyone could read and understand it. Luther's break from the Catholic Church marked the beginnings of what would eventually become known as the Protestant Reformation. The Holy Roman Church had lost favor with Frederick the Wise, Emperor of all Germany, and so the Protestant movement soon became a very popular cause. Before long, there were Mennonites, Calvinists, and many other groups joining in the rebellion. Martin Luther was ultimately able to print and release his common language version of the Holy Bible.

John Wycliffe, an Englishman, had previously issued an English version of the Holy Scriptures around the year 1400, but it was attacked by the Roman clergy and banned in England in the year 1408. Then, in 1525, an Englishman named William Tyndale traveled to Germany to visit Luther, because he wanted to utilize Luther's work to create an English version of the Bible as well as the German version. Tyndale was jailed on orders of the Holy Roman Church. He was later strangled to death, and his body hanged and burned by order of the Catholic bishops of England..

Around this time, England's King Henry VIII became embroiled in a bitter dispute with the Pope over all the women he was continuing to marry and divorce. Henry's many wives were an embarrassment to the Church. It was customary in those days for Rome to approve all royal marriages, but Henry challenged the Church's authority to overrule his personal decisions. This dispute ultimately resulted in a break in relations between England and Rome. Henry then established the new Anglican Church of England with himself as its head, and now, with Rome out of the picture, an English version of the Holy Bible could finally be printed and released. This English version was soon followed by the famous Geneva Bible, printed by exiles in Switzerland, and then later replaced by the popular Bishop's Bible. Many years later, these English bibles eventually evolved into the version we know today as the King James Edition, printed on the orders of King James IV of Scotland. It wasn't until later in the 17th century that this English language Bible was made commonly available to the lower classes. You can imagine everyone's excitement at finally being able to read and interpret the Holy Scriptures for themselves.

The Protestant Reformation sparked a great exodus of Christians from Europe into the New World. Tens of thousands of religious pilgrims left the shores of Europe seeking the religious and social freedoms now available to them in America. America became the new Israel for Europeans with dreams of emigrating to the Promised Land. Practically everyone in America carried a Bible under one arm, and the book provided an almost exclusive source of reading material for those long winter evenings in many New England homes.

New England now stood as the gateway to the New World. As newcomers arrived daily from Europe, they were offered 100-acre parcels of land to homestead; all they had to do was clear the land and build a house on it. Many homesteaders would then sell their property to the next person coming down the road and needing a place to stay. They could then move on westward and begin the process all over again.

New England thus became the pathway for all hopeful new pilgrims to the new Israel. It was in this spirit of hope and promise that Reverend William Miller preached his message of salvation to the world.

As newcomers arrived daily to take up residence in the New World, churches sprang up in every New England town and village. Ambitious church missions were launched into foreign lands by missionaries seeking to spread the gospel to all who would listen, and new churches of every known denomination were constructed in every New England town. There were Congregationalists, Deists, Methodists, Lutherans, Baptists, and churches of every known religious doctrine. Since everyone was free to interpret the Scriptures as he or she wished, it was only natural that all these different churches would emerge. On Feb. 15th, 1782, William Miller was born into this period, the son of a poor farmer in the northwestern Massachusetts hill town of Pittsfield.

When Miller was about 4 years old his family moved down into New York's Hudson River Valley and settled near the town of Low Hampton, New York. William Miller was a boy who loved to read books, and his maternal grandfather, the Reverend Elnathan Phelps, was a source of great inspiration to him. At age 22, Miller married Lucy Smith and moved into nearby Poultney, Vermont, where he became an active member of the Deist church.

Now the Deists were a purist sect that rejected many of the Roman Catholic doctrines taught in the Christian Bible, such as the virgin birth. It wasn't that the Deists rejected the entire Bible; they just thought it had been infected with many pagan doctrines by the Roman Catholic Church; so the Deists worshipped the purest creation of God as reflected in nature and science. The Deist Church was founded upon secular humanist philosophies.

Miller eventually went off to fight in the War of 1812, and served as a captain in the US Army at the Battle of Plattsburg on the West bank of Lake Champlain. After returning from the war, Miller built a farming estate in Low Hampton, NY. The war had exposed Miller to some of the harsher realities of life, which were to have a lasting effect upon the future direction of his career. Miller was thoroughly disillusioned with the state of human society and man's inhumanity to man. Miller became curious about the ultimate destiny of mankind, and decided to begin delving into the great mysteries of the Bible. He studied the Bible in great depth for over two years, and began to undertake the task of deciphering the secret codes that provided the chronology of Bible events. The end-time prophecies of Daniel were of particular interest to Miller, who found a pattern in the numbering system used in Bible prophecy that he believed held the key to the correct calculation of the time of the end. He soon found new spiritual salvation in the teachings of Jesus Christ in the born-again doctrines of the Baptist Church. Miller's discoveries were destined to make him a famous figure in the early Millennium movement in America.

Popular belief at the time held that the Bible contained secret codes that could help to reveal the timing of prophetic events. One of these codes, found in II Peter 3, Verse 8, revealed that a day to the Lord was as if a thousand years to man. Believers therefore held that civilized man's existence here on Earth was limited to a seven-thousand year period, or seven God-days, the first six thousand years witnessing the development of man, and the last thousand years being spent under the personal dominion of the Lord himself.

Since the Adam and Eve event had been calculated by Bishop Ussher as occurring around the year 4000 BC, it was thought that the Lord's return would come at the end of the sixth day, or around the end of the second millennium AD. Miller's calculations for this Second Coming, or "Second Advent" of the Lord Jesus Christ led him to believe that the time of the end was very close. Miller's calculations for the time of the end were based upon the 2300-year prophecy of Daniel Chapter 8, Verses 14 through 23. This prophecy (a day for a year, Num. 14:34, Ezek. 4:6) referred to a time when the last of the biblical beasts, or "transgressors," would have "come to the full." Since the prophecies of Daniel were recorded around the year 457 BC, the 2300 year prophecy would place the time of the end to be near the year 1843.

For those of you unacquainted with the rules of Bible prophecy, the word "beast" in prophecy refers to a world-conquering empire that oppresses God's people. The prophecies of Daniel concerned themselves with these biblical beasts, or world empires, that would come into existence to oppress God's Hebrews.

The Bible tells us that the twelve sons of Jacob fathered the original twelve tribes of God's people. When Jacob bestowed God's special blessing upon his son Joseph, Joseph's brothers became jealous and sold Joseph into slavery in Egypt. But Joseph, blessed with the gift of prophecy, soon found favor with Pharaoh, and rose to a high position in Egypt. As God's punishment for their evil deed, Joseph's brothers and their families eventually found themselves serving as slaves to the Egyptians.

The Egyptians were the first in a long series of empires to oppress God's people. The Egyptian Empire was followed in turn, by the Babylonian, Persian, Greek, and Roman empires. It was mostly the prophecies of Daniel that Miller was concerned with, for the succession of these biblical beasts, or empires, was vital in determining the exact timing of the end.

History tells us that around the year 926 BC, the Israelites decided to give up their farming and sheep-herding lifestyle, and establish a new city-based state in the Holy Land. This city-based society soon caused the Israelites to fall into a state of great moral decay (Judges 2:11). They turned away from God in favor of a politically ruled society. The Israelites abandoned their religious roots and became self-serving, adopting the more politically correct philosophies of their new man-made government. They even began to war with the more orthodox southern tribes of Judah and Benjamin. This angered God greatly, and so, around the year 723 BC, He decided to send the children of Ishmael to avenge His anger upon them. God sent the Assyrians down out of what is now Iraq, to war against the 10 tribes of Israel and take them into captivity.

The sins of God's people continued on however, and a century or two later, even the tribes of Judah and Benjamin ultimately strayed from God's laws. So God again sent the people of Ishmael down to also take the remaining two tribes into captivity. It was during this period, known as the "Babylonian Captivity," that the prophet Daniel recorded his end-time prophecies for us.

Daniel had found favor with Babylon's great King Nebuchadnezzar by accurately interpreting a dream the king had experienced. King Nebuchadnezzar's dream concerned a great statue with a golden head, silver breast, brass belly, iron legs, and ten toes of iron and clay that would not mix together. Daniel told the king that this statue represented his great Babylonian Empire and the four lesser empires that would follow it, which were in turn, the Persian, Greek, Roman, and

"Holy" Roman empires. Miller taught that the exact identity of these empires was vital to accurately tracking Bible chronology.

Later, during the reign of Babylon's King Belshazzar, Daniel received a vision of his own, also concerning four beasts. Miller taught that these four beasts represented those same four world empires. These four beasts are described for us in Daniel Chapter 7.

The first beast was a lion with eagle's wings. Reverend Miller identified this winged lion as the Babylonian Empire. This exact winged lion actually was in fact the symbol that the Babylonians used to represent their empire.

The second beast of Daniel 7 was a bear raised up on one side with three ribs in its mouth. Miller identified this bear as the symbol of the Medo-Persian Empire. Miller taught that all prophecies were represented in more than one place in the Bible to provide the reader with verification from more than one source. He compared the bear raised up on one side in Daniel Chapter 7, to the ram of Daniel Chapter 8, whose second horn came up after the first horn, but grew to be the higher of the two. Miller taught that the Persian Empire rose up after the Median Empire, but was the more powerful of the two, and was therefore represented in this fashion.

The two empires of Media and Persia are represented in prophecy as one, because both came together under the Persian emperor Cyrus. The three ribs in the mouth of the bear represented the Babylonian, Lydian and Egyptian kingdoms over which Cyrus ruled.

The third beast of Daniel's dream was a leopard with four wings and four heads. Miller taught that this leopard represented the Greek Empire, and that the leopard's four wings and four heads represented the four swift armies commanded by the four generals under Alexander the Great. Miller compared this leopard with four heads, to the rough goat of Daniel 8 with four horns, also representing Greece. When Alexander the Great died unexpectedly at the young age of 32, his four generals divided up the Greek Empire into four parts. General Lysimachus was given Thrace, Hellespont and the Bosphorus to the north, General Ptolomy received Egypt, Lydia, Arabia and Palestine to the south, General Seleucious was granted Syria and all Asian lands to the east, and General Cassander was given Macedonia and Hellas (Greece) to the west.

After the three great empires of Babylon, Persia and Greece had disappeared, the most powerful beast of all suddenly appeared on the scene. This fourth beast was dreadful, terrible in strength, and exceedingly powerful. It had teeth of iron, for the Iron Age had now arrived; and with iron weapons to overcome the inferior bronze weapons of its enemies, this fourth empire was able to extend its influence over a much wider area than any of its predecessors.

Miller had no doubt that this fourth beast represented the Roman Empire. He taught that this beast's ten horns represented the ten kingdoms that would eventually arise from the breakup of the Roman Empire. Miller compared these ten horns to the ten toes of King Nebuchadnezzar's statue, five of iron, and five of clay.

When we add the preceding empire of Egypt to this list of empires, we now have the biblical identity of the first six empires (beasts) of the western world.

1. The Egyptian Empire   3400 BC
2. The Babylonian Empire   650 BC
3. The Medo-Persian Empire   550 BC
4. The Greek Empire   330 BC

5. The Roman Empire   170 BC
6. The Holy Roman Empire   313 AD

Miller's calculations were not to be taken lightly, Miller had access to much detailed information about Bible and church history that was in many ways superior to the information available to us today. Miller's calculation for the time of the end was based upon a time when the last of the biblical beasts to oppress God's people will come to its end, or when "the transgressors are come to the full." This statement, recorded in Daniel Chapter 8, Verse 23, led Miller to believe that this same date would also immediately precede the Judgment Day.

Miller followed the trail of these world empires, or beasts, all the way from the ancient Egyptians, to the Holy Roman Empire, and was convinced that the end of the Holy Roman Church would mark the end of the world, and also herald the Lord's return.

The Millerites believed that the bestial Catholic Church had altered the laws of God. They therefore looked to the orthodox Jews for God's true laws because the tribe of Judah had been trusted with the scepter, or law, of God (Gen. 49:10).

Through many elaborate mathematical calculations, Miller determined that the end of the last beast, or Holy Roman Church, was growing very close. Since the Daniel prophecy was given around the year 457 BC, the 2300-year Daniel 8 prophecy set the time for the end of the "last of the transgressors" to be about the year 1843. Miller was convinced that a heavenly Rapture would occur just prior to this date.

Miller had made his original calculations in the year 1818, but would not circulate them until many years later. In 1831, Miller finally began to preach his Rapture theory on the end of the world and the "Second Advent" of Christ, in local churches, and found many people quite receptive to it. Millennium fever was growing rapidly in the 1830's, and Miller was soon overwhelmed with invitations to speak in churches all over New England.

In 1838, Miller wrote his book entitled *"Evidence from Scripture and the History of the Second Coming of Christ."* Miller's book stirred a great deal of interest from those who wanted to believe that the Judgment Day was very near.

Miller's preaching eventually came to the attention of Joshua Himes, a Baptist minister from Exeter, New Hampshire, who saw great potential in Miller's message. Himes became Miller's manager, publisher and public relations director, and soon the Millerite movement was a major force in New England religion. Himes published many books, pamphlets and newspapers on Miller's predictions, and organized evangelistic crusades from Maine to Michigan. Miller was not an ordained minister, but he had obtained a license to preach from his own church, and was soon recognized as a popular source of Bible instruction. Miller had his share of scoffers though, and was sometimes pelted with eggs at public evangelistic gatherings and camp meetings.

Miller and his followers came to believe that the true church of God would be Raptured up to heaven in advance of the Judgment Day. Miller's message appealed to the vanity of his audiences. Everyone wanted to believe that they were the exclusive members of God's elect, and would therefore be granted a special place in heaven. Miller acknowledged that his calculations might not be totally correct, and when his original date came and went with no Rapture occurring, Miller was forced to recalculate his figures.

Miller's new calculations revealed the date of the end to be the year 1845. His calculations were so precise that the

Millerites announced the Rapture would occur at exactly midnight on October 22, 1844, which was the tenth day of the seventh month of the Jewish calendar. Many major newspapers soon ran full page ads ridiculing the fanaticism of the Millerites.

Miller originally had some doubts about this controversial October 22nd date, but the elders of his church convinced him of its veracity. Miller's following had now grown to over 50,000 people, and included hundreds of thousands of others who were extremely interested onlookers. Many of Miller's followers sold all their worldly goods and made final preparations to be Raptured up to heaven on the fateful day. The eyes of all New England were on the Millerites (Adventists) as they prepared for the great event.

On the evening of October 22nd, 1844, as midnight approached, Millerites in churches, private homes, and on hilltops all over the northeastern United States readied themselves to be taken up to heaven at the Lord's return. In the great cities of Boston, New York, Philadelphia and Cincinnati, many loyal followers, some dressed in white Ascension Robes, and others sitting in metal washtubs, patiently waiting to be lifted up to heaven in the upcoming Rapture.

When midnight passed with no Rapture occurring, the disappointed Millerites were forced to return to their homes in great humiliation, as people laughed and jeered at all the fools who'd fallen for "Miller's folly." After what eventually became known as the "Great Disappointment," Miller's following rapidly fell apart, and some of the remaining Millerites (Second Adventists) eventually reformed under the leadership of a woman named Ellen Gould White (Seventh Day Adventists). The Millerite movement was written off as a great failure in the annals of church history.

The Great Disappointment was viewed as just another example of the silly fanaticism of religion. It was the 19th century, and science was rapidly emerging as a much sounder way of revealing the many mysteries of life and of the universe. Religious theory was constantly being shown to be unscientific, and therefore flawed.

There is however, one very interesting fact that should be taken into account before rendering any judgments on Reverend Miller's work. Miller's calculations were based upon a time when the "transgressors are come to the full" (Dan. 8:13-14), or the end of the last beast, occurring 2300 years after the going forth of the commandment to rebuild Jerusalem.

It has recently been discovered that the Vatican copy of the Greek Septuagint (from which our English Bibles were originally copied) records Daniel's Chapter 8 prophecy as occurring 2400 years after this event, instead of the 2300 year figure appearing in our English Bibles. It seems that an error occurred during one of the many Bible transcriptions that took place over the centuries. A pen stroke was apparently dropped from the number by mistake. When corrected for this error, Miller's date for the end of the last empire to oppress God's Hebrews becomes 1945 instead of 1845.

Interestingly, 1945 did indeed mark the end of Adolph Hitler's infamous Nazi Empire, which was in fact dedicated to the complete annihilation of the Hebrews. And so it may be that Miller and his Seventh Day (Saturday) "Sabbath Keepers" were right after all. We will attempt to further explore this complex question on the exact identity and order of the biblical beasts in some later chapters of this book.

CHAPTER 11

HOW CHRISTMAS WON THE WAR

"It would be particularly improper to omit in this first official act, my fervent supplications to that Almighty Being who rules over the Universe, who presides in the councils of nations, and whose providential aids can supply every human defect; that His benediction may consecrate to the liberties and happiness of the People of the United States."

George Washington – Inaugural Address

America's history has often been fraught with peril and strife, but somehow fate has always acted at the last minute to turn the tide of battle and save the day. The following story chronicles a strange but true event in American history. It is sometimes a good thing for us to revisit history in order to gain a better understanding of the many ways in which God has watched over us during difficult times.

In the latter part of the 18th century, a new spirit of independence and adventure was sweeping across the civilized world. European settlers were arriving daily upon America's shores with dreams of finding new freedom and opportunity in the New World. America was rich in natural resources, and could provide a "well of plenty" for anyone willing to work hard in order to make his dreams come true. The early Christian colonists came to America fleeing the class system in place in Europe that allowed wealthy European nobles to economically oppress the lower classes. When England's King

George began imposing heavy tax burdens upon his American colonies, the colonists rebelled.

Most of them were having a difficult enough time just trying to survive in the New World. It was nearly impossible for farmers and businessmen alike to show a reasonable profit for all their hard work and struggles in the New World, and worse, the colonists had no political representation in England with which to address their many grievances to the Crown.

This "taxation without representation" policy soon gave rise to the famous Boston Tea Party, where a group of angry colonists dressed up as Native Americans, and dumped a load of English tea into Boston Harbor to protest the government Tea Tax. This ultimate act of defiance drew a final line between the British colonists and their Monarch. After the Boston Tea Party, King George proceeded to impose harsh new penalties on his American colonies. The stage was thus set for the American Revolution.

In 1775, an armed conflict between the American colonists and British soldiers took place in Boston, Massachusetts, and the historic battles of Lexington and Concord followed Paul Revere's now famous "The British are coming!" ride. On July 4th, 1776 the American Revolution was made official with the issuance in Philadelphia of a document known as the Declaration of Independence.

The task of writing this original founding document was assigned by John Adams to a young man named Thomas Jefferson who authored it alone in a small rented hotel room at the Graff House in Philadelphia, Pennsylvania. Jefferson was the person who would ultimately be credited with the creation of a new form of government based upon the God-given rights of all free men.

From the first symbolic battles in Boston, it quickly became apparent that the American Revolution was not going to be an easy war to win. The British had a well-trained army, and plenty of money with which to finance a war. The British were also more experienced in how to successfully conduct, and win, a conventional war. They were also known to hire professional armies from other nations to do their fighting for them.

The American colonists on the other hand, were poorly trained and poorly equipped to fight in any prolonged conflict; they did however have one thing on their side, and that was the will and determination needed to endure severe hardship.

The American Revolution has many interesting stories to tell. One of the most interesting of them all however, is the story of how the entire direction of the war was changed by the outcome of a single battle. This battle was one of the strangest battles in all of history; its memory is forever preserved for us in the now famous painting of George Washington crossing the Delaware River. The real story behind this battle however, is not often told, and the story needs to be told, because this was the single battle that changed the course of American history. It's also the story of how Christmas won the war. That's right, if it weren't for the Christmas holiday, the United States of America might not exist today.

The American Revolution you see, was a very difficult war for America's colonists to fight. You must remember that they were fighting against the army of their own government. There were also many colonists still loyal and sympathetic to the Crown of England. But King George had levied many severe taxes upon his colonies, and these taxes amounted to an unbearable burden for most people. A small group of American colonists therefore decided it was now time to fight for their independence from the British Crown.

King George however, was not about to allow his colonies to separate from their mother country. Many colonists were hesitant to join in any rebellion, not because of any loyalty to England, but because they considered it foolhardy to attempt to fight against the well-trained troops of the British army. Also, many colonists feared retribution from the British if the war were lost. Anyone caught siding with the revolutionary cause could be branded a traitor and hanged. The American Revolution therefore, did not get off to a very good start. There was much sympathy for the colonial cause, but most people were convinced that this rebellion was doomed to certain failure. The few skirmishes after the 4th of July declaration only served to further reinforce those fears.

England however, had one big disadvantage in this war, and that was distance. The Atlantic was a large, cold expanse of ocean that took many months to cross. It was difficult therefore, for the British to deliver large numbers of troops to put down any rebellion. European armies often numbered 300,000 men or more, but sending an army that size across the Atlantic Ocean was nearly impossible, and so the number of troops and supplies that could be quickly delivered to fight in this war was severely limited. It was therefore very important for the British to maintain their ties with British sympathizers in the colonies, who could provide their troops with food and lodging. The British were known to burn the homes of those not supporting the Crown.

The British launched their first attack at Bunker Hill in Boston. The colonials were routed when they eventually ran out of powder, but the battle ended up little more than a draw. Since New York City was considered to be the economic heart of America, the British decided to launch their first major assault there. A large military force was dispatched from England to carry out this mission.

America's General George Washington had very little experience fighting in a European style war, and with inexperienced troops as well, didn't stand much a chance of defending Long Island against the more experienced British regulars. In August of 1776, a force of 30,000 British troops was dispatched to Long Island. They quickly routed Washington's Colonial Militia, and sent them scrambling for cover. The British had an easy time chasing the Americans off Long Island, and it was clearly evident that the Continental Army was no match for British regulars. General Washington found it nearly impossible to defend New York City from the British, because the city was surrounded by water, and therefore at the mercy of British sailing vessels that could bombard it with cannon fire from all sides.

In October, the Battle of Valcour Island on Lake Champlain in upper New York State did not go much better for the Americans. The colonials gave a good account of themselves, but this battle too, was lost. Another formal battle in White Plains, New York resulted in a similar defeat for Washington. The Colonials clearly lacked the skills and training needed to effectively fight in a conventional style war, so in this battle as well, they lost more ground to the British.

When the British captured Fort Lee, in Westchester, N.Y., General Washington's assistant, General Lee, began competing with Washington, hoping to replace him as commanding general of the Continental Militia. Lee purposely did not move quickly enough to support Washington's army, and thus hastened Washington's retreat. Washington decided to move what was left of his army south into New Jersey to see if he could bolster its dwindling numbers with volunteer forces from the New Jersey Militia. Washington's numerous defeats however, were becoming too well known, and with the British already in New Jersey, about 2000 soldiers from the New Jersey Militia refused to reenlist.

The negative outcome of all these military battles was not doing much for America's morale. Support for the war was beginning to wane, and many people were beginning to think they were right in their original assumption about the effectiveness of the Colonial Militia. Washington's troops were now having a difficult time even begging food or lodging from local farmers.

Washington now headed for Princeton with only about 3000 men left from his original 20,000-man army. By December, things were not looking very good for the Colonial cause, and Washington was involved in a desperate retreat from the British. He personally led his army's rear guard, burning bridges and knocking down trees in order to block the progress of the pursuing British army. By the time Washington reached Princeton, he had only about 400 men with him. Two thousand men from the Pennsylvania Militia however, agreed to join up with Washington when he finally reached the town of Princeton.

Winter was now upon them, and General Greene's troops were also heading for Princeton. Washington's General Lee was slow to respond, and delayed moving his troops. Lee's lack of action however, eventually resulted in his capture by the British. The remainder of Lee's army under General Sullivan continued on to Washington's location. General Greene headed for New Jersey as well, and General Gates came down from Fort Ticonderoga to also join up with Washington's forces.

Washington and his harried continental army now headed for the safety of the Pennsylvania side of the Delaware River. The British were close behind and attempting to overtake them in order to put a quick end to the war. When the Colonial Militia finally arrived at the Delaware River, they needed boats to cross it, and found them at a local business that used heavy boats to ferry its goods across the river. Washington commandeered every boat in the area, not only so he and his men could cross, but also to prevent the British, who were close on his trail, from being able to cross as well. Washington realized that the success or failure of the entire Revolution was now in his hands. His Militia was in a complete shambles, and the British were closing in for the kill.

Washington managed to successfully relocate his army to the Pennsylvania side of the Delaware River, but his men were short on food and supplies; and without proper winter clothing, many were now freezing to death in the cold. Many Militiamen did not even own shoes, and wrapped their feet in layers of rags in order to insulate them from the snow. Morale in the colonies had sunken to a new low, and Colonial troops were no longer able to obtain food or shelter from their own countrymen, who were now deathly afraid of British retaliation.

The British General Howe was well aware of Washington's plight, and not very concerned about Washington's army in its present state. He knew that time would only serve to make Washington's situation worse, and therefore decided to set up winter camp on the New Jersey side of the river, and wait for spring.

Washington's troops were deserting his Militia in droves and heading for home. Everyone was convinced that the Revolution had failed. To add to Washington's plight, half of his troops' enlistment contracts would be up in a few days on

January 1st. Washington needed a miracle, and he needed it fast. If he could not pull off a military victory soon, the American Revolution was over.

Washington sent word to the Continental Congress that he was badly in need of reinforcements, and also food and clothing. Unfortunately, reinforcements were not in the offing; in fact, the Continental Congress itself was now in complete disarray and worried about its own future. Washington's situation was growing more desperate by the hour, but desperate situations often test the mettle of great men, and George Washington was a man of great determination and resolve.

Most of the descriptions of Washington's winter encampment in Pennsylvania begin with the following phrase:

It was a cold, snowy Christmas Eve, but George Washington and his troops had very little to celebrate.......

Well, this is where our story begins, because the truth is, that in 1776 Christmas was not celebrated in America. In fact, if someone were caught celebrating Christmas, they could be tarred and feathered and run out of town on a rail! There were no Christmas trees, no Christmas cards, and no Christmas gifts. Christmas was a Roman Catholic holiday, and not celebrated in Protestant America.

That's right, the biggest holiday of the year was almost unknown in America. In fact, the people who originally arrived on America's shores to found our nation came here specifically to get away from Christmas. They were European Protestants who hated the pagan holidays of the Holy Roman Church.

The pagan Germanic tribes of Eastern Europe had worshipped the evergreen tree for many centuries because of its ability to seemingly defy death and keep its green leaves all winter long. These pagans would go into the forest to cut down an evergreen tree, and then bring it into their homes to decorate it with silver and gold. This was in direct violation of Bible instructions given in Jeremiah Chapter 10, Verse 3. The Christians of America would never think of celebrating such a pagan holiday as Christmas.

The British however, had hired a group of German mercenary soldiers called Hessians to help them fight the Americans, and the Hessians did celebrate all the holidays of the Roman Catholic Church, especially the Christmas holiday. It was this fact that was to spell a great opportunity for the Americans.

The British General Howe had left a force of about 1500 Hessians on the eastern shore of the Delaware River to keep an eye on Washington's army. It was Christmas Day and the Hessians were busy stuffing themselves with food and drink in their traditional Christmas celebration. Outside, it was snowing fiercely, and by late evening most of the Hessians were sound asleep in a drunken stupor.

Thus far, all the battles of the Revolutionary War had been fought in formal military style, with neatly lined up rows of soldiers facing each other on the field of battle in traditional military formations. Washington decided that it was now time for a drastic change in tactics. He decided that from now on he would fight in the style he was more accustomed to, the style of the American Indian. Washington knew that all the successful armies in history moved quickly and surprised their enemies by striking where they weren't expected, at a time when they weren't expected. So from now on Washington would utilize only light cannon and fast horses, and make surprise moves that his enemies would not expect.

Washington was desperate and had to make a move soon. Since it would have been a breach of military etiquette to attack the Hessians on Christmas Day, Washington decided to attack the Hessians on the day after Christmas. This might be better anyway, because most of the Hessians would be hung over from their excess of food and drink the night before.

Washington still had approximately 6,000 troops under his command, and so he devised a plan to cross the Delaware River after dark on Christmas night. He broke his army into three parts, and planned to cross the Delaware River at three different locations in order to completely surround the enemy.

Under the cover of a raging blizzard, Washington attempted the hazardous crossing with his men at a point about nine miles north of Trenton, New Jersey. Washington had commandeered all the large boats in the area, and was in possession of some 50-foot transport boats from a nearby factory that were capable of ferrying his horses and light cannon across the river. Washington planned to surround the Hessians at Trenton, and attack from all sides at dawn, forcing them into a quick surrender.

The river was packed with ice however, and the raging blizzard was making conditions for the crossing nearly impossible. Two out of three of Washington's regiments decided it was much too dangerous to complete their crossing. Only Washington's main force made it across the river, mostly due to of Washington's blind determination. By morning, General Washington and 2400 of his troops, with 18 cannon, had successfully crossed the Delaware River. The crossing took longer than expected however, and by the time it was completed, it was too late for a predawn attack. Certainly no one could have expected that Washington's army would be able to successfully cross the Delaware River in that kind of weather.

Now, with Trenton only nine miles to the south, his army's march to town would take a couple of hours; but Washington had to hope he did not meet up with any Hessian patrols on the road. Blizzard conditions still prevailed, but the heavy snow was actually working in Washington's favor. The blizzard was so intense that the Hessians did not think there was any possibility Washington's Militia would move in this kind of weather. The Hessians therefore, had not even sent out their normal morning patrols.

The blinding snowstorm was covering Washington's moves as effectively as if it were nighttime. No one was able to see anything in the distance, and even the sound of the horses hooves and the cannon wheels, was being muffled by the heavy snow. The sleeping Hessians were totally unaware of the Militia's approach. Washington's troops marched into Trenton totally unannounced, and caught the Hessians by complete surprise.

Most of the Hessian soldiers were barely able to stand, let alone fight, and the Americans quickly and easily overwhelmed them. The Hessian officers had been drinking heavily the night before, and were in even worse shape than their troops. Colonel Rall, the Hessian commander, was awakened from his drunken stupor, and had trouble even getting his pants on. The Americans moved swiftly into town and broke up the Hessian formations as quickly as they formed. Many of the Hessians' muskets would not fire because of the overnight dampness, but Washington's cannon performed perfectly. The Colonials raked the streets of Trenton with close range artillery fire.

The Hessian commander, Colonel Rall, was badly wounded in the battle, and many of his officers were also killed. The

Hessians were now surrounded and confused, and did not know where to run.

There were a total of three Hessian regiments in town. Two of them, under Rall and Lossberg, headed to the east to retreat, but found Washington's General Greene blocking their escape route. With nowhere else to run, and guns that would not fire, they immediately threw down their weapons and surrendered to the Colonials. The third regiment headed south out of town, but was cornered against a creek and also forced to surrender. About 600 remaining Hessian troops ran for their lives through the woods and escaped out of town to the south. The Americans shot and killed almost 100 Hessian soldiers, and took another 900 prisoner

The attack was such a surprise, that not one single American soldier was lost to the enemy, although two of Washington's men had fallen by the side of the road and frozen to death on the short march to town. It was the most ridiculously one-sided battle in the history of warfare.

The Hessians had paid heavily for their Christmas celebration of the previous evening. The Americans were now finally able to raid the British supply depots. They now had the food, blankets, and clothing they needed to keep warm, and when word got out that Washington had captured Trenton without losing a single man to the enemy, Americans were dancing in the streets. The rag tag American Militia had finally proven that it could defeat a force of trained professional soldiers. Men were now lining up to join in the revolutionary cause, and money and supplies were now available from every source. The British had been treating the American colonists very badly, including even British sympathizers, and everyone was hoping against hope for just this kind of victory.

When the British General Howe heard of the Trenton rout, he was absolutely dumbfounded. He just could not believe that three hardened regiments of professional soldiers who fought for a living, had been so easily defeated by a bunch of rag tag American militiamen. Howe immediately dispatched General Cornwallis to retake Trenton. Washington however, anticipated Howe's move, and also the direction from which it would come.

Washington's two remaining armies, still on the other side of the Delaware River, assumed that Washington had also failed to cross. When they heard that Washington had captured Trenton, they were shocked, and hurriedly rushed across the river to meet their general. Washington knew that Cornwallis was on his way however, and immediately ordered all his troops back across the river. Cornwallis finally arrived in Trenton with a small force, but was forced to wait for reinforcements to arrive from the rear. He therefore set up camp for the night.

The British could see the American campfires burning on the other side of the river, and assumed that Washington was preparing for battle the next morning, but Washington had other plans. He slipped around the British during the night, leaving just enough men to keep the campfires going so the British would think he was still there. Washington planned to get behind the British and head for the town of Princeton to the east. The Colonials took a back road so they would not run into Cornwallis' reinforcements coming in from the east. Traveling light and fast, they planned to attack Princeton as they had Trenton, totally unexpected.

With Cornwallis still in Trenton, the Militia launched its surprise attack on Princeton and, with the Trenton victory boosting their morale, were all in good spirits. The battle went back and forth, but finally, General Washington mounted his horse and led a charge into the enemy lines. The sight of Washington bravely charging into battle astride his white stallion was enough to inspire the spirit of every American militiaman. Their battle spirit renewed, they quickly captured Princeton.

When news got out that Washington had captured both Trenton and Princeton, the Colonial Militia was now considered unstoppable. There was suddenly a new spirit of independence in the air, and everyone knew that the outcome of the American Revolution was now assured. Soon afterward at the Battle of Saratoga, the great British General, John Burgoyne, was defeated and captured. This was the final straw for the British. They now realized that America would ultimately win its War of Independence. A new nation would be formed; a nation of free people living in a free society, where the true power would be vested in the people themselves, and not in their government.

Now you know the true story of how it was that Christmas won the Revolutionary War. If it hadn't been for that single Christmas celebration in 1776, there might never have been a United States of America. History unfortunately, is always written by the winners, and the truth is often lost in the telling. The Battle of Trenton was for obvious reasons not the most celebrated battle of the American Revolution, but it was the most important battle just the same.

The pagan roots of the Christmas holiday are well known. It is therefore not so very strange that the celebration of this Roman Catholic holiday should have proven to be the undoing of the pagan forces attacking the Christians of America. The Battle of Trenton was just one more example of the many strange and unusual events that governed the destiny of the American people.

CHAPTER 12

THE BILL OF RIGHTS

"I know of no safe depository of the ultimate powers of society but the people themselves. And if we think them not enlightened enough to exercise their control with a wholesome discretion, the remedy is not to take it from them, but to inform their discretion by education."

Thomas Jefferson

Lately, there has been a renewed interest in America's Bill of Rights. I therefore thought it appropriate to devote a chapter of this book to this historic document that defines the individual God-given freedoms we all hold as citizens of the United States of America. The Bill of Rights is the single founding document that makes the United States truly unique from all other nations on Earth.

In 1776, the thirteen colonies of America were basically independent self-governing commonwealths, with their own legislatures, making their own laws and determining their own future. Their original formation had stemmed from European Protestant religious origins, and most of their laws were based upon religious laws. Many of the colonies once required church membership in order to vote or participate in government, however subsequent rules allowed "all men to follow God in their own consciences".

The original New England colonies consisted mainly of English Protestant Separatists seeking personal freedom through free religious expression. The New York, New Jersey and Pennsylvania colonies were mostly Dutch, German, and Quaker settlers who had emigrated from northern Europe, and the America's Southern colonies consisted mainly of aristocratic English Anglicans (Episcopals), who represented the remains of the Roman Catholic Church of England. This strange homogenization of religious viewpoints made for strange bedfellows, but the leaders of the American colonies also recognized the need for all groups to come together as much as possible to lay a foundation for a revolutionary new form of government.

The task of composing a document that would adequately express the fundamental needs of all free men fell to a solemn young man who sat in a small room in a Philadelphia hotel composing this document that would ultimately alter the future of the entire world. This man's name was Thomas Jefferson, and the document he was composing was America's Declaration of Independence. This document was based upon the masonic principles (see George Mason) of "life, liberty, and the pursuit of happiness" for all mankind, and expressed the purest hopes and dreams of inspired men like Thomas Jefferson and John Adams for a better future for Americans in a free Christian society. The Declaration of Independence served as the single founding document for the United States of America on July 4th of that same year. The nation's Constitution, and Bill of Rights, were later additions to that original charter.

In 1776, America's colonists were suffering terribly under the oppressive dictatorship of their monarch, King George of England, who was using the British army to subjugate his own people. The normal relationship between king and subject had completely broken down, and a state of martial law existed in the American colonies. America's colonists decided that their only recourse was to revolt against their own government. They were prepared if necessary, to establish a new nation where free citizens would be guaranteed their God-given rights to life, liberty and the pursuit of happiness.

Jefferson's original founding document eventually resulted in the formation of a new nation, where every citizen would be guaranteed the rights naturally endowed to him by the Creator. Jefferson was hopeful that sinful men, under the inspiration of Almighty God, would be able to preserve this new Republic forever.

Every nation needs a constitution, but Jefferson wanted his nation's constitution to be different from all others. He knew that every citizen would need to be afforded constitutional protections against the kind of oppression he was now suffering at the hands of his King. The U.S. Constitution, influenced by those favoring a strong federal government, like the federalist John Hamilton, finally appeared in 1789, and John Adams was so disturbed by the document, that he decided amendments needed to be added to it to limit its powers.

Both Jefferson and Adams felt that in the United States of America, every citizen needed to be protected against government tyranny and oppression by rights guaranteed him under the nation's Constitution, and that these rights should never be subject to government interpretation, limitation, or suspension, under any circumstances.

Jefferson, and his mentor John Adams, decided that a Bill of Rights outlining these precious individual freedoms needed to be added to our nation's Constitution. Each amendment to this new Bill of Rights would be written in the common language, and consist of only one single sentence, so as to preclude future interpretation by the government courts. The amendments would define the precious God-given freedoms held by every free citizen against the national government. This special addendum to the nation's Constitution would be a unique undertaking, and would need to be carefully planned, and well thought out.

Just prior to the drafting of this bill of individual freedoms, Jefferson was sent to France as America's Ambassador, to study the new form of government that the French were setting up, and also to review a new French version of a citizen's bill of rights. Jefferson wanted to see if this French document could be used as a basis for America's new bill. Jefferson was much distressed however, to discover that the French had not chosen to found their nation upon faith in God, but had instead chosen to exclude God entirely from their nation's founding documents.

Back in America, John Adams was involved in the final preparations for drafting America's new Bill of Rights. He wrote to Jefferson in France to see what information Jefferson had gleaned from the French document, and Jefferson sent back a list of eleven rights that he thought should be included in the new bill. Adams and his colleagues used Jefferson's letter in drafting the final version of America's Bill of Rights.

While preparing the document however, Adams was forced to reject one of Jefferson's items that concerned protections against business monopolies, because this amendment was a government duty, not a citizen's right. Adams did not want anything to confuse the basic purpose of this document, which was to define individual freedoms held by every free citizen against the federal government. Two other amendments appended to the bill by America's politicians were also rejected before the final bill was approved by all thirteen states. The final Bill of Rights contained just ten amendments, each one defining a specific right that every free individual held against government tyranny.

America's colonists originally came to the New World fleeing religious oppression by the Holy Roman Church of Europe. The Catholic Church controlled most of the continent of Europe, and wielded great power in government circles. Anyone speaking out against Church views could be tortured or killed, and indeed the armies of the Catholic League had piled the dead bodies of Protestant men, women, and children high in the streets of many European cities. The colonists believed in a firm and secure alliance between God and State, but greatly feared any alliances between Church and State. Our nation's founders wanted to provide constitutional protections supporting the exercise of free thought and free speech in order to allow everyone the freedom they needed to interpret the Holy Scriptures on their own.

Jefferson wanted to build upon the laws of the Creator in order to guarantee every individual those God-given rights. He therefore purposely included the words "God" and "Creator" in his original founding document. Every government official, from the highest to the lowest, was required to swear a Christian oath to God with his right hand upon the Bible, to faithfully uphold the duties and responsibilities of his office. Jefferson also wanted to guarantee every individual's right to freely express his own views and to speak the truth, even if those views conflicted with popular opinion or government law. The First Amendment of the Bill of Rights addressed this crucial issue.

1. Congress shall make no law respecting an establishment of religion, or prohibiting the free exercise thereof; or abridging the freedom of speech, or of the press; or the right of the people to peaceably assemble and to petition the government for a redress of their grievances.

The next amendment, the Second Amendment to the Bill of Rights, guaranteed every free citizen the right to keep and bear arms. America's Revolution was still fresh in the minds of the colonists. King George had used the government army against his own people and had ordered the confiscation of firearms and gunpowder. The founders wanted to guarantee American citizens the means to defend themselves against the government army. An armed populace had proven to be the most effective defense against the King's imposition of martial law in America. And so the Second Amendment guaranteed every individual the right to keep a soldier's weapon in his home for the purpose of serving in a freely-formed citizen's militia. The Second Amendment reads as follows.

2. A well-regulated militia, being necessary to the security of a free State, the right of the people to keep and bear arms, shall not be infringed.

The Declaration of Independence listed many specific offenses committed by government troops against private citizens, including the following: "(The King) has kept among us, in times of peace, Standing Armies, without the consent of our legislatures." "(The King) has affected to render the Military independent of, and superior to the Civil Power." "For quartering large bodies of armed troops among us." "For protecting them, by mock Trial, from Punishment for any Murders which they should commit on the Inhabitants of those States." "(The King) is, at this Time, transporting large armies of foreign mercenaries to complete the works of Death, Desolation, and tyranny already begun, with circumstances of

Cruelty and perfidy, scarcely paralleled in the most barbarous Ages, and totally unworthy the Head of a civilized Nation."

The King had permitted government soldiers and barbaric foreign mercenaries to take over the homes of private citizens in peacetime, without the consent of the owners, and to commit crimes against the homeowners and their families without being subject to civil trial for those crimes. The Third Amendment addressed this outrage.

3. No soldier shall, in time of peace be quartered in any house, without the consent of the owner, nor in time of war, but in a manner to be prescribed by law.

The King's soldiers had conducted warrantless searches of private homes, invaded the owners' privacy, and ransacked and seized any item of property they wished, without evidence or probable cause to believe that a crime had even been committed. The Fourth Amendment set down strict rules governing government search and seizure, and the protection of an individual's privacy. It required the government to show "cause" before individuals or property could be detained or seized. Mere "suspicion" would no longer suffice. The Fourth Amendment read as follows:

4. The right of the people to be secure in their persons, houses, papers, and effects, against unreasonable searches and seizures, shall not be violated, and no warrants shall be issued, but upon probable cause, supported by oath or affirmation, and particularly describing the place to be searched, and the persons or things to be seized.

In the King's courts, citizens could be accused of capital crimes on the word of a single complainant. Private property could be seized without warrant and sold at public auction without compensation to the owner, and confidentiality and privacy were totally ignored. The courts often tried people more than once for the same crime by slightly altering the charges, and an accused could even be forced to testify against himself. Trials were often held repeatedly until a guilty verdict was reached.

Even federal soldiers serving in the military were forced to give up their rights as free citizens, and were subject to military trials for offenses not committed during wartime or in a national emergency. The government courts used any excuse to abuse the rights of free citizens. These abuses by the federal courts, including the military courts, were addressed under the Fifth Amendment.

5. No person shall be held to answer for a capital, or otherwise infamous crime, unless on a presentment or indictment of a Grand Jury, except in cases arising in land or naval forces, or in the militia, when in actual service in time of war or public danger; nor shall any person be subject to be twice put in jeopardy of life or limb; nor shall be compelled in any criminal case to be a witness against himself, nor be deprived of life, liberty, or property without due process of law; nor shall private property be taken for public use without just compensation.

Even in the lower courts, a defendant could be imprisoned indefinitely while awaiting trial, or moved to a distant location and tried by people unfamiliar with his personal character or reputation. Judges were allowed to conduct closed-door trials, and defendants were often not even allowed to face their accusers. Rumor and hearsay were sometimes used as evidence, and defendants could be tried without the benefit of legal counsel. These abuses by the courts were addressed under the Sixth Amendment.

6. In all criminal prosecutions, the accused shall enjoy the right to a speedy and public trial, by an impartial jury of the State and district wherein the crime shall have been committed, which district shall have been previously ascertained by law, and to be informed of the nature and cause of the accusation; to be confronted with the witnesses against him; to have compulsory process for obtaining witnesses in his favor, and to have the assistance of legal counsel for his defense.

Since judges were often biased in favor of the government that paid them, citizens would need to be guaranteed the right to a trial by jury, even in the lower courts. The Seventh Amendment reaffirmed the uniquely American concept that the ultimate power and authority always remained in the hands of the people. The courts were therefore granted only the power necessary for them to administer the law as written. The authority to create law was reserved to the State legislatures, and ultimately to the people themselves. The individual always reserved the right to appeal to the people for justice. The Seventh Amendment reaffirms every individual's right to a trial by a jury of his peers.

7. In suits at common law, where the value in controversy shall exceed twenty dollars, the right to trial by jury shall be preserved, and no fact tried by jury shall otherwise be re-examined in any court of the United States, then according to the rules of common law.

In government courts, judges were known to impose high bail or fines in order to keep defendants imprisoned. Judges would often ignore prescribed punishments and invent their own, thereby subjecting individuals to physical injury or public ridicule. These types of judicial abuses were addressed under the Eighth Amendment.

8. Excessive bail shall not be required, nor excessive fines imposed, nor cruel and unusual punishments inflicted.

The Ninth Amendment prohibits the federal government from limiting an individual's rights only to those specified under the Constitution.

9. The enumeration in the Constitution, of certain rights, shall not be construed to deny or disparage others retained by the people.

The founding fathers also wished to reaffirm the superior power of the States to legislate law. Legislative authority was intended to fall first to the people, second to the States, and third to the federal government, in that order. The Tenth

Amendment severely restricts the legislative powers of the federal government.

10. The powers not delegated to the United States by the Constitution, nor prohibited by it to the States, are reserved to the States respectively, or to the people.

Jefferson taught that it was the nature of all governments to eventually oppress their citizens. To prevent this from ever happening in the United States, our founding fathers established this nation as an independent and sovereign Republic, not a democracy. A republic is a form of government based upon higher laws and principles, and the Republic of the United States was founded upon the God-given principals of freedom and justice for all free men. If the U.S. had been established as a democracy, those rights could one day be overruled by popular vote. Jefferson knew that someday Americans might eventually be duped into foolishly giving up many of their freedoms in turn for government promises of security.

To prevent this eventuality, he founded the United States as a free Republic operating under the supreme laws of the Creator of the universe. The words "God" and "Creator" both appear on the document originally used to found our great nation on July 4th, 1776, but the word "democracy" does not appear anywhere in its text. The founders were very careful not to include the Luciferian word democracy (democracy, demos, demon) in any of our founding documents, and would have been shocked to witness modern-day schoolchildren being taught that they live in a "democracy," where a majority vote can overrule even the supreme laws of God. The founders only permitted voting by free, adult, male landowners who obeyed the laws of God. And they would have been especially appalled to learn that the United States of America has now decided to officially recognize an establishment of religion, and presently employs an official Ambassador to the Vatican in papal Rome!

Thomas Jefferson and John Adams were the true founding fathers of our nation, and God saw fit to honor these two men in a very special way. He took them both from us on the same day, July 4th, 1826. This day also happens to be the 50th birthday of the nation they gave birth to and nurtured with their two famous documents, the Declaration of Independence, and the Bill of Rights. It was their unique destiny to be taken up to heaven on this very special day. Jefferson died at his home in Monticello, Virginia, and Adams died at his home in Quincy, Massachusetts. Neither knew of the other's passing.

We owe these two great American heroes a tremendous debt indeed for the many individual rights and freedoms we all enjoy today as free citizens of the United States of America. But as Americans, we must always remember that the price of liberty is eternal vigilance.

CHAPTER 13

THREES

The secrets of the prophecies
Deciphered now with ease,
By seeking out the path to truth
Revealed within the threes.

The significance of numbers in prophecy has not always been clearly understood. In prophecy, numbers are treated as signposts that must be read and followed in order to successfully arrive at a final destination. No prophecy can be accurately interpreted unless all the signposts are read, just as it is impossible to arrive at your highway destination if you miss an exit sign. Numbers therefore, are an important consideration in the accurate interpretation of prophecy. In this short story we'll explore the significance of the number three in prophecy.

Have you ever noticed how things always seem to occur in threes? It's a strange phenomenon that's been observed by many people down throughout history. People often take notice of these strange phenomena that don't seem to make much sense, but happen anyway. This is probably how we came to adopt the many superstitions we're always observing, like not walking under ladders, and avoiding black cats.

Those who study prophecy have also taken notice of this strange phenomenon of things occurring in groups of three. The number 6 for instance, has always carried a bit of an evil connotation to it, but it develops a much more evil connotation when there are three sixes, as in the number 666.

If we search back through history, we can note an interesting historical event linked to the number 666. This event was the great Fire of London that occurred in the year 1666. This fire was one of the most profound tragedies in all of history, and the fact that it occurred in a year of three sixes, did not go unnoticed by those who study prophecy.

The fire started on a Sunday in a bakery shop on Pudding Lane near London Bridge, and rapidly spread throughout most of the old, walled city. The fire burned on for four days, and ended up destroying approximately 80 percent of London. Historians tell us that the fire may have in fact been a blessing though, because it also helped to destroy the rat-infested slums that were contributing to a plague overspreading the city at the time.

Unfortunately, in the 17th century, no one paid much attention to sanitation, because the existence of germs, and their role in disease, was not understood. It would be another two hundred years before a man named Louis Pasteur would come along to discover the long hidden microbe.

The infamous Black Plague had invaded London the year before the fire, and in only a few months had claimed approximately 15 percent of the city's population. The death toll from the fire however, was drastically reduced by the plague, because many of London's citizens had already fled the city for the surrounding countryside in order to escape falling ill.

The fire spread rapidly through most of London's slums, destroying many of the rodents responsible for spreading the plague. The popular children's song "Ring around the Rosie" commemorates the time of the great plague. The line that reads "achoo, achoo, all fall down" refers to the fact that anyone exhibiting the deadly sneeze or cough of the pneumonic plague was destined to fall down dead within the day. The Black Plague was quite deadly, and once symptoms appeared, death could follow in less than 24 hours.

Many of the children's songs and nursery rhymes of that era often contained these macabre themes. There was "Jack and Jill went up the hill," with Jack falling down and breaking his crown, and of course there was also the "Rock-a-bye baby in the treetop" whose cradle fell down when the tree bow broke. When you add these ominous themes to that of an old witch baking little children in her oven, it makes for a terribly frightening world for the young children of those times. If we were to examine all of the grim (pardon the pun) details contained within most fairy tales, we probably wouldn't read any of them to our children.

The phenomenon of "The Threes" has been noted on many other occasions as well. If we check farther back into history, we can note another instance of the phenomenon of "The Threes" that occurred in the year 1333, and it was linked to the 1666 incident. It seems that 1333 was the year that the bubonic plague first made its appearance in Europe. It had finally crossed through the city of Constantinople after taking a terrible toll in many cities of China and India. The bubonic plague had mortality rates as high as 70 percent, and was actually depopulating many large cities. It was mostly confined to cities, because that was where slums and rodent populations most contributed to its spread.

There were two distinct types of plague, and both these plagues were carried by rodents One strain of this plague was called bubonic plague, and the other, pneumonic plague. The bubonic plague was spread by the bite of the Oriental rat flea. The pneumonic plague however, was usually inhaled into the lungs while its victim was sweeping a floor covered with mouse droppings.

Rodent populations were generally spread through the goods traded between nations. The early European bubonic plague of 1333 traveled to Europe along land trade routes that ran through the Middle East. The plague arrived in Europe through the city of Constantinople. The 1665 plague of London however, arrived by sea. By the mid-1600's, London had firmly established itself as a major world seaport, and the city was often ravaged by the plague. The plague arrived by way of British sailing vessels that traveled all around the globe. Wherever rodents traveled, the plague traveled with them.

The first time the strange phenomenon of "The Threes" was noted in the last millennium was in the year 1111. That year marked the crowning of King Henry V of Germany as Emperor of the Holy Roman Empire. Henry received the Crown of Heaven from the Holy Roman Church in 1111. The story of how Henry got his crown is a rather interesting one.

Like most kings, Henry enjoyed wielding great power over his subjects. It was customary in those days for power to be shared by both kings and popes. In the 12th century, the Catholic Church had finally succeeded in gaining temporal powers in Europe. Those temporal powers gave the Church the right to own land. German land barons were soon appointed bishops of the Holy Roman Church, and controlled vast tracts of land in Germany. As bishops of the Church, these land barons swore allegiance to the Pope, and not to the King of Germany. In this way, they could also avoid paying taxes.

Henry however, wanted to rule and collect taxes in his entire domain, not just in parts of it. He therefore resolved to reclaim the lands taken away from him by the Church. Henry first tried to speak to the Pope to see if some compromise could be worked out, but the Pope refused to even discuss the issue. Henry then decided to take his land back by force.

He invaded Italy with a large army, and forced the Pope to crown him Holy Roman Emperor. He also removed the right of the Church to own land. The German land barons immediately revolted, so Henry took the Pope and his bishops prisoner until they agreed to give him what he wanted. Henry was a rather nasty fellow, but his tactics were quite effective, and he finally got his way.

This brings us to the next incidence of "The Threes," which occurred in the year 1222. This was the year that the Mongols launched their military invasion of Europe. The Mongols were a nomadic people who wandered the plains of northern Asia raising horses, in much the same way as they still do today. The sudden appearance on the scene of the great Mongol leader Genghis Kahn however, changed the Mongols' lives forever. Kahn, once known as Temujin, was the leader of one of the warlike Turkic Caucasian tribes that had wandered eastward out of the Caucuses Valley in Turkey, across the steppes of Russia, and into northern Mongolia.

The Mongols had been warring with China for many years, but were never able to defeat the Chinese army. This war had been going on for so long that it was actually responsible for much of the construction of the Great Wall of China, as the Chinese tried to wall out their enemies. Genghis Kahn however, was a very clever and determined man. He trained his Mongol warriors to become an efficient cavalry force that could travel light and fast, and fight very effectively. After Kahn finished training his army, he was able to launch a successful invasion of China, and take possession of China's great wealth and power. With all this newfound wealth, Kahn was able to launch a much larger and more widespread campaign to conquer much of the known world.

Kahn had once been insulted by the leader of the Arab world, and therefore decided to extend his empire into Arab lands first. Kahn made good use of the technology that Chinese gunpowder afforded him, and was then easily able to defeat his enemies. After successfully invading both India and the Middle East, Kahn set his sights on Europe. From the Middle East, he moved northward into Eastern Europe and was able to penetrate all the way to the Russian Ukraine.

Genghis Kahn and his Golden Hordes finally brought the influence of the East to the West. The Mongol language and culture were to have a lasting effect upon eastern Europe. Even today, you can still see traces of Mongol bloodlines in the faces of the Ukrainian people. The great Genghis Kahn however, had overextended his empire, and was unable to penetrate any further into Europe. His reign of terror ended a short time later with his death in the year 1227. Genghis Kahn's fame as a world conqueror however, was permanently sealed within the pages of history.

We then come to the year 1444. In 1444, history took another prophetic turn. For many years the Christian Crusaders had marched through the city of Constantinople, and repeatedly invaded the Holy Land. These many conflicts between Christians and Muslims had gone on for nearly 400 years, and the lives of many Crusaders were lost in these wars, mostly due to the terrible diseases so prevalent in the Near East. In 1444 however, the Crusades were brought to a sudden end when the Ottoman sultan, Murad II, defeated an army of Christian Crusaders at the historic battle of Varna on the shores of the Black Sea. The Roman brand of Christianity had long maintained its hold on the Middle East, but this historic event finally allowed the Muslims to defeat the eastern branch of the Catholic Church at Constantinople and reclaim the Near East for Islam.

During this campaign however, the sultan made the mistake of taking hostage and sexually abusing a 13-year old boy who was the son of the European Prince of Wallachia. The boy eventually escaped his Muslim captors and found refuge in the forests of Transylvania; but he never forgot his encounter with the Turks. Many years later, this same boy, now known as Count Dracula, re-crossed the Danube River and repaid his debt to the Ottomans, by mercilessly slaughtering and anally impaling on wooden stakes over 20,000 Turks, earning Count Dracula a reputation for evil and cruelty undiminished to this very day.

This brings us to the year 1555, when a different type of prophetic event took place. In that year, a Hebrew prophet by the name of Michel de Nostredame (Nostradamus), published a book of prophecy that was destined to become a source of mystery and controversy for the next 450 years. Nostradamus claimed to have received many visions of future events. His book of prophecy, called the *Centuries*, consisted of 10 chapters of 100 prophecies each, describing Nostradamus' brief glimpses into the future. Nostradamus' many followers claimed that he was able to transcend the bonds of time to foretell the coming of future world figures like Napoleon Buonaparte and Adolf Hitler.

Many of Nostradamus' prophecies were truly amazing. One of his prophecies concerning the great scientist Louis Pasteur, actually included Pasteur's name, and told of Pasteur's amazing discovery of the microbe, even going so far as to detail the great scientist's ultimate fate.

Nostradamus' book fascinated men for the next 450 years, as many would try to decode its secret revelations. Nostradamus however, had cleverly disguised his prophecies in much the same way as the ancient Bible prophets. Not one of his prophecies was ever successfully interpreted before its occurrence. To this day however, the prophecies of Nostradamus are still quoted nearly every time a major world event occurs.

We can now leap forward to the year 1777, which brings us into more familiar times. In the year 1777, an event occurred that was destined to alter the course of American history. In that year, a battle was fought that would finally seal victory for America's War of Independence. Until this time, the outcome of the American Revolution was still in doubt, but in this decisive battle in 1777, fought in Saratoga, New York, a large force of Colonial Militia soundly defeated the British army and captured the famous British general, John Burgoyne.

Burgoyne's capture had a demoralizing effect upon the British, and marked the final turning point in America's War of Independence. It was now guaranteed that there would finally be a United States of America, founded upon Christian principles of freedom for every individual. A new nation of free people, living in a free society, could now be established. It marked the first time in history that a nation's power would be vested in its people, instead of its government. The United States of America would stand as a bastion of freedom in a bestial world.

This then brings us to another prophetic year, 1888. This year marked the date of completion for America's famous Washington Monument. This giant Masonic obelisk stands at the very center of our nation's capital, and was erected by our founding fathers as a symbol of American freedom. In 1888, the members of the Masonic Order put the finishing touches on this great masonry structure that now sits at the very center of our nation's Capital Mall in Washington, DC.

This great monument, erected as a symbol of freedom, symbolized the shedding of God's grace upon America, as mentioned in Irving Berlin's well-known song "God Bless America." The height of this giant monument was designed to represent the number of grace. That's right, another case of the phenomenon of "The Threes." The Washington Monument was built to stand exactly 555 feet tall!

All this brings us to the year 1999. Not many people can remember a prophetic event occurring in the year 1999, but there was one, and it was linked to the events of the year 1555. It seems that the great prophet Nostradamus, in his famous book on prophecy, included a prediction of an event that was to take place in the year 1999 during the month of July. This prophecy was unique in Nostradamus's vast collection, in that it gave an exact date for the prophecy's occurrence.

The prophecy eventually became known as the "King of Terror" prophecy, because many Nostradamus "experts" had misinterpreted the prophecy as describing an invasion of the Middle East by a Mongolian antichrist, setting off the final battle of Armageddon. This ominous prediction fit right in with all the other "end of the world" predictions that preceded the arrival of the year 2000. More Nostradamus books were sold at this time than at any other time in history. Nostradamus suddenly became a household word, as people rushed out to buy movies, books and videos about the great prophet's famous prediction.

When the month of July passed without incident, all the Nostradamus "experts" were shocked and disappointed that their prophecy had not come true. They quickly came up with all sorts of excuses for why the prophecy had not occurred, not realizing that the prophecy actually had come true exactly as Nostradamus predicted it would. If you'd like to find out what Nostradamus really predicted would happen in July of 1999, you can find the answer to that question in another chapter of this book under the title "Angolmois."

Nostradamus' great "Angolmois" prophecy marked the end of a Millennium of amazing prophetic events, each one occurring in a year of "The Threes."

CHAPTER 14

THE "BEAST"

He marked the ones that bought and sold
Within the marketplace,
Then swept them off to Hecatomb
To purify his race.

There is much controversy in the religious world today over the identity of the biblical antichrist. He has been identified as everyone from the Pope of Rome, to the head of the European Common Market. He has also been identified as the beast of Revelation Chapter 13. Many religious leaders still preach on the future arrival of this greatly feared antichrist. The Bible however, tells a different story.

The Bible tells us in Mark Chapter 13, Verse 22, that there will be more than one antichrist coming to mislead the world. The Bible speaks of a series of beasts, or kingdoms, coming to oppress God's people. Beasts in prophecy represent kingdoms, or empires, that oppress God's people. There have been many world empires that have appeared throughout history, but the Bible concerns itself only with those that oppressed the Hebrew people.

If we are going to accurately identify these many biblical beasts, we must first review their history, which is carefully chronicled for us within the pages of the Holy Scriptures.

In the book of Revelation, Chapter 17, Verse 10, near the very end of the Bible, an angel tells us that there will be a total of seven kings, or kingdoms, that will appear on Earth to oppress God's people. The angel says that five of these kingdoms, or beasts, had already fallen, and that a sixth beast was just coming into existence at the time of this prophecy, which was given around the second century AD. The angel then tells us that a seventh beast, or empire, was yet to come, and that it, in turn, would be followed by an eighth beast.

It also mentions the fact that this seventh beast "is," then "is not," then "is" again, so its spirit apparently appears, then disappears and reappears once more as the eighth beast. This eighth kingdom is said to be "of" the seventh kingdom preceding it. This curious relationship between the seventh and eighth beasts is also mentioned in the book of Revelation, Chapter 13, where we are told that the second antichrist, or second beast, exercises all the powers of the first beast before him.

The first five beasts, or empires, to oppress God's people are well known. They are the five great empires of history, the Egyptian, Babylonian, Persian, Greek and Roman empires. The prophecies of Daniel give us even more details concerning these beasts.

Daniel Chapter 2 tells us about King Nebuchadnezzar's heavenly dream of a great statue with a golden head, silver breast, brass belly, iron legs, and ten toes of iron and clay that will not mix together. When the prophet Daniel is called upon to interpret King Nebuchadnezzar's dream, he explains to the king that this statue represents his Babylonian kingdom and the four kingdoms that will follow it, which are in turn, the Persian, Greek, Roman, and Holy Roman empires. Note the metals that are used to represent these great empires, which reflect the Golden Age, Silver Age, Bronze Age and Iron Age. When we add the preceding empire of Egypt to this list, we now have the identity of the first six beasts of Bible prophecy.

Daniel Chapter 7 tells us about Daniel's dream of four beasts, a lion with wings, a bear raised up on one side, a leopard with four heads, and a terrible fourth beast with great iron teeth. This fourth beast in the last days gives rise to a little horn (antichrist), who plucks up three of the horns before him. A horn in prophecy is a general or the commander of an army.

The winged lion was the symbol of the great Babylonian Empire, the bear raised up on one side represented the Kingdom of Persia, the four-headed leopard was the great symbol of Greece, and finally, we have the appearance of the Roman Empire with its terrible weapons of iron.

Daniel Chapter 8 tells us about a dream that Daniel has, of a two horned ram that is overcome by a he-goat which fathers four kingdoms, one of which gives rise in the latter days to an antichrist. The angel Gabriel explains to Daniel that the ram represents the kingdom of Media-Persia and the he-goat represents the kingdom of Greece. We should note that the ram with one horn higher than the other compares to the bear of Daniel 7 with one side higher than the other, denoting the fact that the Persian Empire rose later than the Median Empire, but proved to be the more powerful of the two. Both these empires came together as one under the Persian emperor Cyrus. The four-horned he-goat also compares to the leopard with four wings of Daniel's first vision, representing the kingdom of ancient Greece led by the four generals of Alexander the Great.

We should note that the sixth empire, or "Holy" Roman Empire, was the result of an internal takeover of the Roman Empire by the forces of Christianity. This new empire, part Roman and part Christian, lasted for 1500 years and flowered in the 16th century with the Italian Renaissance, or "rebirth," of the Roman Empire. The Holy Roman Empire, by then called

Italy, eventually split up into ten pieces, five existing as independent Roman kingdoms, and five existing as provinces of the Church, thus forming the ten toes of iron and clay of King Nebuchadnezzar's dream, that would not mix together. The identities of the seventh and eighth beasts were not to be revealed until the last days.

These last two beasts, or antichrists, are discussed in great detail in Revelation Chapter 13. John's vision of these last two beasts was received while he was being held prisoner on the Greek Island of Patmos, in the Mediterranean Sea.

In a previous chapter, we explored the many details surrounding the identity of the seventh beast (first antichrist), or Napoleonic Empire, which conquered the Holy Roman Empire in the year 1806. These first seven beasts, or empires, were consecutive empires, and therefore quite easy to verify by following the record of history.

We should note however, that this seventh empire differed from those before it, in that it was the empire of a man instead of a nation. Daniel 7, Verse 8, tells us that this seventh kingdom has the eyes of a man, and a mouth speaking great things, marking it as the kingdom of an antichrist. This first antichrist is also described in great detail in Revelation Chapter 13. Napoleon's empire was unique in that it was the first time in history that one man was able to take complete control over both church and state and declare himself both religious and military ruler of the world.

Napoleon's identity was first revealed to the world by Tsar Alexander I of Russia. Tsar Alexander identified the Emperor as the first antichrist "Napollyon," leader of the biblical army of locusts, through various Bible references to him. When Napoleon decided to invade Russia in 1812, Tsar Alexander vowed never to allow Napoleon and his "army of locusts" to invade the Russian motherland. Alexander followed biblical instructions on how to defeat this antichrist and his locust army. Alexander burned everything in Napoleon's path. Tsar Alexander's locust-destroying tactics worked perfectly, and Napoleon's entire army of over a half million men was completely destroyed. It was therefore Tsar Alexander who single-handedly destroyed the first antichrist, and removed him from his European throne. If not for Alexander, the world would be a much different place today.

Alexander was the grandson of Catherine the Great, Queen of Russia, and Catherine was cousin to the Queen of England. Catherine therefore carried the royal bloodline of the House of David, seated on the thrones of Europe at the time. She passed on her royal inheritance to her grandson Alexander. It was therefore Alexander's prophetic destiny to defeat the first antichrist Napoleon. The Napoleonic Empire exactly fulfilled all the prophecies of Daniel and the book of Revelation concerning the seventh empire, or seventh beast to oppress God's people. The trail of history provides us with clear evidence of the first seven empires of the western world. But we still do not know the identity of the mysterious eighth empire, the empire of the second antichrist.

THE WORLD'S GREAT EMPIRES

1.	Egyptian Empire	3400 BC
2.	Babylonian Empire	650 BC
3.	Medo-Persia Empire	550 BC
4.	Greek Empire	330 BC
5.	Roman Empire	170 BC
6.	Holy Roman empire	313 AD
7.	Napoleonic Empire	1796 AD
8.	8th Beast?	Date?

After the fall of Napoleon's empire, Revelation 17, Verse 8 tells us that there is a period of time when there "is not" an empire. The antichrist spirit of Napoleon disappears for a time, but then reappears sometime in the future as the dreaded eighth beast.

This final eighth empire is that of the second antichrist, or eighth beast, the most evil of all the beasts. His empire appears near the time of the end, when there are terrible technologies available with which to wage war.

In the book of Revelation, the prophet John has great difficulty describing his visions of these marvels of modern technology that give this second antichrist the power to make fire come down out of the sky onto his enemies in faraway cities, and perform other miracles unheard of in John's time. We find a detailed description of this eighth beast (second antichrist), in the second half of Revelation Chapter 13.

A unique sentence in Rev. 13, Verse 10, neatly divides Revelation 13's descriptions of these two antichrists. As mentioned previously, the first half of this sentence describes only the fate of the first antichrist Napoleon, which was to die in captivity; and the second half of the sentence describes the fate of the second antichrist, or eighth beast. The second half of this sentence tells us that this eighth beast causes God's Hebrews to be killed with weapons, possibly on a massive scale, and that it is therefore this second antichrist's fate to also be killed by such a weapon. You may notice that the weapon mentioned is a sword, which was the soldier's weapon of John's time. But this weapon might be a gun if this second antichrist were to appear in the 20th century, or maybe even a phaser, if he were to appear in the 23rd century. In any case, the prophecy tells us that since he lives by the phaser, he dies by the phaser. And thus we know that this second antichrist causes

God's people to be killed with weapons, and that it is therefore his fate to also be killed by such a weapon.

The next verse of Revelation 13 tells us that this second antichrist does not rise up from the sea like the first beast before him, but instead rises out of the Earth. The principal landmass populated by God's people after the fall of the Napoleonic empire, was Europe. We can therefore surmise that this second antichrist, or eighth beast, rises out of the continent of Europe. John then tells us that this second antichrist has two heads, and two horns.

For those of you unacquainted with the rules of Bible prophecy, heads represent nations, and horns represent military leaders. This means that this eighth beast's empire consists of two nations led by two military leaders. John says that the two horns of this beast are like those of a lamb, symbolizing the fact that this antichrist represents himself as a messiah, coming to lead his promised people into a thousand years of peace. The prophecy then goes on to say that he speaks with the mouth of a dragon (Serpent), which means that he deceives his followers by tempting them with lies they will want to hear.

The next three verses were very confusing to ancient Bible scholars, because these early scribes had no understanding of the terrible technologies John was attempting to describe in these verses. The first technology this beast possessed, was the power to make fire come down out of the sky onto his enemies. This was John's attempt to describe the aerial bombs and rockets he saw in his vision, that were the product of technologies not understood in the second century AD. John next talks about seeing an image having the power of speech. An image, or idol, in Bible prophecy, is a creation, or invention, of the hands of man. John says that this invention has the power of speech, and that anyone refusing to listen to it, can be delivered up to the government and sent off to certain death. John also tells us that this second antichrist numbers the people who buy and sell in the marketplace, and that he places these numbers on their arms or heads.

The last thing John tells us is that this beast's number is 666, and that it is the number of a man. All numbers in prophecy have meanings; 777 for instance is God's number, 555 is the number of grace, 999 is the number of Judgment, and 666 is the number of sinful men. Every number has significance. Since this beast's number is 666, it is a man's number, and since it is repeated three times for emphasis, we know that we are dealing with a male antichrist. This is another reference to the fact that the seventh and eighth beasts, or empires, were not the empires of nations, but were instead the empires of men. Both the seventh and eighth empires carried this distinction, since each was led by a male antichrist.

Now let us list all the information we learned about this dreaded second antichrist who leads the eighth and final empire to oppress God's people.

1. We know that his empire is not a part of the unbroken chain of the world's first seven empires.

2. We know that his empire utilizes modern technologies with which to wage war.

3. We know that he deceives his followers by telling them that they are his chosen people and that he will lead them into a thousand years of peace.

4. We know that he causes God's Hebrews to be shot, possibly on a massive scale.

5.   We know that his ultimate destiny is to be killed by a gun or other hand-held weapon.

6.   We know that he rises out of the continent of Europe

7.   We know that his empire consists of two nations, led by two military leaders.

8.   We are told that he spreads his lies through a man-made device having the power of speech.

9.   We know that anyone refusing to listen to this invention may be carried off by the government to face certain death.

10. We know that he numbers the people who buy and sell in the marketplace by placing numbers on their arms or heads.

Have you figured out who this second antichrist is yet? If not, you might simply walk up to any stranger on the street and ask him to name the most evil man ever to walk the Earth. The answer you receive will often be the name of this infamous second antichrist.

History records for us the fact that it was Tsar Alexander I of Russia who identified the first antichrist. But what is not so very well known, is that Tsar Alexander was also aware of the identity of the second antichrist as well. When Alexander died, his coffin was supposedly placed in a tomb in Moscow. In 1926, a group of Russian revolutionaries opened Alexander's tomb in order to desecrate it. When these evil socialist revolutionaries invaded Alexander's tomb, they were met with a big surprise. His tomb was empty! You see, Alexander was aware of many events scheduled to occur in the future, and he knew of the coming of a second antichrist who would try to complete the work of the first antichrist before him. Alexander wanted to protect the Russian people from this eighth beast by leaving them the information they would need to defeat this most evil of all the beasts. The secret of what became of Tsar Alexander may provide us with another clue as to the identity of this last beast.

In a previous chapter we explored the works of the Reverend William Miller. Miller's work in deciphering the prophecies of Daniel centered on the date when "the transgressors are come to the full," or the date marking the end of the last beast of Revelation. This biblical reference, contained in Daniel Chapter 8, Verse 23, led Reverend Miller to believe that the date for the demise of this last beast was the year 1845. We also revealed that an error had occurred in the transcription of the King James version of the Holy Bible as it was being copied from the text of the Greek Septuagint. This error involved the number of years between Daniel's prophecy and the death of this last beast. The number quoted in our King James Bibles is 2300 years (Dan. 8:14), but the number quoted in the Vatican copy of the Greek Septuagint, from which our English Bibles were copied, is 2400 years. When corrected for this error, Miller's 1845 date for the death of this eighth beast, or second antichrist, becomes 1945, and that was indeed the date that marked the demise of Adolph Hitler and his Nazi Empire. Hitler's Nazi empire did in fact commit the last and greatest oppressions against the Hebrew people.

There are some very interesting facts that should also be taken into account concerning Adolph Hitler's empire if we are to determine its significance in prophecy. Not only did it come at the exact time predicted in Daniel's prophecy, but it also fulfilled the false Messiah prophecy of a man coming to lead his chosen people into a thousand-year empire. Hitler conducted his evil campaign under the sign of the cross. The famous Nazi Iron Cross was proudly worn by many German soldiers, and the crooked cross, or Nazi swastika (Hellas cross), became famous as the official emblem of the Nazi regime. The new messiah, Adolf Hitler, promised his loyal followers that he would lead them into a glorious thousand-year Reich, or empire.

Hitler's family tree is very important to the revelation of his biblical identity. Some of our earliest records trace Hitler's family history from his paternal grandmother, Maria Anna Shicklgruber, who worked as a housemaid for the Frankelbergers of Graz, Austria. Maria, who was unmarried, became pregnant while working for the Frankelbergers. Her illegitimate son, Alois, was destined to one day become Adolph Hitler's father. It may be possible therefore, that Hitler's paternal bloodline extends from the city of Graz. The Frankelbergers, a wealthy Jewish family, reportedly made regular payments to Maria for support of her son Aloise until his 15th birthday. Adolf Hitler long remembered his grandmother's plight, and in his Jewish Edict of many years later, he would include a law forbidding Jewish families from hiring German housemaids of less than 45 years of age.

Aloise Hitler's fourth child was born on April 20th, 1889 at approximately 6:30 PM in the small town of Braun am Inn in northwestern Austria, near the German border, in a building once used as a convent. As a child, young Adolph was sent to a religious school operated by Benedictine monks, and headed by an abbot named Theodoric Von Hagen. The Von Hagen family crest, a "hagenkreuz," or "hooked cross," was emblazoned everywhere on the walls of the monastery. Adolf dreamed of one day becoming an abbot himself, and adopted the hagenkreuz, or "swastika" as we now know it, as his personal symbol. This strange symbol was also identified as the "Hellenic Cross" by the German archeologist Heinrich Schlieman, who originally unearthed it in the remains of the ancient Hellenic city of Troy.

As a young man, Hitler lived in Bohemia, often associating with the rich Jews of that region. He admired their ability to make money and live an idealistic lifestyle. Hitler dreamed of one day becoming a great artist or architect himself, and designing great statues and tall buildings. Hitler's talents however, were not very impressive, and he failed miserably in these endeavors. Once, he briefly left Germany to visit his brother in Liverpool, England, but for the most part, Hitler spent nearly all of his life in either Germany or Austria.

When World War I broke out, Hitler joined the German army as a dispatcher, marking the beginning of his 27-year war with the world. He eventually worked his way into the German Workers Party as an undercover agent, and greatly enjoyed working as a political activist. Hitler was a liberal idealist, defending the rights of the common German worker, and dreaming of a greater destiny for Germany. Hitler eventually grew to hate all Jews and Catholics, and any others who rejected him. He blamed the Jews for manipulating the stock market and destroying the German economy. And with so many Germans now out of work, it was not very difficult for Hitler to find sympathy for his cause. Hitler was easily able to influence the common German worker with his dreams for a glorious rebirth of the German Republic.

All names have meanings, and they can reveal much about the people who carry them. The name Adolph Hitler (actually Heidler) in the German language, means "pagan wolf-leader"; and Hitler was indeed a clever leader of his Nazi pack of wolves. Hitler's headquarters in Poland was known as the "Wolf's Lair", and his eastern headquarters in the Russian Ukraine was nicknamed "Werewolf," The site of the KDF manufacturing plant for Hitler's "peoples' car" is "Wolfsburg," and Hitler's submarine "wolf packs" successfully terrorized the world's oceans for the entire Second World War.

Hitler carefully studied the empire of his predecessor Napoleon, and thought that perhaps Napoleon's blood even ran in his veins, since the Emperor had passed through that part of Austria a century earlier, and was known to entertain young German maidens in his tent each evening. Hitler thought it was his manifest destiny to complete Napoleon's task of creating a unified New World Order in order to enlighten modern society, and rid the world of the genetically inferior races. Hitler would succeed where Napoleon failed; he would successfully invade Russia in the winter. When Adolf Hitler was elected leader of the German people, the newspaper headlines read "ex-corporal leads 62,000,000 Germans," and so it seemed that the "little corporal" (Napoleon) had once again returned.

Hitler launched his Russian invasion on the same day as his predecessor Napoleon, but 129 years later, and followed Napoleon's exact route to Moscow. Hitler's Russian campaign was code-named Barbarossa (Red Beard), after the great German emperor Frederick Barbarossa, who'd once led Germany to greatness. Tsar Alexander however, was waiting for him. Alexander had not died and been buried in a tomb in

Moscow after all, but had instead become a hermetic recluse in the service of the Russian Orthodox Church. Alexander spent the last few years of his life in the service of God, and left careful instructions for Russian Church hierarchy on what to do when the inevitable invasion of the second antichrist finally came.

When Hitler launched his attack on Russia, the Russians were ready for him. Russian leaders instructed their people to destroy and burn everything in Hitler's path, exactly as they had done 129 years earlier when Napoleon had invaded. Every home, field and forest was set on fire, and every factory and power-generating dam was blown up or destroyed. Nothing was left for Hitler's "locust army" to use. This "scorched earth" policy worked perfectly for a second time, and Hitler's army was halted in its tracks due to severe shortages of food and supplies. The Russian front eventually proved to be Hitler's undoing. He'd squandered his military forces capturing over 500,000 square miles of Russian territory, and received absolutely nothing of value for his efforts.

The NAZI cause was now failing, and the allies, supplied by the United States with endless military equipment and supplies, were soon closing in on Berlin. By the end of April, the Russians were approaching Hitler's bunker in Berlin. Hitler had seen what happened to Mussolini in Italy, whose body was hung upside down on display for the Italians to spit on. He was determined that he and his mistress would not suffer a similar fate. When the Russians finally reached Hitler's bunker, they found a burned body lying near the bunker that looked like "der Fuhrer," but was in fact the torched body of Hitler's double that had been left for the Russians to find.

With God's help, Alexander was able to posthumously help defeat the second antichrist as well, and save the world from a second horrible fate. Daniel's prophecy for the time when "the transgressors are come to the full," described in Daniel 8, Verse 23, was fulfilled right on schedule in 1945, just as Reverend William Miller had predicted. The eighth and final beast met his biblical fate of being killed with a hand held weapon exactly as the apostle John had prophesied (Rev. 13:10). The world owes a great debt to Tsar Alexander, who saw to it that the era of the beasts was finally brought to an end.

The events foretold in the book of Revelation now seem to be slowly unfolding exactly as predicted within the pages of the Holy Scriptures. What new prophetic events are yet to take place, still remains a mystery. The intricate movement of the great timeclock of the universe however, still continues to tick away the minutes of man's brief time here on Earth.

CHAPTER 15

LYME DISEASE

The only laws that are truly just, are the laws of God and nature.

It seems that America has recently been bombarded with a rash of new diseases. These diseases have been popping up everywhere, threatening the health of many Americans and their families. Our medical professionals are often at a loss to explain where all these new diseases are coming from, and why they have appeared so suddenly.

Due to the many medical advances of recent years, most Americans now feel they've gained a great degree of control over their own personal health. This has unfortunately caused many of us to lose sight of the fact that the natural world around us is a complex system with intricate mechanisms for perpetuating its own existence. In this story we'll examine the origins of a modern-day disease that is still affecting the health of many Americans today.

In the late 1960's, an economic boom in the New York City area resulted in the sudden appearance of many new suburban communities in the nearby state of Connecticut. This occurred as urban commuters from New York City moved into this rural, farming state. These upper class New Yorkers had very little exposure to the agricultural lifestyle of the Connecticut locals. This sudden influx of New Yorkers brought with it many economic and social changes for Connecticut farmers and their natural ecosystem.

The farmers of Connecticut had always held full control over their state's natural environment. But as more and more New Yorkers moved in, many farms were forced to close down, and that control was ultimately lost. Native white-tailed deer populations soon began to increase dramatically in number, and the New Yorkers were treated to the sight of wild deer feeding in their backyards every morning. It was a novelty for them to have their city friends visit and see these wild deer feeding under the bird feeders. Many people also began to feed the deer in order to keep them coming close to their homes. It was soon a common sight to see deer feeding by the side of Connecticut's roadways.

Unfortunately, many of these deer suffered from distended abdomens, due to the large quantities of grass they were now forced to consume, because of a shortage of natural forest foods. Their wild food supplies were now being rapidly depleted, due to severe overpopulation and overgrazing by the large deer herd. Without farmers around to cull excess deer numbers, there was nothing to prevent Connecticut's deer herd from growing totally out of control.

By the mid-1970's, Connecticut Fish and Game officials, charged with the responsibility for managing deer populations, tried to encourage deer hunting in the state in a desperate attempt to reduce white-tail numbers. The liberal New Yorkers however, wanted nothing to do with deer hunting. The sight of a dead deer in the back of a pickup truck with its tongue hanging out, was more than most of them could stand. Connecticut wildlife officials soon found themselves under attack by groups of New York City animal rights supporters, who considered deer hunting to be cruel and inhumane.

Deer populations continued to expand, and soon, deer fences over 7 feet high had to be erected around most homes to prevent wild deer from devouring the shrubbery. Deer droppings on the forest floor were nearly ankle deep in many places. The health of Connecticut's deer herd began to decline rapidly as well-intentioned, but misinformed, New York City animal lovers attempted to impose their brand of logic upon God's natural world.

Then, in 1975, an unusual outbreak of "Juvenile Rheumatoid Arthritis" was recorded in the small town of Lyme, Connecticut. Local doctors documented over 50 cases of this debilitating disease in a small three-town area of the state. Since these cases were so unusually concentrated, public health officials decided to conduct an investigation to see if some common denominator could be found for the outbreak.

The first thing Connecticut medical officials noticed was that most of these cases seemed to be occurring in the summer when children were playing outside. They also noticed that many of the cases were occurring in homes located near wooded areas. When doctors ran tests on the children to screen them for a common bacterium, they uncovered an unidentified spirochete bacterium in all the test samples taken.

When the children's parents were questioned about any unusual symptoms that had occurred just prior to the appearance of the disease, they found that most of the children had exhibited a rash just before the onset of symptoms. Parents were then asked to bring their children in immediately if they exhibited such a rash. It was soon determined that in all cases the children had been bitten by a tick just prior to disease symptoms developing, and that a rash had formed in a bulls-eye pattern around the site of the tick bite. Apparently the children were being infected with this crippling disease by ticks. The specific tick identified as the culprit was the Eastern Deer Tick, a tick normally hosted by white-tailed deer.

Diseases have always been an important part of our natural environment. Their presence is necessary in order to restore order to the natural system if things begin to slide out of control. For instance, when animal populations are allowed to grow beyond the ability of the environment to support them, disease mechanisms will naturally activate in order to cull excess animal numbers, and thus restore balance to the system. Disease organisms have always been a vital part of our natural ecosystem. They only rear their ugly heads when their presence is necessary to correct an imbalance in that system. They therefore serve as a useful tool for maintaining balance and order within the natural environment.

The 1975 outbreak of "Juvenile Rheumatoid Arthritis" in Connecticut was a typical example of this natural process. The tick responsible for the outbreak of this disease in Lyme, Connecticut was Ixodes Scapularis, a tick commonly hosted by white-tailed deer. As white-tail populations were allowed to grow out of control in southwestern Connecticut, nature's population control mechanisms were naturally activated to bring a plague upon the deer herd, and thus reduce its numbers. This plague was very efficiently spread throughout the herd by the common deer tick.

White-tailed deer have been native to Connecticut woodlands for centuries, and served as fine table fare for American colonists for over two centuries. They are still harvested for food today by modern deer hunters, although not in sufficient numbers. The early New England colonists obeyed the biblical instruction that animals with cloven hooves and chewing the cud were good for food (Lev.11:3).

Unfortunately, some of these early colonists were also guilty of abusing God's natural system. In the 19th century, greedy upper-class American land speculators encouraged New

England farmers to clear almost every acre of land in New England in order to sell the land for profit to immigrants pouring in from Europe. At one time in the 1800's, it was possible to travel all the way from Boston to New York City without ever encountering a decent patch of woods. The infinite, and uninterrupted pattern of stone walls that still covers New England today, stands in stark testimony to this massive deforestation of the New England landscape by people more respectful of personal profit than of the natural environment. These rich business tycoons left almost no natural habitat to support wild creatures, and as a result, many native birds, plants, and animals were all but eliminated from the New England ecosystem.

It wasn't until the early 1900's, when farming was replaced by industry, that our woodlands began to recover from this terrible deforestation. White-tail deer suffered massive destruction of their habitat in the 18th and 19th centuries, and now are suffering once again due to the meddling of New York City animal lovers possessing university degrees, but very little common sense. Man it seems, is still blind to the intricate workings of God's natural universe, and still continues to attempt to impose his will upon it. It is now estimated that a case of Lyme disease exists in every third household in some areas of suburban New York and New Jersey.

Animal rights supporters have suggested feeding the deer food laced with birth control pills, but that solution is a purely non-selective method of population control, and does not allow for survival of the smartest and fittest animals, as does the more natural solution of predation. Some have also suggested re-introducing the gray wolf to the Northeast to control deer populations, but the western gray wolf (first discovered by explorers Lewis and Clark) was never native to the Northeast.

Its larger cousin, the eastern (red) wolf, was a wolf that terrorized America's early colonists, because it much preferred to devour children and domestic animals, as they were much tastier, and easier to catch.

As an example, in the year 1782 in the small town of Shelburne, New Hampshire, Mr. Hope Austin dropped off a hitchhiker named John Peter at a familiar fork in the road. But when John Peter failed to show up at his next destination, the townsfolk conducted an extended search for him, and finally located his remains.

John Peter's bloodied clothing and bones, along with the carcasses of seven large dead wolves, were all that remained to attest to a grisly event. John Peter had put up a good fight, but was ultimately overcome and eaten by a large pack of hungry eastern red wolves. Wolf packs are driven by hunger, and during times of short natural food supply, will not hesitate to hunt down and eat humans. The most recent incident of a pack of wolves devouring a human occurred in Saskatchewan, Canada on November 8th, 2005.

Most animal lovers consider the predation of the modern hunter to be cruel and inhumane. But I wish they could experience the agonizing screams of a young deer fawn having its intestines ripped out by a pack of coy dogs while it's still alive and its mother looks on helplessly from a few yards away. They would then have something to compare to the more responsible predation of the deer hunter, who kills quickly and cleanly with his gun, taking reasonable care that animals do not suffer unduly in the process. Hunters by the way, do not kill deer fawns.

The animal lovers of New York City, through their bold and irresponsible actions, have now brought a terrible disease upon themselves and also upon the deer they originally sought to protect. The modern plague of "Lyme Disease" is now spreading across America, causing untold suffering for thousands of humans and animals alike. This degenerative, crippling disease slowly damages the body's organs over time, resulting in slow suffering and premature death for many of its victims. This disease is from the family of spirochetes, like syphilis and leptospirosis, that have the ability to linger undetected for long periods of time in the human body. There are now over 17,000 new cases of Lyme Disease being reported in humans every year in the United States.

Man has a long history of attempting to impose his will upon God's natural order, and in every case has paid a terrible price for his meddling.

CHAPTER 16

THE GREAT SOCIETY

'The Vietcong are going to collapse within weeks. Not months, but weeks!"

W. Rostow, 1965, US National Security Advisor

The above statement, made by President Lyndon Johnson's National Security Advisor in 1965, was the supreme example of an idealistic and unrealistic assessment of a decade-long war, that would ultimately result in the United States of America being unpleasantly introduced to the disappointing realities of world politics.

The preceding decade of the 1950's had ushered in an era of technological advancement and economic growth not previously experienced at any other time in American history. The "happy days" of the 1950's had produced a wave of exuberant optimism and confidence in the future of the nation. The old-fashioned "ice box" was now giving way to the modern electric refrigerator, and television sets were rapidly invading America's homes. The nation was experiencing a few of the many miracles of modern technology that would eventually completely revolutionize the American culture.

Inventions such as automatic clothes washers, pop-up toasters, and countless other modern time-saving household devices were now freeing up mom from the drudgery of her everyday household chores. America was growing ever more confident in the ability of technology to solve the problems of human society, and it genuinely seemed as if nothing was beyond our grasp.

The newly invented portable transistor radio was keeping modern Americans in constant touch with the outside world, and an era of mass communication was slowly being ushered in, as modern technology was creating a social revolution in America.

In 1951, pediatrician Dr. Benjamin Spock had published his famous "Baby Book," introducing America's parents to the exciting new field of Child Psychology. It would now no longer be necessary for Americans to follow the biblical instructions of "spare the rod and spoil the child," as modern psychology offered a more progressive and intelligent alternative. Dr. Spock's book on child rearing would soon outsell every other book in print except the Bible, and would continue to hold this position for the following half century.

In 1953, technology scored another first, as Dr. Jonas Salk released his famous Polio vaccine. Salk's new vaccine quickly eradicated this terrible debilitating disease that had struck down more than 50,000 Americans the previous year. Polio had left thousands crippled, and more than 3,000 dead. America would no longer need to rely upon God to heal the sick, it now had modern vaccines, antibiotics, and countless other medical miracles with which to treat and cure illness, and all these things were the product of modern technology. Disease itself promised to soon become a thing of the past.

America was also ready for drastic changes in its national leadership. The long, unbroken chain of White, Anglo-Saxon Protestant (WASP) presidents who'd ruled the White House for nearly two centuries, was about to be broken. For the first time in American history, a member of the Roman Catholic faith had a realistic chance of becoming President of the United

States. He was a young, dynamic Irish Catholic senator from Boston named John F. Kennedy.

This young man from Massachusetts was exactly what the liberal Democrats in Washington were waiting for. Kennedy was the son of a ruthlessly ambitious father who'd worked his way up through the Boston Irish community and, courtesy of Democratic President Franklin D. Roosevelt, finally arrived in the world of international politics. The young JFK was an enthusiastic supporter of new, liberal changes in American government.

To have any real chance of winning the election however, Kennedy would need to select a running mate from America's South in order to attract the more conservative southern voter, and so he chose a former Texas schoolteacher by the name of Lyndon Baines Johnson to be his running mate.

John F. Kennedy was indeed young and idealistic, but his charm and humor greatly pleased many of America's younger voters, and Kennedy was ultimately successful in his 1960 presidential bid. His victory was boosted by the rather vain antics of his Republican opponent Richard M. Nixon, and also by a clever marketing campaign financed with dad's money.

John F. Kennedy entered the U.S. presidency with an attitude of extreme idealism, but he unfortunately lacked the real world experience necessary to address the hard political realities of that office. One of his first official acts was to approve an invasion of the island of Cuba by a group of young and enthusiastic Cuban exiles, who'd been trained by America's CIA to invade the island nation and reclaim it from its new dictator Fidel Castro.

Unfortunately for Mr. Kennedy however, his "Bay of Pigs" invasion ended in complete disaster, as Castro quickly overwhelmed the invaders, humiliating the Kennedy administration, and giving the Russians a unique opportunity to establish new relations with the island nation.

President Kennedy then proceeded to attack many other national and international issues with the same wild abandon that had marked his Bay of Pigs fiasco. The Kennedy administration quickly created many enemies for itself with its Don Quixote style attacks on everyone from organized crime to southern white extremists.

FBI Director J Edgar Hoover was not very impressed with this new young president, and in fact considered him to be a stain upon the American presidency. Hoover began to have Kennedy followed in order to document and expose his many loose moral habits, and illicit sexual liaisons.

The Kennedy years would spark a complete social and moral revolution in America, as many Americans swept away the religious taboos of the past in favor of a more "progressive" society based upon principals of "free love" and "humanism". The many religious based Puritanical laws of the past were soon ignored, as lawyers anxiously sought to rewrite the archaic "blue laws," that allowed such practices as closing businesses on Sundays, and prayer in public schools.

In 1961, the Kennedy administration was surprised to discover that the Russians were installing medium-range nuclear missiles on the island of Cuba. This action sparked one of the most dangerous nuclear confrontations in world history, as Russia's premier Nikita Khrushchev mistakenly assumed that Kennedy's response to his actions would be purely political. But the young Kennedy's bold and courageous actions during the Cuban Missile Crisis caught Khrushchev completely off guard. The Russians ended up embarrassed and humiliated, thereby adding one more powerful enemy to the list of Kennedy foes.

When President Kennedy decided to travel to Dallas, Texas in 1963, he sent Ambassador Adlai Stevenson on ahead as his advance man. Angry southern white extremists spat upon Stevenson to make their views crystal clear on Kennedy's upcoming visit.

On November 22, 1963, while President Kennedy was riding in a parade through Dallas in an open limousine, he was shot and killed by assassin Lee Harvey Oswald.

The sudden death of President Kennedy left a huge void in the hopes of America's liberal elite. This void however, was quickly filled by the next person in line for the presidency, Vice President, Lyndon Johnson.

Lyndon Baines Johnson was a former Texas high school teacher, and truly represented the world of liberal academia. Johnson received his Bachelor of Arts degree from Southwest Texas State Teachers College, and always dreamed of changing the world. Johnson eventually decided to enter the world of politics, and ambitiously supported President Roosevelt's New Deal. Johnson was soon appointed head of the Texas National Youth Administration where he was now able to influence the curriculum taught in Texas schools.

When WWII began, Johnson knew he would need military experience to advance himself in politics after the war, and so he joined the Navy, but was given non-combat duty. He then asked his good friend James Forrestal for a combat mission and was assigned to act as an observer for General MacArthur on a bombing mission to New Guinea. Johnson said his aircraft came under fire and was forced to turn back, and so he received the Silver Star for his mission. A later examination of flight records however, would show that the plane turned back not because it came under fire, but because of generator trouble, and also that Johnson was the only person on board the plane to receive a decoration.

Lyndon Johnson first began his attack on Christian America in 1954 with passage of the so-called "Johnson Amendment," which prohibits religious leaders from having a voice in matters of American politics. This first political act however, would represent only the beginning of Johnson's ongoing campaign to change the American way of life.

On November 22, 1963, Vice President Lyndon Baines Johnson was suddenly catapulted into the most powerful position on the face of the earth. The death of JFK would finally give Johnson the opportunity he needed to pursue his dream of changing American society. In the following year's election, Johnson would garner the largest plurality of any president in American history, as liberals now realized their ultimate dream of a true liberal idealist occupying the Oval Office. Johnson's ideology mirrored that of America's liberal elite, reflecting the purest hopes and aspirations of attaining world peace through the universal application of science and education. It now seemed possible that America could finally be molded into the perfect human society.

On July 30th, 1964, President Johnson signed into law the sweeping new 1964 Medicare Act, setting up the first government sponsored healthcare insurance program in American history, providing healthcare insurance for all Americans age 65 or older. Johnson funded his new social programs by initiating new payroll deductions from worker's paychecks and removing the silver from America's coinage. Johnson's new program would eventually be expanded to include a free new Medicaid healthcare program and Food Stamp subsidies, marking the beginning of what would later be dubbed the "Welfare State." The Johnson administration was quickly chastised by America's economists however, when the following year New York City's welfare rolls swelled to over 480,000 people, as the poor signed up for welfare benefits now made available to them through Johnson's new government programs.

Then, on August 20th, 1964, as part of his newly announced "War on Poverty," Johnson signed into law the Economic Opportunities Act, creating a new Office of Economic Opportunity, and assigned Kennedy's brother-in-law, R. Sargent Shriver to the task of coordinating the Job Corps, the Neighborhood Youth Corps. VISTA Volunteers and Head Start, in a national attempt to improve the education and health of America's poor.

President Johnson, being a former schoolteacher, realized that in order to fully achieve the goals of his new "Great Society," he would need to influence the thinking of all future Americans. He therefore decided it was time to replace the "outdated" conservative curriculum taught in America's schools with a new, more liberal, and gender sensitive curriculum from new sources in California. He also gave liberal schoolteachers much greater control over what could be taught in America's classrooms. The authority of local school boards was now usurped by the Federal government, as Johnson passed his new Elementary and Secondary Education Act of 1965.

Books labeled "Modern" Math and "Modern" Science soon began to appear in America's schools. The old tried-and-true textbooks relied upon by America's schools for decades, quickly became a thing of the past. There were now newer and more "progressive" theories on how to educate America's schoolchildren. An educational revolution was now underway.

On the larger international scene, communist revolutionaries from North Vietnam were attempting to infiltrate South Vietnam, and unseat the American-supported capitalist South Vietnamese government. President Kennedy had originally sent in U.S. ground advisors to aid the South Vietnamese in fighting off the communists, but the conflict was not going very well, and the North Vietnamese were now attacking U.S. ground personnel, and also American naval vessels on the high seas. President Johnson therefore decided to order U.S. forces to attack the communist aggressors in the North, and the Vietnam War was officially on.

The following year witnessed an alarming increase in the Vietnam conflict that could only be addressed by an even greater involvement of U.S. ground troops. By the middle of 1965, 125,000 U.S. troops had been ordered to South Vietnam, and the U.S. military draft had to be re-activated. The draft resulted in the largest increase in enrollment in U.S. colleges in more than a century, as America's liberal elite sent their children off to college in order to avoid their being drafted into the Army.

President Johnson's rather idealistic attitude on the Vietnam conflict was also reflected in the views of many of the members of his Democratic cabinet, who were assuring him that this war would be over in just a matter of weeks. But as in the U.S. "Bay of Pigs" invasion, things did not go very well in the field, and the conflict continued to expand.

On the home front, the U.S. Civil Rights movement was also beginning to cause some serious problems for President Johnson. Black Muslim militants had assassinated the moderate black leader Malcom X, as he was preparing to make a speech about the need for blacks and whites to peacefully co-exist in the U.S. This Black Muslim movement was rapidly gaining in popularity, as blacks now concluded that Islamic style militarism was their best choice for affecting change in American society.

On August 12, 1965, the Watts section of Los Angeles erupted in mass rioting by over 10,000 blacks, who burned down 500 city blocks, and destroyed nearly 40 million dollars worth of property. This was soon followed by similar rioting and destruction in many other major U.S. cities The great Dr. Martin Luther King quickly expressed his disdain at this movement away from Christianity and toward Black Muslim militancy.

In the public services arena, electric utility companies in the Northeast had formed themselves into a massive cooperative electric power grid, stretching from southern Ontario to New York City, over which they intended to share the distribution of electricity in the Northeastern U.S. This plan was approved by the U.S. government and was intended to lend stability to electric utilities that had previously suffered from periodic power shortages and blackouts. Utilities could now temporarily borrow power from each other during times of excess electrical demand.

Government oversight of the project however, had been typically shortsighted, and on November 9th, 1965, a circuit breaker failed in Ontario, Canada, causing a chain reaction that resulted in the largest electric power blackout in all of U.S. history. This event exposed a huge security breach that was overlooked by government regulators, and now left the United States vulnerable to acts of sabotage by its many enemies.

On the domestic front, America's leaders in the new Women's Rights Movement, had also decided to take advantage of this new liberal trend in U.S. politics by launching a campaign of their own. The previous year, topless bathing suits had been introduced on many of America's beaches, as women now began to "burn their bras" in protest of the traditional role of women in American society.

In 1966, the Marxist raised Ms. Betty Friedan founded the National Organization for Women (NOW) to affect new political and social change in the structure of the American family, thus carrying out Khrushchev's famous prophecy that Russian Marxists "do not have to invade the United States, we will destroy you from within." The modern American woman would now exit her home and enter the workplace, demand total equality in her marriage, and no longer promise to love, honor and "obey" her husband. Her youngest children would now be dropped off at the local daycare center (a Soviet style day-care nursery), and her older children would come home after school to their now locked and unoccupied house.

The Johnson administration was also a firm supporter of social diversity. Johnson was the first president in history to be sworn in by a woman, and he would later appoint his friend Abe Fortas, the son of orthodox Jews, and Thurgood Marshall, a black, to positions on the U.S. Supreme Court. Marshall was the first black man to serve on the Supreme Court. Johnson's friend Abe Fortas however, would later be pressured into resigning his position on the Supreme Court as a result of an ethics investigation.

Eventually, some of the liberal ideals of President Johnson's "Great Society," would begin to unravel, as the idealistic plans of America's academic elite would crumble in the face of many harsh realities.

All that extra time that mom had gained from the use of those modern time-saving household appliances, was soon replaced by a 40 hour-a-week job, as Betty Friedan's women's liberation had now sent American housewives into the workplace to help support their families. Many of America's largest corporations were overjoyed at now being able to extract 80 hours of labor each week from the average American family, and quickly adjusted wages accordingly.

And the famous "Baby Book" written by Dr Benjamin Spock, had not produced a generation of well-adjusted young adults after all, but had instead produced a host of new problems for America's youth. Juvenile gangs soon began to take over many of America's major cities and crime was on the increase. The twin problems of teen pregnancy and teen alcohol abuse were now raging totally out of control. With mom now off at work, the American family slowly and inexorably began to dissolve, as witnessed by the sudden appearance of "latchkey" children, and a rapid rise in divorce rates. Even Dr. Spock, considered to be such an expert in solving complex problems in human relationships, was unable to resolve the problems in his own marriage, and ended up divorced. America's dysfunctional youth would soon begin to fill up American prisons. By 2005, the U.S. would have 10 times as many of its citizens in prison as it did in 1960, and would now incarcerate a larger percentage of its population than any other nation on Earth.

The promise of modern medicine to eliminate all disease from society had also not developed exactly as planned. Those new, powerful, antibiotics that had originally been shown to be so effective in the treatment of disease, were now actually being shown to make disease organisms stronger and more resistant to treatment. Apparently the very short life cycles of these tiny microbes, allowed them to quickly develop immunities to the modern antibiotics being used against them. In fact, these modern antibiotics were now producing "super bugs," against which doctors had few defenses. America's chemical manufacturers responded quickly by substituting new and more powerful drugs to react to the crisis, but many of these new drugs produced side effects even more dangerous than the diseases they were designed to treat.

The ongoing conflict in Vietnam was also not going very well. The Vietnam War was poorly managed due to constant interference from liberal politicians in Washington DC, who were now dictating field tactics to army generals. Army officers were now being told what targets they could and could not attack, based purely upon political considerations.

Modern technologically advanced bomb guidance systems allowed the precision bombing of exclusively military targets, thereby avoiding residential areas. The citizens of North Vietnam therefore did not have to worry about having their homes destroyed or their personal lives unduly disrupted by the war. They thus had little reason to change their minds about the form of government they'd chosen to live under. Military supplies were coming in from outside sources anyway, and so the U.S. bombings were having very little effect on the ability of North Vietnam to wage war. The Vietnamese conflict eventually witnessed American soldiers fleeing in panic from the southern city of Saigon, as an embarrassed United States of America lost its war with the tiny Asian nation of North Vietnam.

And as for America's educational system, the liberal changes introduced in the 1960's had also failed to produce the desired results. Students' academic scores began a long and slow negative slide, whose effects are still being felt today. In 2003, the Organization for Economic Cooperation and Development released the initial results of a study by the Programme for International Assessment, that ranked 15 year-olds in 29 modern industrialized nations in the areas of mathematics literacy and problem solving. Their survey concluded that the United States now ranked 24th on a list of 29 industrial countries in mathematics literacy. America's schools were now rated at the bottom of a list that they had once been at the top of.

Up until the 1960's, the history of the United States of America had documented nearly two centuries of unbroken economic and technological successes. These achievements had improved the quality of life for millions of people all around the world in nations whose economies were dependent upon our own. The socialist changes introduced in 1960 had unfortunately ended the control of local governments over their own affairs, and effectively destroyed the strength and Christian values of the American family.

If we were to closely examine the history of the many societies of the past, we would find a similar pattern in their successes that ultimately led to their demise. The greatest enemy to human society seems to be human nature itself. We humans are most content when we are working our way up the ladder of success. When we do finally arrive on the top rung of the ladder, we invariably assume that our position was achieved through some inborn superior qualities of our own. We then proceed to overindulge ourselves in food and drink, occupy our free time with carnal pleasures, and instruct others on how they should follow our lead; all the time ignoring the fact that our "superior society" is presently crumbling under our feet.

Nowhere is this phenomenon more observable than in modern-day America. It seems that material wealth still has the power to corrupt the human soul. Our economic wealth has allowed us to isolate ourselves from the realities that the rest of the world must face. This isolation robs us of the ability to deal effectively with life's harsh realities. As we drift into a state of apathetic isolation, we concentrate only upon momentary pleasures, and ignore the plight of others around us

Like the ancient Mycenians on the doomed island of Stronghyli, we flock into our gambling houses, relax in our hot tubs, and sink into apathetic isolation, totally unaware of the horrible fate that is about to consume us. There may yet be some truth to the statement that "those who fail to study history, may find themselves doomed to repeat it."

CHAPTER 17

DISEASE

'Tis ignorance that stalks the halls
of universities,
As mankind fails to understand
God's purpose for disease.

What is disease and where does it come from? For thousands of years man has been attempting to solve the complex riddle of disease. Disease has always been a hidden enemy that strikes without warning, wreaking havoc on our everyday lives. For almost all of man's civilized existence on Earth, the underlying cause of disease remained a complete mystery. It was not until the latter part of the nineteenth century that a French chemist named Louis Pasteur finally revealed to us the long-hidden world of the microbe. Pasteur discovered that diseases were caused by tiny living organisms, too small to be seen by the naked eye.

By the time of Pasteur's famous discovery, the world's diseases had already killed or maimed more human beings than all the wars in history. Throughout the entire period of the European Crusades, more Crusaders lost their lives to disease than to battle. When the Christian Crusaders left Europe's pristine forests to venture into the hot, dry climate of the Middle Eastern deserts, they were quickly overwhelmed by the many deadly diseases residing in the polluted water wells of that region. It seems that man has always been helpless to defend himself against the ravages of disease.

For centuries, the world's largest cities were a breeding ground for all sorts of terrible diseases. In the 14th century, the infamous bubonic plague wiped out nearly one quarter of the population of Europe. In most cities, the plague claimed the lives of nearly 70 percent of its victims. This was mainly due to the fact that city dwellers were already weakened due to poor diet and nutrition, and repeated attacks of cholera. No one could explain why the plague seemed to be confined mostly to cities, and particularly to the poorest areas of those cities.

Europe's large cities drew many people from the surrounding countryside with the promise of instant riches. Those who ventured into these cities however, usually found themselves living in the filth of the slums, where clean water and proper sanitation were practically non-existent. Most large cities lacked adequate provisions for clean drinking water and the sanitary disposal of sewage. Rats quickly overran slum areas, feeding off the refuse of human society. When rats overpopulated an area, nature's natural population control mechanisms were soon activated to bring a plague upon the rat population, thus reducing its numbers.

Rat plague, also known as bubonic plague, was efficiently spread throughout the rat population by a tiny flea whose technical name was Xenopsylla Cheopis. This tiny flea could also transfer the plague to humans. During the 14th century, the bubonic plague killed almost 25 million European citizens. The First World War by comparison, accounted for only 9 million deaths.

The infamous bubonic plague first appeared in northern China, then crossed into Europe through the city of Constantinople in the year 1333. The disease attacked the lymph system, causing large black and blue marks, or "bubos" to appear under the armpits of its victims. This condition gave rise to the popular term "boo-boo," still used today to describe a black and blue spot.

The plague normally appeared in one of two forms, rat plague and mouse plague. Rat plague, also known as bubonic plague, attacked the lymph system, and mouse plague, or pneumonic plague, attacked the lungs. Both forms of this disease were caused by rodents, but bubonic plague generally entered its victim's bloodstream through the bite of a rat flea. Pneumonic plague on the other hand, was usually inhaled into the lungs while the victim was sweeping a floor covered with mouse droppings, or sometimes it was contracted from the cough or sneeze of another infected person.

Pneumonic plague was the deadlier of the two varieties and could kill within 24 hours of the onset of symptoms. It still occurs in the U.S. today in the Desert Southwest, where it is now sometimes called "Hanta" virus. Pneumonic plague appears wherever mice have been allowed to overrun an area, and the disease kills so quickly that there is not enough time for modern antibiotic treatments to take effect.

It was most likely that this pneumonic form of the disease was responsible for the 1665 plague of London. Pneumonic plague was also known as the "Black Death" because the bodies of its victims turned blue from lack of oxygen. The London plague gave rise to the popular children's song "Ring Around the Rosie." The line "achoo, achoo, all fall down" refers to the fact that anyone exhibiting the deadly cough or wheeze of the pneumonic plague was destined to fall down dead within a day. The great Fire of London that occurred in 1666 combatted the plague by reducing the rodent population.

The bubonic plague still survives today in many parts of Asia, Africa and the Americas. It also still occasionally occurs within the United States. About a dozen or so cases of the plague are reported each year in the continental US. These cases do not come from overseas, but occur quite naturally right here in our own nation, in areas where sanitary conditions have been allowed to slip, and rodents allowed to become too numerous.

We are sometimes told that these deadly diseases arrived here from some distant country, but this is often not the case. We experience many incidents of rare and deadly diseases occurring spontaneously, right here in the United States every year. We were told in 1999 that West Nile Virus arrived in the United States from Africa, but this type of encephalitis is actually quite common here in the U.S. Many cases of infectious deadly encephalitis occur every year within our nation's borders.

West Nile Virus is known to be hosted by aquatic birds, and can become epidemic in locations where waterfowl populations have been allowed to proliferate. When this type of encephalitis is diagnosed in America's lower Midwest, it's called "St. Louis Encephalitis," and cases occurring in the upper Midwest are labeled "La Crosse Encephalitis." If a case is found in the northeastern United States, it is generally diagnosed as "Eastern Equine Encephalitis." The reason that this eastern strain received its unusual "equine" label was due to the fact that state laboratories in the Northeast closely monitor the horse racing industry, regularly testing the blood and urine of racehorses to screen them for illegal drugs. When a few expensive racehorses in the northeastern U.S. died unexpectedly of encephalitis, the disease was given the name Eastern Equine Encephalitis. Believe it or not, these American strains of encephalitis can often be deadlier than the African strains.

When the first few samples of West Nile Virus in New York City were sent off to national laboratories for testing, they came back testing positive as Eastern Equine Encephalitis. Routine laboratory diagnoses are often inaccurate. Nationally, we have experienced many situations where sick patients at various hospitals were diagnosed with a confusing variety of serious illnesses, only to find out later that all these victims had attended the same business conference, and were actually all victims of a mass food poisoning incident. Medicine unfortunately, is not an exact science.

In 1880, Louis Pasteur's revolutionary discovery of the microbe caused the medical profession to reject the previous religious concept of the "spontaneous generation" of disease. It was the 19th century, and that knowledge stolen by Eve so long ago was finally beginning to bear fruit. The miracles of God were slowly being replaced by the miracles of science.

It was never Louis Pasteur's intent to destroy this "spontaneous creation" theory; he merely wished to further clarify it. Pasteur demonstrated that diseases do spontaneously appear in response to the sudden creation of conditions conducive to their growth. Pasteur taught that disease organisms naturally existed everywhere within our environment, and that there were reasons why they would suddenly begin to breed out of control. Pasteur showed that disease was caused by large quantities of microbes infecting a host animal, and establishing living colonies within the body of that host.

Pasteur's discovery allowed 19th century doctors to make significant improvements in the control and treatment of many diseases. Doctors soon began to associate poor sanitation with the development and spread of disease. Government officials were then charged with the responsibility of isolating disease outbreaks and preventing their spread.

Many diseases were eventually controlled through the use of improved sanitation, medical quarantine, and the use of antibiotic drugs and chemicals. Recently however, some diseases we thought we had eliminated, have staged an amazing comeback. It seems that disease organisms possess the unique ability to develop resistance to the drugs and chemicals we use against them.

Due to their extremely short life cycles, disease organisms are able to rapidly adapt to radical changes in their environment. When a disease is treated with an antibiotic for instance, many disease organisms are immediately killed off; but a few always manage to survive. These survivors quickly pass on their genetic drug resistance to their offspring, thereby creating new, drug-resistant, strains.

The dreaded disease tuberculosis is presently staging an amazing comeback in America's prisons. This disease, caused by inadequate ventilation in overcrowded buildings, had been the scourge of the 19th century. Tuberculosis strains that are now appearing have proven highly resistant to the antibiotics we once successfully used to control them. Drug-resistant strains of many other diseases are now frustrating the best efforts of our medical professionals to control them. Many former "miracle drugs" have now been rendered almost completely useless in the treatment of certain diseases, and in fact only serve to make the disease organisms stronger.

This situation occurred because our medical professionals failed to recognize the true nature of disease itself. In the natural world, disease organisms serve a very useful function. When animal populations begin to grow out of control, it is disease that steps in to correct the situation. Disease organisms kill off excess animal numbers, thereby helping to restore the balance between animal populations and their supportive environment. Disease thus serves as an important tool to help maintain order and balance within God's natural system. As animal populations are allowed to increase in numbers, the opportunity for disease increases proportionately.

Diseases have sometimes also been known to jump the species barrier and infect other animal species. In today's world, our medical professionals often have to deal with these zoonotic diseases that jump the species barrier in this manner. Tularemia, or "rabbit fever" for instance, can jump the species barrier and infect people who handle the remains of diseased rabbits, or who mow lawns containing infected rabbit droppings.

When any disease strikes, it initially kills off many members of the particular species it attacks. At first glance, this appears to be a horrible disaster, but in the long run the disease brings that animal species back into balance with its supportive environment. Disease therefore, is not always an enemy, but often acts as a friend by maintaining this balance within the natural system. Diseases can easily be avoided by obeying the laws of God's natural order. We can illustrate this with a hypothetical situation.

If we were to send a group of people into the Rocky Mountains to live in a community that is completely isolated from the outside world, we should normally expect them to remain relatively healthy and disease free. There would be no reason for us to expect them to contract diseases from other humans, due to their extreme isolation.

If however, these people suddenly decided to dig a new drinking water well too close to their septic system, it is likely that an epidemic of cholera would soon ensue. The cholera would not come from any outside source; it would instead be generated quite naturally, in response to the sudden creation of conditions conducive to its growth. Cholera, like any other organism, merely responds to changes in its environment. In other words, the cholera appears as soon as the conditions suitable to its growth appear. Disease organisms are always activated whenever conditions conducive to their growth are suddenly created.

Many times in history, man has unwittingly created the conditions suitable for the growth of deadly microbes. In the mid-1800's for instance, cholera was a common disease in the city of London, England. A British physician named John Snow decided to examine the pathology of this deadly disease.

Snow was a London anesthesiologist who had a talent for gathering and studying information. He began to keep detailed documentation on all the cholera cases reported in London by the many physicians he worked with. When Snow examined the data he'd collected, he was surprised to find that most of the cholera cases were confined to very specific areas of the city.

Snow laid out a map of London and marked the locations of cholera outbreaks on the map. To his surprise, he found that the cholera cases were distributed over the city in the exact same pattern as the public drinking water supply. Sections of the city that received their drinking water from the Thames River for instance, would all suffer cholera outbreaks at the same time; and when a case appeared in a section of the city served by a public well, everybody using that well would soon develop cholera.

The medical community was already aware of the fact that cholera could be transmitted from person to person through contaminated food and clothing, but this water-borne link had never been previously demonstrated.

Snow soon determined that London's drinking water intakes on the Thames River were located too close to the sea. Due to the influence of ocean tides, the river water flowed backwards twice each day, often allowing raw sewage dumped into the river downstream, to back up and be sucked into the city's clean drinking water intakes upstream.

Snow's pioneering work resulted in the Lambeth Company of London digging new sanitary water wells on the outskirts of London, and installing new piping into the city. Areas served by these new clean drinking water wells soon had their incidence of cholera reduced by over 90 percent when compared to the rest of the city. It was finally clearly demonstrated that the primary source of cholera in London was contaminated drinking water being drawn from the Thames River.

The work of medical pioneers like John Snow and Louis Pasteur did much to contribute to our understanding of the pathology of disease. In spite of their discoveries however, many of our modern medical professionals still fail to recognize the true nature of disease itself.

Since disease was always considered to be man's enemy, it was always man's ultimate goal to eliminate disease from the environment. This was a rather lofty goal, but many great strides were made in that direction. For a time it even seemed as if man might someday eradicate all disease from his environment.

But man's efforts to eliminate disease from the environment turned out to be no more successful than his efforts to eliminate insects from the environment. This was due to the fact that man failed to recognize disease as an essential and vital part of

God's natural order. Disease plays an important role in the complex system of checks and balances that sustains life on our planet. Disease is but one of many mechanisms that exist within nature for the purpose of controlling and correcting unnatural conditions and behaviors.

In reality, disease organisms are always present everywhere around us in the natural ecosystem, and only present themselves as disease when the delicate balance of that system is disturbed. Diseases will then naturally activate in order to restore order to the system.

Disease organisms are universal. Some of the world's deadliest diseases naturally occur right here in the United States every year, in spite of all our efforts to prevent them. In short, most disease epidemics are not merely accidental occurrences; but are instead the result of human ignorance of natural law.

It seems that humans still continue to bring disease upon themselves through their ignorance of the laws of nature. When we fail to observe the laws of God's delicately balanced natural order, we always pay a price for our ignorance. Science is only now just beginning to understand the true complexity of the universal system in which we all live.

CHAPTER 18

EDUCATION

"The schools in our area have come a long way since the one-room schoolhouse I attended as a child.. There are some who feel that our nation's schools and teachers need to be held more accountable.. I strongly oppose both a national curriculum – which could accompany a national test – and a federally unfunded mandate for testing that would be forced upon states."

Professor and Congressman, Ted Strickland

Should there be a strict school curriculum in the U.S.? And should schoolteachers be tested for competency? Would such a thing be fair? In this chapter we'll attempt to more closely examine the history of America's educational system, and review the many changes that have taken place in it over the past century or two.

America's early colonists were often educated in rural settings, utilizing textbooks read by candlelight after a long day's work. Their curriculum was a Bible-based curriculum, and designed to instill high moral character and high personal integrity within the soul of every American child. And indeed, in the American colonies it was not normally necessary to employ a written contract between Christians, for a man's word was his personal bond, and an oral contract was generally just as good as a written one.

The early settlers who first came to America's shores, did so to escape the corrupt social system in place in Europe that allowed the upper-classes to profit from the labors of the poor. The Bible had promised all free Christians that in the world of the future they would reap the fruits of their own labors. The colonists considered it necessary to instill within all future Americans those high moral values that would allow them to rise above the level of being the usurpers of the labor of others. Americans wanted their children to grow up to be farmers and tradesmen, not entertainers or salesmen. The educational system in the United States would therefore need to be a system of the highest quality, for the colonists knew that the standards of a society were always determined by the moral integrity of its future citizens. Courts and prisons were not necessary in a society where all citizens were of high character and obeyed the laws of God.

Many New England towns and villages eventually constructed one-room schoolhouses in which to educate their children, and hired local schoolteachers of high moral character to instruct the children in a single classroom environment made up of multiple grade levels, often numbering 35 or more students to a class. Every day, each class would begin with a prayer to the Almighty for spiritual guidance.

Modern educators would find it difficult to conceive of any education at all taking place in the primitive conditions that existed within colonial America's schools. Most one-room schoolhouses had no central heat, poor ventilation, and no modern lighting for overcast days. They utilized tattered textbooks, and were constantly running short of common school supplies like pencils and paper. Also, the children in these one-room schoolhouses were often underfed and overworked at home, and were required to perform many difficult manual chores both before and after their school day.

Our modern schools in contrast, are well ventilated and well lighted, and serve their students well balanced school lunches planned by licensed nutritionists. They also utilize modern textbooks, designed by top educational professionals from recognized universities, who are considered to be experts in their fields. The most difficult chore that many modern American schoolchildren must perform when they get home is to get out their computers and play a video game.

Small wonder then that the education received by today's schoolchildren is so superior to that received by the children educated in the one-room schoolhouses of the past.

This is the picture that modern parents receive when they question their local school officials about the quality of the education their children are receiving. But is this an accurate representation of the evolution of America's educational system over the years? Are we still instilling within our students the same high quality education they received more than a century ago?

When one examines the personal letters sent home by Civil War soldiers, and compares them to similar letters sent home by modern soldiers, one cannot help but be struck by the stark differences in the quality of the letter writing. Letters written by Civil War soldiers contain well-structured sentences that flow smoothly like the lines of a sonnet. They are nearly devoid of misspellings and grammatical errors, while similar letters written by modern soldiers are often littered with misspellings and mistakes of grammar. But how could that be, if the education of our modern soldiers is so superior to that of soldiers who fought during the Civil War? Could it have something to do with the quality of the education they received?

An examination of historical records reveals many significant changes taking place in America's educational system during the 20th century. Many of these changes were initiated during the 1960's under the administration of President Lyndon Baines Johnson, who was himself a former schoolteacher.

During the Johnson Administration, America's school curriculum was totally replaced by a more "progressive" curriculum from a new source in California. This was done as part of President Johnson's master plan for his so-called "Great Society".

Local school boards soon lost the ability to hire and fire teachers and determine school curriculum, and a federal program was instituted to place control of local school systems into the hands of the educators themselves. This program resulted in a gradual reduction in class size, and a slow but steady rise in teachers' salaries over many years. Pupil-to-teacher ratios soon began to shrink, as educators fought for more "individualized" instruction for students.

This trend has continued into present times, and it now takes two teachers to instruct the same number of students that were formerly instructed by one teacher in the 1950s. Teachers' salaries have also reached a level high above that of the average American wage earner. President Johnson's theory was that if educators were allowed more control over their own environment, the quality of America's educational system would improve.

So how can it be that the underpaid and overworked schoolteachers of the past were so able to impart such superior writing skills to their students? Exactly what were the qualifications required of these teachers who taught in America's one-room schoolhouses?

In order to better answer that question, we may want to take a look at a test that was required of teachers wishing to be certified to teach in the one-room schoolhouses of the 19th century. Since the one-room schoolhouses of the past employed only one teacher, it was necessary for that teacher to be proficient in nearly every subject, at all grade levels, in order to teach successfully in the crowded environment of the one-room New England schoolhouse.

Most modern schoolteachers would choke at the idea of being required to read, write, and interpret sheet music, but that was indeed a requirement for candidates wishing to be certified to teach in New Hampshire schools. It was considered necessary for all students to be educated in every area of social appreciation, in order to serve as responsible citizens in a free Christian society. Teachers were therefore required to be skilled in a wide variety of scholastic disciplines.

The following test was taken directly from the records of the New Hampshire Department of Education in the year 1896. This skills test was required of those wishing to be certified to teach in New Hampshire's public schools in the late 19th century. Below are the questions teachers were required to correctly answer:

ALGEBRA

1. Multiply $a^2 + b^2 + c^2 - ab - bc - ac$ by $a + b + c$.

2. Divide $4a^4x^2 - 4a^2x^4 + x^6 - a^6$ by $x^2 - a^2$.

3.   A man is now twice as old as his son. 15 years ago he was three times as old as his son. Find the present age of each.

4.   Resolve into factors the following:

(a) $x^4 + x^2 + 1$ (b) $x^2 + 2x - 15$

(c) $14x^2 - 11x - 15$ (d) $a^3 + 64$

5.   A cistern can be filled by two pipes in 25 and 30 minutes respectively, and emptied by a third pipe in 20 minutes. In what amount of time will the cistern be filled if all three pipes are running together?

BOTANY

1. Define and give an example of each of the following: thallophyte, endogen, gynosperm, legume, tuber.

2. a. What is meant by chlorophyll? What are its uses?

   b. Describe the most important ways in which leaves are arranged on a stem. What governs their arrangement?

3. Name the parts of an ordinary flower, and state the uses of each.

4. Describe the principal contrivances for the dissemination of seeds.

5. Tell what you can of bacteria, and the germ theory of disease.

6. Write a careful description of the plant given you.

7. Give a list of a dozen plants that you could make use of in teaching Botany, and state what special use you would make of each.

8. Write an outline of a lesson on the uses to the plant of its leaves.

ENGLISH GRAMMAR

1.   Slave of the dark and dirty mine,
            What vanity has brought thee here?
        How can I love to see thee shine
            So bright, whom I have bought so dear?

   a. Give the modified subject, the predicate verb and the object of the first sentence.
   b. State the entire object of the verb *love*.
   c. What does the clause *whom* to *dear* modify?
   d. What is the antecedent of *whom*? The case of *whom*? Give the reason.
   e. What part of speech is *shine*? Give its construction.

2. Write the possessive plural of each of the following nouns: *lady, fox, woman, sheep, ox.*

3. Write a synopsis of the verb *go* in each of the tenses, third person singular, indicative mode, active and passive voices.

4. Analyze the following sentence without diagram: *Therefore all things whatsoever ye would that men should do to you, do ye even so unto them.*

5. Punctuate and capitalize properly the following sentence: *is the earth the only planet that has a moon asked philip mercury and venus have no moon mars has two and jupiter has four but we can see them only when we look through a telescope replied frank.*

6. Correct the following, giving full reasons for the correction in every case:
   a. *The fox had sprang the trap.*
   b. *I saw six ships lying at anchor.*
   c. *I cannot think so mean of him.*
   d. *Those sort of people are never happy.*
   e. *Which of the twins is the fattest?*

HISTORY OF EDUCATION

1. State the essential features of the so-called Abstract Theological Education which developed after the Reformation, and flourished during the latter half of the sixteenth century and the seventeenth, and state the character of the reforms urged by Bacon, Ratich, Comenius, and others.

2. The characteristic educational movement of the eighteenth century was Humanism. Define it, state the claims made for it

as a rational system of education, and state in what classes of schools its influence is still strongly felt.

3. Briefly summarize the educational work of Pestalozzi, and state those principles of his which are strongly influencing modern education in this country.

4. Explain the object of Kindergarten. Ought it to form a part of our system of free public education? Why?

5. Describe the educational system that prevails in the United States. Of what classes of schools does it consist? How are they supported? By whom administered, etc…?

6.   Describe the essential features of the common German School System. In what important ways does it differ from our own?

7. Give a brief account of the educational system of *one* of these countries: China, Ancient Greece, Egypt.

PHYSICS

1. a. Give an outline of the molecular theory of matter.
   b. State some evidence in support of this theory.

2. a. What is meant by *specific gravity*?
   b. Describe an experiment in which the *specific gravity* of a substance is determined.

3. a. At what rate does sound travel in air?

b. Distinguish between *pitch, intensity,* and *quality* of tones.

4. a.   Give the three laws of motion, and illustrate each by example.

b. A clock loses time. What change will you make in the pendulum to remedy the defect, and why?

5. a. What *is* the *heat* of a substance?

b. What constitutes the *temperature* of a body?

6. a. Why is hot, damp weather more uncomfortable than hot, dry weather?

b. Why does the use of a fan in hot weather make one feel cool?

7. State as many ways as you can think of in which a railway train may be used as an illustration in the explanation of physical principles.

8. Write an outline of a lesson on the barometer and its uses.

So how well would your child's teacher do on the above test questions that were required to be answered by schoolteachers wishing to be certified to teach in the one-room schoolhouses of the 1890's? These are just a few of the many questions that were required to be answered correctly on the teacher certification test held in the State of New Hampshire in 1896.

As you can see, these questions clearly demonstrate that the schoolteachers in 1896 were required to achieve an extremely high degree of technical proficiency in many subjects in order to successfully pass such a test. These questions are only a sample of the many challenging questions required to be correctly answered by candidates seeking certification to teach in New Hampshire's schools in the 19th century.

The typical applicant taking this test was an unmarried female, who was expected to handle nearly every aspect of the difficult task of educating school students in the small town environment. She was totally on her own, and received very little help from local school officials when she ran into a practical problem in the classroom.

It is evident from this test that the schoolteachers of 100 years ago were a truly independent and highly competent group of individuals who'd devoted a great deal of effort to their education in preparation for instructing the future citizens of America. One wonders how the schoolteachers of today would fare if the clock were suddenly turned back 100 years.

The schoolteachers of today might take a lesson from the capable young schoolmistresses who operated the one-room schoolhouses of the past. The ingrained qualities of personal integrity and public duty have seldom achieved the level attained by these hard working individuals, who selflessly dedicated their lives to the education of America's children. America's colonists knew that only a person of high moral integrity would be able to impart those same qualities to the future citizens of the United States of America.

The plan of our nation's founders was based upon the principle that power and control would always remain in the hands of the people. It does not appear that President Johnson's decision to remove the power from local elected school boards and place it in the hands of government has worked very well.

When local schools boards had the power to determine their own curriculum, examine students, and hire and fire teachers, they were able to deliver a high quality education to America's schoolchildren.

In the 1950's the U.S. ranked at the top of the educational scale for modern Industrialized nations. But in 2003, the results of a study conducted by the Programme for International Assessment, ranking 15 year-olds in 29 modern industrialized nations in the areas of mathematics literacy and problem solving, concluded that the United States now ranked 24th on a list of 29 industrial countries in mathematics literacy.

Perhaps things would have been different if President Reagan had gone through with his threat to eliminate Education as a cabinet level position, thereby placing education back into the hands of parents and locally elected school boards. It is clear that something has to be done quickly to save America's educational system from a total meltdown.

One possible solution for America's educational system may lie within the Internet. It was once predicted that within a few decades the education of all children and adults would be conducted online, and that America's school buildings would serve only as monthly examination centers where proctored exams would be conducted in order to accurately track and certify student progress.

This change would allow for a customized education for each individual student. Advanced students would no longer be held back intellectually, and would be able to obtain accelerated degrees much more quickly and easily. And with mom's help, special needs students would be able to study at home, learning at their own pace, in a secure home environment, utilizing educational techniques tailored to their specific needs. The result of such changes would be a superior education for all students, and drastically lower tax bills. And best of all, our children will no longer be bringing home the flu!

CHAPTER 19

WEST NILE VIRUS

And when you are gathered together within your cities, I will send the pestilence among you….

(Lev. 26:25)

If you're the kind of person who is not satisfied with the fact that something happened, but also want to know why it happened, then you may find the following story very interesting. In this world of modern technological miracles like organ transplants and genetic cloning, it is easy for us to forget the basic realities that govern the operation of the ecosystem that surrounds us. We do so however, at our peril.

History records for us the fact that many disease epidemics began in cities. It seems that people living in modern metropolitan areas sometimes tend to lose touch with the world of nature. The disease known as West Nile Virus has been the subject of many recent newspaper and magazine articles, and all sorts of opinions have been rendered on the causes and origins of this deadly disease. I therefore thought it appropriate for us to take a closer look at the history of West Nile Virus to see if we might be able to reveal any clues as to its true origin.

In 1999, a few isolated cases of Eastern Equine Encephalitis were reported in certain communities along the New England coast. This disease was known to affect horses, but could also infect human beings as well. Since mosquitoes were known carriers of this deadly virus, public health officials immediately began a program of mosquito trapping in coastal towns in order to examine the mosquitoes for this deadly disease. Tests soon confirmed that many mosquitoes were indeed carrying Eastern Equine Encephalitis.

Encephalitis is a disease that causes inflammation of the brain and spinal cord. It can affect almost any warm-blooded creature, but is especially dangerous to humans. In persons with suppressed immune systems, the disease can cause serious symptoms that include high fever, stiff neck, mental confusion, muscle weakness, coma, and in extreme cases, death. The disease is especially dangerous to the very young, and the very old.

Encephalitis is not a new disease, and is found all over the world, but cases most commonly occur on the continent of Africa. In the fall of 1999, public health officials in New York City however, reported an outbreak of deadly encephalitis in the United States.

This deadly virus was first identified in the West Nile region of Uganda many years ago, and can be transmitted to humans through the bite of a mosquito. The first reported cases of West Nile Virus occurred in Africa in the year 1937, although it is very likely that the disease existed long before that time. Since that first outbreak in Uganda, cases have been documented in many other nations as well. In the 1950's an outbreak was recorded in Egypt, and another outbreak occurred in some elderly patients in a nursing home in Israel in 1957. As the disease gained greater recognition, new cases were reported in France and Egypt in the 1960s, and in South Africa in 1974. Romania recorded an outbreak in 1996, and Russia recorded a few cases in 1999. The disease is known to be hosted by migratory waterfowl, and can be easily transferred to humans and other animals by the bite of a mosquito.

New York doctors initially had a difficult time trying to identify the virus. It was more than once confirmed through laboratory analysis to be Eastern Equine Encephalitis. It is quite common for such diseases to be very difficult to diagnose, even by the nation's top laboratories. It is only when a disease rises to epidemic levels that it is it given the attention necessary to arrive at a more accurate diagnosis. When this viral outbreak in the United States was finally classified as having epidemic potential, more accurate genetic tests were performed on it. Scientists were then able to determine that this strain very closely resembled the West Nile variety of encephalitis, and so it was agreed that this outbreak would be classified as West Nile Virus.

Since birds were known carriers of the disease, people were asked to bring in any dead birds found in affected areas. Crows and Blue Jays were brought in most often, since these birds are at the bottom of the food chain. Laboratory tests however, soon confirmed that many other species of birds were also carrying West Nile Virus.

It is likely that there was West Nile Virus activity in the United States long before these 1999 incidents, but the disease is very difficult to diagnose because its symptoms are so similar to those of the flu, and may include fever, headache, muscle aches, stiff neck and other flu-like maladies. It's possible that many people suffering from West Nile Virus in the U.S. were never properly diagnosed.

The first few confirmed cases of West Nile Virus in the United States were recorded in New York City in 1999, where 62 people came down with the disease, exhibiting its classic symptoms. These 62 cases resulted in 7 deaths. The death rate from diagnosed cases of West Nile Virus currently stands at approximately 9 deaths for every 100 serious cases. The number of West Nile Virus cases has risen steadily each year as the disease has spread across the United States. The current North American case count as of 2006 is approximately 9000 serious cases, and will probably continue to rise in the summer of 2007 as mosquitoes come out of their winter hiding places and begin to multiply. Approximately 850 deaths have occurred in the United States so far as a result of these 9000 cases, and many people have also suffered permanent neurological damage from the disease. The disease seems to be most dangerous to the elderly, the very young, and persons with suppressed immune systems. The disease therefore has the potential to wreak havoc on the residents of nursing homes and elderly communities.

The first few cases of West Nile Virus in the U.S. were reported in 1999 in New York City, but the following year many more cases were reported over a much wider area that extended from Connecticut to Maryland. By 2001, the disease had spread to most of the eastern seaboard, and new cases were being reported all the way from Maine to northern Florida.

By 2002, West Nile Virus had successfully jumped the Mississippi River and more cases were being reported from Michigan to Texas. The disease is still spreading westward, and by 2007, West Nile Virus will be a serious problem everywhere in the continental United States.

There is, as of this date, no effective human vaccine for West Nile Virus. There aren't even any effective treatments for the disease except for normal supportive therapies. It is therefore advisable for most people to try to avoid being bitten by mosquitoes.

The common North American House Mosquito is a known carrier of this virus, but it has recently been discovered that two new species of mosquito have invaded our nation and also become carriers of West Nile. These new species are the Asian

Tiger Mosquito, and the Asian Japonicus Mosquito. These two new Asian invaders are much more efficient at transferring the virus from one host to another, as much as 5 times more efficient! Both species have dark bodies with distinct white stripes, or scales, running along the sides of their abdomens. Be especially careful of these two new Asian invaders.

It is now feared that migratory birds may be spreading West Nile Virus across our nation. Health officials have been experiencing many problems recently with Canada Geese, due to a severe overpopulation of this species. Canada Goose populations have more than tripled in the last twenty years, and are still growing at a rate of over 5 percent a year. The number of geese taking up permanent residence in the U.S. has also increased by a factor of 12 over the last thirty-five years. Exploding populations of these wild geese, particularly in the New York City area, have caused significant problems for public health officials.

Large flocks of Canada Geese have been observed landing on public reservoirs and depositing their feces in great quantities, thereby causing large surges in the coliform levels of public drinking water supplies. Water department officials have been hard pressed to keep chlorine levels high enough to control all the bacteria.

In many areas, Canada Geese have also been congregating in public parks where people tend to feed them. This situation encourages the geese to interrupt their normal migration cycles and take up permanent residence in these parks. Only twenty years ago, it was rare to see a Canada Goose in a city park or on a public beach or golf course. Canada Geese were most often seen in their familiar V-formations flying south, or were sometimes seen in cornfields feeding on the corn left over from a recent cutting. For centuries, farmers had always left a tenth (tithe) of their harvest in the field to be gleaned by animals, and cornfields were a principal food source for Canada Geese heading south. But now cornfields are harvested with equipment so efficient that not a single ear of corn is left on the ground for wild geese to glean. Canada Geese have therefore been forced to turn to grass as an alternative food supply, and without enough energy to fly south, they are now taking up permanent residence in many city parks, cemeteries and golf courses.

In the greater New York City area, public parks have now become so severely overpopulated with Canada Geese that residents visiting those parks must often wear boots in order to walk around. Goose feces is nearly ankle deep in many places, and often coats the bottoms of men's trousers and ladies' long dresses. Park visitors can no longer allow their children to play in the grass, or on the beach, and people visiting cemeteries and golf courses also must be very careful where they step. This threat to public health has been totally ignored by thousands of animal lovers who enjoy seeing the large flocks of geese move out of the way of their vehicles as they enter these parks.

Disease mechanisms have always been a natural part of our environment. Their presence is necessary in order to restore order in the natural world when things begin to slide out of control. Disease organisms have been around for millions of years, and are a vital part of our natural ecosystem. They only rear their ugly heads when their presence is required to correct an imbalance in that system.

The recent outbreak of West Nile Virus in the U.S. is a classic example of this natural process. The hunting of wild geese was severely restricted in the northeastern United States due to political pressure from New York City animal rights groups, and also that fact that many hunters were sent off to wars in the Middle East. Canada Goose populations, once labeled as "threatened," soon rose to unmanageable levels. Fish and wildlife officials in New York, New Jersey and Connecticut found themselves under constant attack by animal rights groups who considered the hunting of wild geese to be cruel and inhumane. New York City residents witnessed goose excrement growing nearly ankle deep in their public parks, but still failed to grasp the consequences of allowing these unsanitary conditions to exist.

West Nile Virus has a very long history. When populations of wild geese began to grow out of control in Europe due to a drop in the popularity of goose hunting, many new cases of West Nile Virus were reported along goose flyways that extended from Northern Europe, down through the Middle East, and into Africa.

In nature, when animal populations are allowed to increase beyond the ability of the environment to support them, disease mechanisms appear quickly as a natural form of population control. These diseases act quickly to cull excess animal numbers and thus restore the natural balance between animal populations and food supply.

Mosquitoes are still actively spreading West Nile Virus today in many parts of Europe, the Middle East, and Africa. And now that populations of wild geese in North America have also been allowed to grow out of control, the disease is appearing in the U.S. as well. West Nile Virus has now become epidemic in many parts of the continental United States. New West Nile Virus cases are turning up all along the Atlantic goose flyway that runs from Labrador to Virginia, and are also now appearing along the central and western goose flyways that run from Northern Canada to Mexico. This deadly disease is spreading rapidly across our nation wherever geese travel, infecting animals and humans alike.

Our desire to create the perfect world can sometimes blind us to the harsh realities of the natural world around us. We tend to ignore what we don't wish to see, and concentrate instead on what suits our pleasure. The Canada Goose has recently been elevated to near iconic status by numerous admirers of the natural world who now place Canada Goose decoys on their lawns. and flock to state parks and beaches to both feed and view these magnificent birds. Canada Geese are indeed beautiful birds, and the thought of a hunter shooting one may run against our grain, but a world knee-deep in goose excrement is not exactly a desirable alternative. We may wish to change the laws of nature to suit our own personal desires, but the realities of the life and death struggle going on in the natural world around us will eventually come knocking at our door. God's natural world is already a perfect world. It was here long before we arrived, and will be here long after we are gone.

This West Nile Virus (EEE in horses) epidemic currently spreading across our nation is the direct result of man's ignorance of the laws of the natural system. It appears that the efforts of animal lovers to save the Canada Goose may have ultimately had exactly the opposite effect. The current overpopulation of Canada Geese in the United States is the direct result of our meddling in the laws of the natural world. The laws of nature are supreme, and we meddle with them at our peril.

Man has had some 6000 years in which to educate himself on the complex workings of the natural system that surrounds him, but somehow in all that time, we humans have still failed to grasp the concept that we are also an integral part of that system. God's universal system is a circle without beginning or end, and any alteration made to the system ultimately affects everything else in the system. We must always suffer the consequences of meddling in its operation. Once again, it seems that we've allowed the genie to escape the lamp, and are now paying the price for our ignorance.

CHAPTER 20

HALLOWEEN

"From ghoulies and ghosties and long-legged beasties,
and things that go bump in the night,….
Dear Lord deliver us!"

A Scottish prayer

The annual fall Halloween celebration is slowly and steadily growing in popularity across America. It is even beginning to replace our more traditional holidays. This unusual situation has been aided by recent U.S. Supreme Court decisions against the celebration of religious holidays in America's schools and public buildings.

Halloween is therefore rapidly gaining in popularity in America's school systems, where young, impressionable schoolchildren are quickly attracted to its "trick or treating" candies and sweets, and the wonders and magical symbolism of its witches, ghosts, and goblins. This childhood fascination with the occult has been boosted by the recent release of some popular films and videos emanating from the Druidic past of the British Isles.

The American Halloween celebration originally drew its beginnings from the ancient Druid New Year that was celebrated in England on November 1st, and later corrupted into All Saint's Day by the Catholic Church. Halloween was originally celebrated all over Europe the evening before All Souls Day, on October 31st. This pagan holiday has also been variously referred to as All Hallowed Eve, Hallowmas, Hallowmesse, and Hallowed-Soween.

The evening before this autumn holiday marked the Celtic and Wiccan religious holiday of Samhain (pronounced *soween*), honoring the end of summer, when the souls of the dead were thought to wander from door to door looking for new bodies to inhabit. If a "souls eve" wandering spirit could be satisfied by a trick or a treat, it would then go on to the next house to seek another unsuspecting victim.

These ancient pagan rituals were nearly always connected to the end of the summer growing season. The pagans of ancient Europe believed that the most important portion of the year was the food-growing season. They therefore celebrated many of their major festivals based on this summer growing season which began May 1st, and ended on or about the last day of October.

It was considered prudent to please all the evil spirits in order to guarantee a successful food crop in any given year. The beginning and end of the growing season therefore, witnessed many popular pagan festivals.

The spring planting celebration of "Ister," was eventually corrupted by the Roman Church into the modern-day Christian celebration we now know as "Easter". This pagan holiday honored the Babylonian fertility goddess Ishtar (Eoster), daughter of the Babylonian Moon god, and was celebrated at the beginning of the spring growing season around May 1st. The early Saxon people represented Ishtar with a faceless statue of the female body in its most fertile state, and the Catholic Church eventually used this pregnant female statue to represent the pregnant body of the Virgin Mary.

When the Holy Roman Church was in the process of expanding its influence into northern Europe during the Dark

Ages, it would often attempt to compromise its way into these pagan festivals by turning them into Christian religious holidays. It was this habit of compromising on the meaning of religious holidays that was to result in much confusion over the true meaning behind these ancient pagan customs and rituals that have survived into modern times.

The practice of "Trick-or-Treating" for instance, arose from the ancient European custom of "Souling," where young children would travel from door to door begging for little "soul cakes," or bread topped with currant jelly (hot-cross buns). These pagan traditions were then gradually introduced into Christian tradition by the hierarchy of the Roman Catholic Church.

The Holy Roman Emperor, Charlemagne for instance, compromised the date for celebrating All Souls Day from May15th to November 1st in order to please the Saxons, and bring more of them into the Catholic faith.

Many of these pagan customs originally stemmed from Low German or Celtic tradition, which originated from many traditional Babylonian and Roman practices.

The carrying around of a Halloween Jack O'Lantern for instance, arose from the Celtic tradition in Britain and northern France that involved someone known as "Stingy Jack," who'd been denied entrance into heaven due to his stinginess. His spirit was therefore condemned to being borne around as a glowing ember taken from a human or animal bonfire (bone-fire), and carried about inside of a hollowed-out gourd.

It was also a common custom at Celtic weddings to have unmarried females "bobbing" for apples. The first young lady to successfully bite into an apple would then be the next one to marry. This custom eventually translated into the "Bouquet Toss" performed at modern-day weddings.

At one time, the December 25th Christmas holiday was the most popular holiday celebrated in America's schools, businesses, and retail stores, but recent Supreme Court decisions have allowed American school administrators to ban the Christmas holiday from the public school system. America's businesses and retail stores soon began to follow along with this new, and more politically correct, policy and now the October 31st Wiccan Halloween holiday has replaced Christmas in many venues across American society.

On October 31st in schools all over America, the walls and windows of school classrooms are decorated with ghosts, human skeletons, and numerous other pagan symbols normally associated with the occult. If you look closely, you will see symbols that include gravestones, caskets, the bones of the dead, werewolves, vampire bats dripping blood from their jaws, witches hats, amulets, and sometimes even Satan himself in his bright red suit.

America's founders formed their new nation to cleanse themselves of these many ancient pagan rituals celebrated all over Europe when they exited their former domicile. The founding fathers did not even permit the Christmas holiday to be celebrated in America due to its pagan roots. The Germanic pagans had worshipped the fir tree because of its ability to defy death and retain its green leaves all year long. Their tradition of cutting down a fir tree and bringing it into the homes to decorate it with silver and gold was specifically forbidden by the Bible in Jeremiah Chapter 10. The founders believed that once you started down the pagan path, it would eventually lead you to Satan's lair.

The 20th century annual Easter parade along New York's Fifth Avenue would have been an aberration to America's founders, who only permitted one parade to be held each year.

America's 4th of July Independence Day parade was always the main holiday parade held to celebrate America's war heroes who fought for our freedoms. The parades held on America's streets today are a far cry from the parades of 200 years ago.

All and all, the modern Halloween holiday is probably representative of the new direction in which our nation is moving in the 21st century. In my long career I have had the opportunity to participate in many afterhours tours of the offices of school systems, retail stores and various government buildings, and have observed wall decorations slowly evolving from American flags, to Christmas trees, and eventually to the satanic themes of Halloween ghosts and goblins. The founding fathers would most certainly have been shocked and dismayed to witness how far Americans have traveled down the road to paganism. It is truly amazing how far the public can be led down the path of deception, as long as the steps to that path are introduced slowly and gradually enough.

CHAPTER 21

MAD COW DISEASE

In the fading twilight I could barely make out the profile of the large, hulking bovine standing over the carcass of the sheep it had just killed. Its cold, black eyes glared madly at me, as it ripped into the bloody intestines of the dead animal. Instantly I knew what to do, "Mad Cow" I yelled, "Ma-a-a-ad Cow"!

In some previous chapters, we learned how unnatural conditions, such as overpopulation, overcrowding, and poor sanitation, can lead to the development and spread of deadly diseases. But can unnatural behavior also lead to disease? It would seem that cows devouring sheep would be a most unnatural behavior for cattle, but who knows what goes on out in those dark pastures after nightfall.

In this short chapter we'll be taking a closer look at another new disease that has been making newspaper headlines recently. It's a disease known as BSE, or Bovine Spongiform Encephalopathy, also popularly known as "Mad Cow" disease. Mad Cow (CWD) disease is one of a larger group of diseases known as TSE's, or Transmissible Spongiform Encephalopathies.

TSE's are a type of degenerative brain disease that can turn healthy brain tissue into a soft, spongy mass. These diseases gradually eat away at brain tissue, creating thousands of tiny holes, causing the brain to take on the appearance of a sponge, hence the name "Spongiform".

This disease was first observed in the mid-1700's in sheep, and was called "Scrapie" because of the strange behavior of affected sheep, who would scrape their bodies on rocks or fence posts in mad attempts to rub off their wool. These sheep eventually lost the ability to stand or walk, and would eventually die within a few months of the onset of symptoms. This disease however, did not seem to be transmissible to human beings.

Then, in the early 1920's, two German neurologists, Dr. Hans Gerhard Creutzfeldt, and Dr. Alphonse Maria Jakob, described a form of TSE disease that occurred in humans. This form of TSE was so rare that it had only been observed in about one out of every one million people. A few cases of the disease had also been documented in certain cannibalistic tribes living in New Guinea, who had the unfortunate habit of eating the brains of their deceased relatives as an act of religious symbolism. This particular disease was known as "Kuru." or "Cannibalism Disease".

Then, in 1985, a cow in Britain was diagnosed with something called "Mad Cow" disease. This cow had apparently ingested the remains of dead sheep that had been mixed in with its animal feed. The feed was manufactured through a process that involved exposing the feed to high temperatures in order to neutralize any bacteria that might be present in the feed mixture.

Since the 1950's, meat-rendering companies had been collecting bones, and other meat by-products, from local butcher shops, and passing them on to food processing plants to be cooked, ground, and dried into dry dog food and other types of animal feed. This process was big business in the newly emerging economy of the second half of the 20th century. No significant problems with this new technology had been observed, except for a few minor cases of food poisoning due to toxins generated by certain molds or yeasts in feed that had been stored in moist environments.

Feed manufacturers soon began experimenting with adding fibers and fillers to their feeds, such as wheat or soy protein, in efforts to improve their bottom line profits. Manufacturers were constantly streamlining their operations and looking for ways to recycle and therefore eliminate waste. Many people however, were beginning to become concerned about what sorts of products were being mixed into cattle feeds, since the entire industry was relatively unregulated when compared to the human food processing industry.

When the first few cases of Mad Cow disease in cattle were diagnosed in Britain, it was ultimately revealed that sheep by-products had been mixed in with the feed being used to raise these cattle. But why would anyone feed ground up sheep body parts to cattle? This fact led to the immediate institution of a ban on the use of ruminant by-products in animal feeds. TSE disease had also been observed in people who'd eaten beef products that were contaminated with BSE. Mad Cow disease soon made the front pages of major newspapers all around the world, sparking numerous investigations into the pathology of TSE.

TSE disease had first appeared in sheep as Scrapie. It was now appearing in cattle as BSE, and in deer and elk as CWD or "Chronic Wasting Disease." In humans it was called "Creutzfeldt-Jakob Disease," or "Cannibalism Disease." TSE's had also been found in ranch-raised mink, and certain other animals consuming commercial animal feeds.

In 1985, Dr. Stanley Prusiner, of the University of California San Francisco, accurately diagnosed the disease through the presence of certain deformed proteins in brain tissues that he named "prions". These deformed proteins could be found in the tissues of the brain, spinal cord, eyes, tonsils, and lower intestines of infected animals. The disease was known to cause a slow, progressive degeneration of brain tissue, resulting in confusion, loss of muscle control, drooling, prostration, and ultimately, death for its victims.

One way this disease could be transferred from one host to another, was through the ingestion of infected tissue from dead animals. In one experiment conducted in England, brain matter from Scrapie-infected sheep was injected into the brains of cattle. Eighteen months later the cattle developed a form of TSE.

Transmissible Spongiform Encephalopathy was also recorded in some people who'd received Human Growth Hormone injections from material collected from the brains of human cadavers, and also in persons who'd received eyeball transplants from cadavers.

After the disease was first identified, and a number of cases of BSE were confirmed in cattle from the UK, a ban was enacted in 1988 on the use of ruminant proteins in the preparation of animal feeds. Almost immediately, more animal-feed bans, and bans on the importation of live animals and/or animal by-products, were enacted by many other nations all around the world.

A total of 150,000 cases of BSE in animals were eventually identified worldwide, with many of those cases being traceable to the UK. A cattle feed ban in the United States in August of 1997, banned the feeding of cattle to cattle, sheep, or goats. Cattle could still be used as food by certain other animals such as chickens or pigs. And a ban was also considered for certain cattle killing systems that involved mechanically striking the brain.

A cow slaughtered on December 9, 2003 in the State of Washington tested positive for Mad Cow disease. This marked the first case of Mad Cow disease in the U.S. Unfortunately, meat from this animal had already found its way into the U.S. food processing system. This particular cow was born in Canada prior to the 1997 feed ban, and apparently originally came from the province of Alberta, the same place that produced the only Canadian cow found to be infected with BSE.

BSE develops very slowly, and its symptoms often do not appear for 4 to 5 years after original exposure. Many people were also wondering how many cases of Alzheimer's might actually be BSE. On Dec 30, 2003, the U.S. government decided to ban the use of "downer cattle" (cattle unable to stand) from the processing of human food. Also banned were the use of brain, spinal cord, and certain other bovine tissues for human consumption.

The modern process of manufacturing animal feed from meat by-products includes a sterilization process capable of destroying most common viruses and bacteria that might be present in the feed mixture. This sterilization procedure includes high temperature boiling or steaming of the feed mixture. This process was known to destroy any disease-causing microbes that might be present in meat by-products.

There was a slight problem however when it came to the prions (spores) involved in BSE. It was soon determined through scientific experimentation that BSE prions were able to withstand these high temperature processes and survive intact. Experiments demonstrated that prions were able to successfully endure temperatures as high as 600 degrees Fahrenheit, thereby allowing them to survive most normal sterilization procedures.

In addition to infecting sheep and cattle, TSE's were also known to infect other ruminants as well, such as wild deer and elk. In the State of Wisconsin in the year 2000, an investigation was conducted into the operation of 550 captive game farms in that state. Many of these game farms used commercial animal feeds to raise their animals, and a few cases of CWD were confirmed in some of these game animals.

This Wisconsin investigation revealed that one farmer had lost an undetermined number of deer into the wild from his CWD-infected captive herd. Several other farmers reported the escape of captive deer or elk that were never recovered. Two other farmers even admitted to game wardens that they had released their entire herds into the wild.

A researcher with the National Institutes of Health announced that "Given these reports of escapes and releases of game farm deer, and given the findings of CWD infected animals on Wisconsin game farms, it is highly likely that these game-farm animals are the source of CWD in wild deer."

Does the mixing of sheep by-products into animal feeds violate a natural law? And did this newly created unnatural behavior (i.e. bovine cannibalism) cause God's natural system to respond with a disease to destroy the offending animals? Only time and more investigation can provide us with an answer to this unusual question.

CHAPTER 22

ANGOLMOIS

THE LAW OF PROPHECY AGAINST INEPT INTERPRETERS: "May whoever reads these verses think carefully. Let the impious and the ignorant not attempt them. Seers, idiot astrologers, the simple-minded, and evildoers, stay way! Whoever does otherwise must be priest to the rite!

Nostradamus Q. 6-100

The above Nostradamus quatrain served as a warning to the impious and inept, who might foolishly attempt to interpret his prophecies before their time. In the last 100 years many people have been guilty of misinterpreting Nostradamus prophecies, and their actions have only served to discredit the great prophet.

One of the most famous examples of this type of misinterpretation concerned a Nostradamus prophecy that eventually became known as the "King of Terror" prophecy. This prophecy was unique from most other Nostradamus prophecies, in that it contained an exact date for the prophecy's occurrence.

Prophecy #10-72 was actually an experiment set up by Nostradamus to see if anyone in the 20th century would be smart enough to figure out one of his prophecies before its occurrence. It was a challenge to the greatest minds of the 20th century.

This prophecy, found in Chapter 10, Quatrain #72, of Nostradamus' famous book, the *Centuries*, actually contained both the month and year that the prophecy was scheduled to take place. The date was July of 1999.

If this prophecy could be correctly interpreted before it happened, it would be the final proof needed to dispel the doubts of unbelievers everywhere. All this created quite a stir in the world of prophecy just prior to the year 2000 Millennium.

The arrival of a new millennium had always generated a great deal of anticipation and fear in the common people. The arrival of the previous millennium in the year 1000 AD had created great panic in Europe, as Christians all over Europe and Asia nervously anticipated the arrival of the great Day of Judgment, and the end of the world.

As was also the case with the modern year 2000 millennium (Y2K), there was no shortage of those aiming to profit from the widespread panic generated by the great event. The Holy Roman Church encouraged its members to do everything they could to improve their standing with the Lord as the dreaded Judgment Day approached. In 999 AD, European Christians, and Byzantines from the Eastern Church, flocked by the thousands into their great cathedrals carrying armloads of gifts in the form of money, jewelry, deeds for land, and wagonloads of valuables, in order to fill up church coffers.

Then on December 31st, 999 AD, peasants and landlords alike from all over the Christian world, crammed into their churches and cathedrals to await the arrival of the dreaded Judgment Day. When midnight passed with no Judgment occurring, Catholic priests suddenly announced that all their offerings had apparently been sufficient to forestall the great Day of Judgment, and the Church was able to erect many new churches with all the money and valuables that it had received during the great fiasco.

As with previous millenniums, the year 2000 Millennium also generated worldwide fear and panic. The media joined in the frenzy, and billions of dollars were spent as the world prepared for something called "Y2K," which was expected to shut down the entire computerized world at the stroke of midnight on December 31st, 1999.

As Nostradamus' dreaded July 1999 date grew closer, interest in his prophecies also increased, and more Nostradamus books were sold at this time than at any other time in history. The original prophecy #10-72 was a four-line poem known as a "quatrain". A rough English translation of the quatrain reads as follows:

QUATRAIN #10-72 (original translation)

In the year 1999 and seven months,
From the skies shall come an alarmingly powerful king
To raise again the great King of the Angolmois,
Before and after, War shall reign at will.

The key to the correct interpretation of this famous prophecy was the word "Angolmois." Nostradamus was known to anagram certain words or names in order to disguise their meaning, and many Nostradamus fans decided that the word Angolmois was actually an anagram of the word Mongolois. They therefore concluded that a great Mongolian antichrist was going to come down out of Asia to invade the Middle East, setting off the final battle of Armageddon. This particular interpretation of the prophecy fit in perfectly with all the other ominous predictions of the time.

When the month of July finally arrived, Nostradamus followers all over the world were anxiously awaiting this Mongolian antichrist's invasion of the Middle East. But the first week of July passed with no unusual events occurring. Then the second and third weeks of July also passed without incident. When the entire month of July passed without the appearance of a Mongolian antichrist, Nostradamus followers everywhere were shocked and disappointed that the prophecy had not come true. They just couldn't believe that nothing at all had happened. They quickly came up with all sorts of excuses to explain their embarrassment, not realizing that the prophecy actually had come true.

The word Angolmois you see, was not really an anagram after all. The word Angolmois in Old French simply means "Angol-people," or "Angol-nation," but who in the world are the Angol people, and where is their nation? The word Angol, spelled A-N-G-O-L, does not exist in any known language. There are also no Latin or Greek roots for this word. The only word in any known language that contains the exact spelling "A-N-G-O-L" is the word "Angola". Angola is a Portuguese trading colony located on the West coast of Africa.

In the late 1400's, the Portuguese established a trading relationship with a nomadic African tribe located in present-day Angola. They traded for such things as ivory, animal skins, gold and diamonds. The leader of this nomadic tribe was called the "n'gola," or king. Thus the name "angola" was given to the colony. So in Old French, the word Angolmois was actually a word meaning "Portuguese African nation."

These Angolan nomads later moved farther north to establish a second trading colony known as Portuguese Morocco, located much closer to Portugal and therefore much more convenient for trading, thereby creating two Portuguese "angolas," one known as Portuguese Angola, and the other, Portuguese Morocco (El Jadida).

Nostradamus' prophecy referred to a world leader possessing a frightening amount of power who would arrive out of the sky into one of these two Portuguese trading colonies to witness the resurrection of an African king upon his native throne. But which colony, Angola or Morocco? And who was this powerful world leader?

Well, the world's most powerful leader in the year 1999 was America's president Bill Clinton. This meant that prophecy #10-72 might actually be predicting that in July of 1999, America's president Bill Clinton would arrive out of the sky (on Air Force One, of course) into either Angola or Morocco to witness the coronation of a king of one of these two African nations. The last line of the prophecy mentioned that the President would also acknowledge a war that had recently been fought for a "bon-heur," or "good-cause".

But as late as June of 1999, President Clinton had no plans to fly into Africa to attend any coronation. On July 23, 1999 however, Morocco's King Hussan unexpectedly passed away. His son, Prince Hussan, had to be immediately crowned as Morocco's new king. Since President Clinton was already planning a trip to Sarajevo, he decided to make a side trip to Morocco on July 25th to attend Hussan's coronation.

And so, on July 25th, 1999, President Clinton and other U.S. officials did in fact arrive out of the sky on Air Force One into the former Portuguese African trading colony of Morocco to witness the resurrection of Morocco's Prince Hussan on the throne of his deceased father, King Hussan. After attending King Hussan's funeral and acknowledging Hussan's resurrection to the throne of Morocco, President Clinton a few days later stepped back into Air Force One and flew off to

Sarajevo to recognize the bravery of American troops who'd just fought in the Kosovo War for the "good-cause" of preventing a human genocide.

President Clinton's unanticipated trip to Morocco was totally unplanned, and prompted by a debt of gratitude Clinton owed to King Hussan because the king had been instrumental in negotiating an earlier Arab-Israeli peace agreement.

This truly incredible feat of modern prophecy went totally unnoticed and uncredited, even though it came true exactly as Nostradamus predicted it would. Nostradamus' followers, by misinterpreting his prophecy, had discredited their great prophet.

The scientific world may scoff at the idea of seeing into the future, but the following Quatrain can be found in numerous books in libraries and bookstores all over the world. And all of these books were published many years in advance of the July 1999 event. For your convenience, I've included a glossary of the Old French and Latin terms for reference.

CHAPTER 10, QUATRAIN 72 (Old French)

In the year nineteen hundred ninety nine, 7th month,
L'an mil neuf cens nonante neuf, sept mois,
From the sky comes a great Leader of frightening power
Du ciel viendra un grand Roi de-ffrayeur
To resurrect the great King of the Angol-people.
Ressusciter le grand Roy d'Angol-mois.
Before and after, a war reigns for a good-cause.
Avant apres, Mars regner par bon-heur.

OLD FRENCH (O.F.) AND LATIN (L.) DEFINITIONS:
 Angolmois – (O.F.) Angol-people
 Avant – (F.) before
 Apres – (O.F.) after
 Bon-heur – (O.F.) good-hour, good cause
 Ciel – (O.F) sky
 Cens – (O.F) hundred
 De-ffrayeur – (O.F. frayeur) of frightening power
 Grand – (F.) grand, great
 L'an- (O.F. an - year), in the year
 Mars – (O.F. Mars, god of war) war
 Mil – (O.F. mille) one thousand
 Mois – (F.) month
 Neuf – (F.) nine
 Nonante – (L. nonagin) ninety
 Par – (F.) for
 Regner – (F.) reign
 Ressusciter – (O.F.) resuscitate, resurrect
 Roi, Roy – (O.F) Leader, King
 Sept – (F.) seventh
 Viendra – (O. F. venir - viendra) will come

This quatrain represents another truly incredible feat of modern prophecy by the Hebrew prophet Nostradamus. It is sad to note however, that Nostradamus' experiment to see whether men of the 20th century would be smart enough to figure out one of his prophecies before it occurred, proved a great failure. Apparently an additional four hundred and fifty years of human evolution had not improved the IQ of mankind one bit, certainly not much of a tribute to the intelligence of so-called "modern" man.

CHAPTER 23

EVOLUTION

"We have been the recipients of the choicest bounties of heaven, we have been preserved in peace and prosperity, we have grown in numbers, wealth and power as no other nation has ever grown. But we have forgotten the gracious hand which preserved us in peace, and multiplied and enriched and strengthened us, and we have vainly imagined, in the deceitfulness of our hearts, that all these things were produced by some superior wisdom and virtue of our own. Intoxicated with unbroken success, we have become too self-sufficient to feel the necessity of redeeming and preserving grace, too proud to pray to the God that made us."

Abraham Lincoln

The above words were written by a man who applied the word of God to help free a race of individuals considered by many to be too uncivilized to serve in a free Christian society. Born on February 12th, 1809, to poor parents in the small town of Nolin Creek, Kentucky, Abraham Lincoln was destined to become one of the most influential world figures in the ongoing battle between the views of God and the views of man.

Born on the EXACT SAME DAY in Shrewsbury, Shropshire, England, was another famous person named Charles Darwin, who was also destined to become one of the most influential world figures in this very same philosophical battle.

The Theory of Evolution has long been a source of great controversy in the religious world, and the man credited with developing this controversial theory was the famous British naturalist, Charles Darwin.

At the age of 22, shortly after graduating from the University of Edinburgh, Scotland, Darwin decided to embark on an ocean trip to circumnavigate the globe to study nature on the world's major continents. In December of 1831, he set sail aboard the HMS Beagle on a five-year voyage around the world. Darwin was originally planning to make religion his chosen field of endeavor, but he had some questions about the true nature of Creation, and wanted to settle them with this trip.

When Darwin returned home from his famous excursion in October of 1836, he immediately canceled his plans to go into the church, and decided instead to further explore the world of science. During his long ocean voyage, Darwin had visited a tiny group of islands located off the West coast of South America called the Galapagos Islands. On the Galapagos, he documented the existence of many strange and unusual animals that differed greatly from similar species on the nearby South American mainland. Darwin was convinced that these remarkable differences resulted from a process he called natural selection, that is, survival of the animals most fit for their particular environment. Darwin theorized that animals less fit for their environment were eliminated through this natural process, and thereby prevented from passing on their inferior genetic traits to the gene pool of their particular species.

Actually, Darwin was not the first person to recognize this natural process of "survival of the fittest". This phrase originally came from another British naturalist named Alfred Russel Wallace, who wrote the phrase down in a letter he sent to Darwin long before Darwin published his famous theory. Actually both these men were outdone by America's great scientific genius, Benjamin Franklin, who also described this process many years before either Wallace or Darwin.

This line of thinking was certainly not new. The science of genetics had been recognized and utilized by man for thousands of years. The ancient Chinese for example, had noticed that some of their carp exhibited a faint color when held up to the sunlight. They found that when they bred these carp together, they were able to produce fish of even brighter color. They then destroyed any fish of poor color, and bred only the most brightly colored fish together. After hundreds of such breeding cycles, they were eventually able to produce the type of carp we know today as the goldfish. The Chinese utilized this same selective breeding process with many other animal species as well, in order to please the refined tastes of their emperors.

In more recent times, this process of genetic selection, whether natural or artificial, has also been observed and utilized by modern man. Modern farmers for instance, often breed their animals for specific traits. Milk farmers will selectively breed their cows to produce more milk, while beef ranchers selectively breed their cattle to gain more weight. Dog breeders for many centuries have selectively bred their animals for specific tasks like hunting wild animals, or herding sheep.

The science of animal husbandry (Grangers) has long been a useful tool for improving and modifying many animal species. It was always understood however, that genetically inferior animals needed to be destroyed as a normal part of this process. The process of Natural Selection has always been recognized as a powerful tool used by nature to refine its various animal species.

Darwin theorized that it must have been this same process that was responsible for the genetic development of all species, including man. Darwin theorized that modern man must have evolved from the lesser apes into the present-day species known as Homo sapiens. Darwin's theory infuriated many people in the church world of America, particularly those who believed in the literal translation of the book of Genesis that described God's "spontaneous creation" of mankind. Even those who thought the creation story to be a figurative tale, had great difficulty accepting the insult that they were originally descended from apes.

Darwin's controversial theory however, found favor with many of the liberal-minded members of the academic community, who began to teach the controversial theory in America's schools. Eventually a legal battle developed between Evolutionists and Creationists. The battle culminated in the famous "Monkey Trial" of 1925, involving attorneys William Jennings Bryan and Clarence Darrow, to prevent the teaching of evolutionary theory in public schools. Tennessee schoolteacher John Scopes had defied a state law preventing the teaching of evolution in Tennessee public schools. The Scopes trial made newspaper headlines all around the world, and resulted in a temporary victory for the Creationists, and a $100 fine for Scopes. Scopes' conviction however, was eventually overturned on a technicality in the Tennessee Supreme Court.

Many liberal educators continued to teach the "science" of evolution in America's schools, as scientists everywhere anxiously sought evidence to support Darwin's controversial theory. Archeological digs were initiated all over the world to locate the many "missing links" between ape and man. Every major science museum had on display a series of human-like figures, representing the many gradual changes taking place in the evolutionary development of modern man from lesser, ape-like, creatures.

Archeologists soon discovered many human-like bone fragments from different periods of time that did seem to support the slow and progressive evolutionary development of the human species from its early ape origins. These remains were dated as far back as two and one half million years on the evolutionary scale. These early hominids however, all possessed skulls that were clearly ape-like in structure, and all possessed large canine teeth. Their skulls did not at all resemble the skull structure of modern human beings.

The first truly human-like skull to achieve any notoriety was the famous "Java Man" skull discovered in the 1890's on the island of Java by archeologist Eugene Dubois, a student of the famous German biologist, Ernst Haeckel. Java Man however, did not come into existence until the most recent million year period of human evolutionary development. Java Man's skull had distinct human-like characteristics, but its brain case was only about 850cc's, as compared with the modern human brain case of 1490cc's. And Java Man still exhibited the large canine teeth of his ape-like ancestors.

Another famous discovery made in 1929 of an even more human-like skull, belonged to "Pekin Man." This discovery was made in China by a Chinese paleontologist named Pei. The skull of Pekin Man was clearly more human-like in its construction, and it had a brain case of approximately 1100cc's. But Pekin Man had lived very recently, only 500,000 years ago.

The next significant discoveries of even more modern hominids living as recently as 250,000 years ago, were labeled "Heidelberg Man" and "Rhodesian Man."

Finally, scientists brought us down to the last 100,000 years of man's development with their discovery of "Neanderthal Man." Neanderthal Man possessed a low forehead and small canine teeth, but some of the larger male specimens were found to possess brain cases in excess of 1500cc's (note: male brains are approx. 10%. larger than those of females). This meant that some male Neanderthals possessed larger brain cases than many modern humans. This development was an unexpected surprise for Evolutionists.

Neanderthals were then closely followed by Cro-Magnon man, appearing only about 75,000 years ago, and finally by modern Homo Sapiens, who came on the scene around 40,000 BC.

There were many important indicators that scientists used in determining where each of these many archeological finds was to be placed on the human evolutionary scale. Canine tooth development for instance, was considered to be an extremely important consideration. Chimpanzees, man's closest relative in the ape family, had long, well developed canines, as opposed to humans, who exhibited only slight canine development. It was theorized that the canine teeth of modern Chimpanzees were a holdover from a time in the distant past when Chimpanzees were meat-eaters instead of herbivores. But in the early 1960's, the scientific community was shocked to its core, when a group of wild Chimpanzees was observed in the wild, eating a small monkey. Further investigations revealed that these cute little chimps had actually hunted down and killed this monkey in order to eat it. Evolutionists were greatly embarrassed to find out that the Chimpanzee's long canine teeth were not a vestige from the past after all, but served a very useful purpose in their present-day diets.

By 1967, all scientific and archeological evidence had conveniently demonstrated a long and slow evolutionary development of mankind from early ape-like creatures who walked on their knuckles, possessed long arms, short legs, large canine teeth, and feet designed for grasping tree limbs. The evolutionary development of man did indeed appear to have occurred exactly as Darwin described, over a period of approximately the last three million years. However the most significant changes had clearly taken place in the most recent 500,000 years of the evolutionary process. Mankind had definitely slowly and gradually evolved from early apes into more human-like creatures that finally arrived in the most recent half of the last million years. Modern man ultimately made his appearance on Earth approximately 40,000 years ago, just as Darwin had predicted he would. Scientists and archeologists felt they had now proven Darwin's controversial theory, and in 1968, a U.S. Supreme Court decision finally legalized the teaching of evolutionary theory in public schools, and effectively outlawed the teaching of religious based Creation science. God had now been officially flunked out of America's schools.

Eight years later however, a shocking development in Africa suddenly threw a large monkey wrench (pardon the pun) into Darwin's evolutionary theory. An archeological dig in Tanzania had revealed a clear set of human footprints casually strolling across a mudflat in an ancient layer of geological sediment. The problem was that this layer of muddy sediment was located at the 3.3 million-year level of the geological strata! This was just about as far back as you could get on the human evolutionary scale. How was it possible that a human being could have walked across a mudflat over three million years ago?

It turned out that these early hominids, known as Australopithecus afarensis, actually walked totally upright on two feet, just like modern human beings. Not only did they walk completely upright, but when scientists examined them for canine tooth development, they found absolutely none at all. Their teeth were as normal as the teeth of modern humans, exhibiting not even the slightest hint of canine tooth development. This discovery put a huge crimp in Darwin's theory. Up until now, all early "missing link" finds had possessed large canine teeth, and were dated at less than two million years old! And it was common knowledge that all hominids even remotely resembling modern human beings, were considerably less than a million years old.

Another important indicator of human evolutionary development was the construction of the foot. Apes had feet shaped like hands, since they were used for grasping tree limbs while climbing. It was therefore thought that the anatomy of the feet of all "missing links" would exhibit a gradual evolution from the hand-like foot of the ape, into the modern human foot structure of today, designed for walking upright. But the feet of these three and one half million year old pigmy African people were exactly like the feet of modern human beings, with not even the slightest hint of the thumb-like big toe, so characteristic of monkeys and apes. Also, the design of their hip joints indicated that these early people walked fully upright, just like modern humans. Scientists and anthropologists were shocked to find out that the only significant difference between these early hominids and modern African pigmies, was their brain size.

By the year 2000, a detailed examination of an entire range of hominid remains found over the last three and one half million years, actually indicated that many of the steps of evolution had occurred completely out of order. Australopithecus africanus, who lived about two and one half million years ago, had a more ape-like body than Australopithecus afarensis which appeared nearly a million years earlier. And Homo habilis, who lived as recently as one million years ago, had proportionately the same length legs, but much longer arms than the oldest Australopithecus afarensis specimens dated almost 2 million years earlier at the very beginning of the evolutionary cycle!

Suddenly, all scientific evidence was leaning away from Evolutionary theory, and toward Creation theory. The Creationists had long held that evolutionary influences were only valid when they concerned the refinement of a species, but were invalid when they concerned the creation of new species. It was now quite clear that tooth shape was actually determined by diet, and foot and hip construction by mode of travel. Creationists had always held that the creation of species was through the will of God, and that evolution merely served to refine and adapt a particular species to its unique environment. It was too late however, to reverse the 1968 decision of the United States Supreme Court. Darwin's theory was now an official part of the curriculum in America's schools.

The Theory of Evolution was also causing some other problems as well. At the start of the 20th century, scientists began to notice a disturbing trend. It seems that modern advances in the field of medicine were beginning to have an adverse effect upon the process of human evolution itself. The genetically weaker members of human society, formerly eliminated through the process of natural selection, were now surviving due to technological advances in the field of medicine.

Evolutionists were becoming concerned about the future genetic integrity of the human race itself; after all, the genetically weak were now surviving to pass on their inferior traits to the general human population. It was now a fact that the genetically inferior members of the lower classes were breeding at a much higher rate than the genetically superior members of the upper classes. The process of evolution itself had now essentially been reversed! And the speed with which the process was happening would place us back into a Neanderthal world in just a few more generations. Evolutionists therefore felt it their duty to take immediate action to eliminate this threat to the genetic integrity of the human species, and so a new science, called "Eugenics," was born.

Supporters of this new Eugenics movement lobbied the government to seek out the genetically inferior members of human society and take immediate action to ensure that their genes were not passed on to the general population. In America's Midwest, it had long been a common practice to sterilize the mentally ill, or "mental defectives," as they were known, in order to prevent them from producing children. This practice enjoyed the widespread support of the government. In fact, the State of Indiana in 1907 enacted a law that legalized sterilization of the mentally ill.

Not much happened with this Eugenics movement until around the year 1920, when the economic and social successes of that era gave rise to a rebirth of liberal idealism, and generated new support for social changes to improve the future of the human race. Drunken with the economic successes and technological achievements of the Industrial Revolution, wealthy intellectuals now set their sights upon improving the genetic integrity of the human species, through the new science of Eugenics.

The Eugenics movement enjoyed the enthusiastic support of the members of white, upper class society, who felt that their superior intellect had endowed them with the responsibility for making such decisions. Eugenics supporters overwhelmingly favored social engineering for the lower classes in order to safeguard the racial integrity of America.

The Eugenics concept, now renamed "Social Darwinism," was heartily embraced by America's academic elite as holding great promise for the future of all mankind. The United States government would now be able to address the many issues that threatened the genetic purity of our nation. Issues such as immigration would need to be addressed immediately.

Immigrants to America's shores would now have to be screened for mental IQ, and other physical factors, before being allowed to enter the country. America's genetic purity could not be compromised by the genetically inferior castoffs of other nations. Strict mental and physical standards would need to be established for all future immigrants to America.

The many accomplishments of America's Eugenics movement did not go entirely unnoticed. The members of Adolf Hitler's NAZI party in Germany were very impressed with the many successes of America's Eugenics movement. The Nazis had long been seeking a workable program to help them maintain the genetic purity of their superior Aryan race and eliminate the "genetically inferior races."

Darwin's theories had been popularly supported by many Germans during the First World War through the writings of the German biologist Ernst Haeckel, whose great works helped to justify the right of the superior Caucasian race of Germany to lead the way in the development and improvement of human society. Social Darwinism now promised to be the key to unlocking the full potential of the German people.

The original seed planted by Darwin had now produced its ultimate fruit. And as the Serpent had so long ago whispered to Eve, "In the day that you eat thereof (of the Tree of Knowledge) then your eyes shall be opened, and you shall be as gods," (Gen. 3:5). Now, with this god-like power endowed through knowledge, Hitler and his Nazis could finally realize their dream of creating the perfect human society. The Enlightenment had now given birth to another great world-conquering beast.

As had occurred so many times in the past, the secular dream of the liberal elite for a society unfettered by the laws of God, was once again loosed upon mankind. Millions of followers of the new messiah, Adolph Hitler, failed to realize that such men are driven only by their own insatiable lust for power. The greatest of all the beasts would not now be satisfied until he had claimed more human lives than any world conqueror before him.

Darwin's name could now be added to the long list of social reformers, like Karl Marx and Leon Trotsky, whose liberal ideas on how the world should be run, eventually brought them into conflict with God. Their idealistic dreams for a politically-ruled society that would improve upon the laws of God, had given birth to men like Lenin and Stalin, who sought to bring their sinful ideas to fruition. Like small children playing with matches, foolish men believed that knowledge, and its resultant technologies, would ultimately allow mankind to create the perfect human society.

The ancient Hebrew prophets had taught that man's only path to Eden was always through belief in, and subservience to, the supreme laws of God. Man's quest for the perfect human society, launched by Eve's original sin, has brought much death and suffering to the world. Four million years of evolutionary development has still not allowed mankind to peacefully coexist with his neighbor, or to live in harmony with the natural world around him.

With human fossils demonstrating clear-cut cases of reversed evolution, and Neanderthals possessing larger brains than modern humans, it is evident that the processes of Creation and Evolution are far more complex than Darwin ever imagined. And we may now have to be careful when calling someone a "Neanderthal," it might prove to be a compliment!

CHAPTER 24

THE FIRST THANKSGIVING

"Whereas it is the duty of all nations to acknowledge the providence of Almighty God, to obey His will, to be grateful for His benefits, and to implore His protection and favor,...Now therefore I do recommend and assign Thursday, the Twenty–Sixth day of November next, to be devoted by the people of these States to the service of that great and glorious Being who is the author of all the good that was, that is, or that will be.

George Washington - Thanksgiving Declaration

The purpose of this chapter is to record the true story of the First Thanksgiving for those who wish to avoid the politically correct versions of history presently being taught to America's schoolchildren. Not many Americans are aware of the true reasons why we celebrate our Thanksgiving holiday. I therefore thought you might enjoy hearing this true story of the many interesting events that led up to the original celebration of this uniquely American holiday. We owe a great debt indeed to the small group of English Pilgrims whose struggles in the New World first paved the way for the Christian colonization of America.

In 1620, a small group of Protestant Separatists from Lincolnshire and Nottinghamshire, England, who had been recently living in exile in Holland, decided to undertake a dangerous ocean crossing to the New World in order to establish a new Christian colony in America. After many tears and humble supplications to the Lord, these hardy adventurers set sail in a small ship from the city of Leyden, in Holland, to Southampton, England in order to meet up with a larger ship they'd also hired for the voyage. Their smaller ship, the Speedwell, leaked very badly, and so it was sailed to Dartmouth for repairs. It was determined however at the Dartmouth shipyard, that the small ship was not up to such a long ocean voyage, and it was therefore decided that it should be sent back to England with a few members of the journey who were not firmly committed to this long and difficult trip.

After this unexpected delay, it was in the first week of September that the Pilgrims finally set sail from Plymouth Harbor in England on their long and dangerous journey across the Atlantic Ocean. The good ship Mayflower met with many severe storms on the voyage, and at approximately the halfway point of the trip, a heavy support beam cracked amidships, threatening the safety of the vessel and its passengers. An emergency meeting was held to decide whether or not to continue the journey, and it was decided that a screw jack brought along by one of the passengers could be used to support the sagging beam, and that the trip should continue. All members of the group were firmly committed to the establishment of this new Christian colony in America.

After a few more weeks of perilous sailing, the crew and passengers began to sight small groups of water birds feeding on schools of fish. This was a good sign, for it meant that land could not be far away. On the morning of November 9th (Old Calendar) at around daybreak, the crew of the Mayflower caught their first sight of land in over two months. The narrow strip of land they sighted was known on the sailing charts as Cape Cod.

The Mayflower immediately altered its course to seek out a river named the Hudson, known to lie south of the Cape, but the winds were against them, and Captain Jones decided it was best to head for the safety of the Cape Cod (Provincetown) bay. This bay provided shelter for great flocks of water birds on their annual flight south for the winter. Never before had these Christian Pilgrims seen so many birds in one place at one time. It was a truly magnificent sight to behold. Every day aboard ship, they were treated to the sight of great whales frolicking about in the bay. The Pilgrims had no means aboard their ship to harvest these whales, which could have been a good source of food, and also valuable whale oil for their lamps.

After their long journey, the Pilgrims were sorely in need of replenishing their rapidly dwindling supplies of firewood and fresh water. The Cape Cod bay was very shallow, especially near shore, and it was necessary for them to wade a great distance through the cold water in order to reach shore. This proved to be a serious problem in cold weather, and caused many in the group to later fall ill.

It was decided that sixteen armed men should be sent ashore to gather necessary supplies. The men embarked upon the bay side of the cape. The cape turned out to be a rather narrow strip of land, bordered on one side by the bay, and on the other side by open sea. The shoreline of the New World was heavily wooded with huge oaks, pine, juniper, sassafras, and other sweet woods. The edge of it consisted of seemingly endless sand dunes. The interior of the land was thickly forested by trees with foliage so dense that not a trickle of light penetrated through. Without light, there were no smaller trees or underbrush growing beneath this forest canopy. It was therefore open and unrestricted underneath so that a carriage could freely be driven about under it. Its soil was rich and black. Never before had the Pilgrims seen a land so rich as this place.

A few members of the group decided to venture ashore to repair the ship's small sailing skiff, which was used to ferry them to and from shore. The repairs took longer than expected however, and it was decided that a group of armed men should be sent out to see if they could contact any of the native inhabitants of the area.

A group of sixteen armed men, under the command of Captain Miles Standish, was sent out along the shoreline to seek what they might find. After traveling only about a mile, they spied a group of 5 or 6 people with a dog, walking toward them along the beach. The Pilgrims shouted to these natives, but the savages quickly ran into the woods and called their dog in after them. Standish and his men rushed into the forest after them. They knew they had no hope of catching up to the natives, but thought that perhaps they might follow them to a nearby village. After tracking them for nearly ten miles, they saw where the savages had climbed to the top of a hill to see if they were being followed. With heavy armor weighting them down, the exhausted Pilgrims decided to set up camp for the night.

In the morning, the party once again picked up the native trail and followed it farther into the woods. After a short time it led them into a thick patch of briars and tangles, and it soon became evident that they had been deliberately led on this wild goose chase. The party continued on however, and eventually came to a small valley filled with many deer trails. These deer trails led them to springs of fresh water where the thirsty Pilgrims had their first drink of icy cold New England water. They drank it with great pleasure, for they were tired and thirsty, and sorely in need of this refreshment.

The men then decided to head farther south to pick up the shoreline again. When they finally reached the water's edge, they lit a signal fire to let the Mayflower know of their new location. They then decided to explore another nearby valley, where they soon stumbled upon a fresh water pond about a quarter mile in length. Near this pond they located an open field of approximately 20 acres that had been previously cultivated by natives. Not far beyond this field they encountered a strange mound of earth covered with straw matting and topped with a large wooden mortar. At the end of this earthen heap, they found a small native cooking pot sitting in a hole that had been dug into the ground. Some members of the party decided to dig into the mound, and soon located a partially rotted set of bow and arrows, a knife, a pack-needle and some strings of fine white beads. It then occurred to them that this might be a native grave, and so they restored it to its original condition, and continued on their way.

After traveling a bit farther, they came upon a small field that was filled with corn stubble from this current year. Passing by another opening, they came to a place where a native house had once stood, with four or five wooden planks laid together on the ground, and an old iron kettle from some ship's galley. They then spied another heap of earth, but this one was much smaller than the first, and not covered with any matting or decoration. They dug into this mound as well, and uncovered a native basket filled with corn from a previous year's harvest. Digging even deeper, they came upon another basket containing fresher corn from the current year. It was a large basket of Indian corn, some yellow, some red, and some mixed with blue, a very welcome sight to the weary travelers. They decided to take the corn with them, and also the kettle, and later return the kettle to the natives, and settle with them for the corn.

Not far from this place, the party came upon a large wooden palisade fence. The palisade was located near where a river was supposed to be. The men quickly located the river and then followed it back to the sea. Along the way they stumbled upon a native canoe hidden on the riverbank, and also spied another canoe on the opposite side. They once again set up camp for the night, and posted a guard. It was raining, and the group tried to sleep as best they could in the cold and wet conditions.

The following morning they were able to locate another trail that led to the east, and soon came upon a young sapling bent down over the trail with a pile of acorns on the ground underneath. One of the men said it was a native trap to catch deer. When William Bradford, following up from the rear, tried to walk around the trap, it sprang up and caught him by the leg. After freeing an embarrassed Mr. Bradford, the party marveled at the fine quality of the rope, and took it along with them as they continued on their way.

When they finally reached the open sea again, they had some distance to travel before they sighted their ship. They then fired off a few signal shots, and a lifeboat was dispatched to pick them up. The ship's skiff was now fully repaired, but it was decided that another skiff needed to be built, and so the ship's carpenter was set to that task. The weather was now growing much colder, and trips to and from shore were becoming a real problem. These trips could only be undertaken at high tide, and the group had to wade great distances to shore in thigh-deep water, which caused many of them to catch coughs and colds that later resulted in many deaths.

When the new skiff was finally completed, a second expedition was undertaken to further explore the native settlement where the corn was found. This time, thirty-four men, including ten from the ship's crew, set sail in the lifeboat and skiff to relocate the river where the native village was located. The weather on this trip was very bad. It was snowing, and the wind was blowing fiercely. The skiff soon began to take on water and had to be sent ashore. The men in the lifeboat continued on, but the wind blew all that day and night, and more men fell ill from this trip. The bay (Truro bay) was finally located, but it was found to be much too shallow to accommodate such a large ship as the Mayflower.

The group then decided to further explore the site where the original native village had been found, to see if more food could be located. They discovered the native canoe still resting on the bank of the creek, and also sighted a large flock of geese. The men shot six of the geese and fetched them with the canoe. They also made use of the canoe to cross the river. It was a large canoe, and could easily carry 7 or 8 men at a time. The party soon relocated the native village and proceeded to dig up more earthen mounds that were found to contain large stores of corn, wheat, and beans.

The Pilgrims thanked God for guiding them to these large stocks of food, grain, and seed, for without them they would not have survived their first winter in the New World. The ground was now covered by snow 6 inches deep, and was also frosted to a depth of 6 inches, and so it became nearly impossible to dig into it. Many of the men were now feeling ill, and it was decided that those men should be sent back to the ship. Only about half of the group stayed on to further explore the area.

They soon located another earthen mound, but this one was much larger and much more elaborately decorated than any previously discovered. It was found to contain the body of a person with blond hair, and also the body of a small child. The party was surprised at this unusual find, because it was known that the native people all had black hair. Was this a Christian who had lived among them?

A further search of the area yielded a small group of native houses (wigwams) that had been recently dwelt in. The houses were constructed of green saplings bent into an arch, with both ends stuck into the ground. The houses were round, and covered on the outside with matting. The matting consisted of two layers, with the inner layer being of a much finer weave and much newer than that on the exterior. The doors to each house were located on opposite sides, and consisted of a flap about 30-inches square, and there was a hole in the roof that served as a chimney. One could stand fully upright inside the structure, and in the center of the floor there was a pit for a fire. There were double layers of matting laid round in a circle inside for sleeping, and outside there were piles of reeds for weaving more matting. There were also numerous baskets, bowls, trays and dishes, all filled with various items including clams, crab shells, acorns, and pieces of smoked herring and venison.

It was now December, and winter was rapidly closing in. A decision had to be made soon about where the group would settle. Some wanted to settle at the present location because of its cleared land and fresh water, but others wanted to explore an even larger bay, called Agawam, that was said to lie north along the coast. It was thought however, that Agawam might be unsuitable because it was too large and too far away, and so a third expedition was launched to see if a more suitable nearby location could be found.

An expeditionary group was sent out in the lifeboat and skiff to explore further north along the coast. The weather was extremely cold and damp, and the men's clothing was soon frozen hard from the icy sea spray. After traveling approximately 40 miles, they spotted a group of savages on the beach gathered around a large black object. It was late in the day, and so the party decided to set up camp for the night. They could see the native campfires burning about 4 or 5 miles distant.

In the morning, they set out for the location where they had spotted the natives, and soon came upon a grampus, or small whale, that had been washed up on the beach. When they arrived at the location where they'd seen the natives, they saw where the savages had been stripping the body of another grampus. There were numerous bare footprints all around the carcass. The party then decided to travel inland, and soon came upon a large wooden palisade that contained many native graves. Some of these graves even had houses built over them. The hour was growing late though, and so they decided to set up camp near the graveyard for the night.

At around midnight, a loud, whooping cry was heard coming from the forest. The men shot off their muskets and the sound stopped. The next morning around daybreak, they again heard the whooping cry, and this time arrows were seen to fly at them from the woods. They could plainly see one of the savages standing about a half a musket's shot away. He shot three arrows at them, but the men ducked his arrows and returned a round of musket fire, wounding him in the arm. The savage and his men then ran off into the woods. The Pilgrims picked up some of the native arrows and continued on their way.

The party set out to sea once again to explore further up the coast. After traveling about another 40 miles, they ran into some bad weather, but continued on, and were at the last minute able to find shelter in another large bay (Plymouth Bay). They spent all night on an island in the middle of the bay, and in the morning were able to determine by depth sounding that this bay was indeed suitable for large ships. Further explorations of the area revealed many cleared fields and numerous sources of fresh water, and so the party quickly sailed back to the Mayflower with good news of their find. In the third week of December 1620, the Mayflower finally set anchor at Plymouth Harbor.

Stormy weather continued to plague the weary travelers, but in a few days they were finally able to go ashore to begin cutting the lumber they would need to build their new settlement. They chose to build the settlement upon a high hill that would be defensible from the savages, and also provide good views of the harbor and the open sea. The Pilgrims often saw native campfires burning in the distance, but the savages never approached their settlement.

The area was a perfect spot for a farming settlement. There were many cleared fields and numerous fresh water streams filled with fish. There were also cherry trees, and plums, and strawberries, as well as great stores of leeks and onions. By January, construction of the settlement was well underway.

A few days later, two men from the settlement were walking their dogs in the forest when one of the animals ran off after a deer. The men soon became lost in the woods and were forced to spend a night in the forest. They found it necessary to climb a large tree in order to escape hungry mountain lions that were roaring nearby. Predators in the New World were extremely plentiful. An area of only 5 miles square would often contain as many as 100 wolves, 40 mountain lions, and 20 black bears.

The next morning, the men ascended a high hill and successfully relocated the bay. They eventually arrived back at the settlement cold and frightened, but none the worse for their adventure.

The following week, Master Goodman was walking his spaniel in the woods when the dog was accosted by two large wolves. The dog ran between its master's legs for protection, and Master Goodman held the wolves off with a large stick. The wolves soon tired of the standoff and retreated back into the forest.

A day or two later, another member of the group was hunting in the forest when he spotted a group of savages heading in the general direction of the settlement. He waited until they had all passed, then ran back to sound an alarm. The workmen, who were in the forest, ran back to the settlement to arm themselves. The natives however, never showed. When the workmen returned to the forest, they found that many of their tools were missing. The Pilgrims resolved never again to assume that they were not being closely monitored by the natives.

Many more native houses were eventually located in the area, but none had been recently dwelt in, and the Pilgrims were unable to successfully establish contact with any of the local inhabitants. Winter was now upon them, and food was growing scarce. Their first winter in the New World was a severe trial for the Pilgrims. Food supplies were dwindling, and many of them were dying from colds and pneumonia. More than once their hastily built cabins were set afire by stray sparks from the fireplaces.

Of the 102 original members of the group, one had died on the voyage, and six more died of pneumonia during the month of December. In January eight more were lost to illness, and seventeen additional in February. On any given day during their first winter, only six or seven members of the group possessed enough strength to nurse the sick or bury the dead. An attack by the natives was a constant fear, and in their present condition, a single attack could have easily overwhelmed them. But that attack never came, and after losing thirteen more of their number during the month of March, the first signs of spring finally began to appear.

By March 1st, the snow had finally started melting, and warmer temperatures were beginning to arrive. Then, two weeks later, on a Friday, a tall, unclothed savage boldly walked up to the gate of the settlement and greeted the Pilgrims in English. He said his name was Samoset, and he spoke a broken English he'd learned from the many English vessels that frequented the area. He said he was not of these parts, but was of the Moratiggon, a tribe to the far north (Penobscot Bay), and was one of the Sagamores thereof. He was a tall man with long black hair falling behind, and short hair in front. He had no hair at all growing on his face (Native Americans couldn't grow beards), and was naked except for a leather skirt bound about his waist, with a fringe at the bottom. He said that he'd been in these parts for about eight months. The Pilgrims greeted him as a friend and invited him into the settlement, but all the men kept their muskets at the ready.

Samoset proved to be an excellent source of information concerning the local area. He told them that the place they now occupied was called Patuxet, and that it was previously inhabited by a native tribe totally wiped out by a plague that had come through about 4 years earlier. The plague had killed all the Patuxets, and about 90 percent of the members of other tribes in the area. He also told them that their land was therefore free for the taking. The Massasoits, their neighbors to the west, who once numbered nearly a thousand, now numbered only about sixty, and the Nansets to the southwest, were about a hundred strong. The Nansets were the tribe that had attacked the Pilgrims in their first unfriendly native encounter.

All the tribes in the area were angry with the British because of the English Captain Hunt, who had deceived them and sold about twenty of their number into slavery to the Spanish. The natives had already killed three Englishmen in retaliation for this despicable act. The Pilgrims sincerely apologized for Howe's unchristian behavior, and assured Samoset that not all Englishmen behaved in this manner. Samoset was then entertained with food and drink, both of which he heartily enjoyed. The following day he returned to the Massasoits but promised to return soon with other natives to trade animal skins.

The very next day Samoset returned with five other savages who were also very tall, and clothed in deerskin trousers. Their faces were painted black, and they wore feathers in their hair. Their chief carried a wildcat's skin over one arm and wore a fox tail in his hair. They left their bows, arrows, hatchets, and wooden war-clubs, known as "tomahawks," about a quarter mile outside the settlement as had been previously arranged with Samoset.

The Pilgrims fed and entertained their native guests, and the natives likewise danced around the campfire in their strange antic manner. They had brought only five animal skins with them however, and so the Pilgrims sent them away to fetch more skins, and also requested that they return the tools they'd stolen from the woods. The natives returned the tools the very same day, and promised to return soon with more animal skins.

In a few days Samoset returned once again, this time accompanied by another savage named Tisquantum (Squanto), who was the only surviving member of the Patuxets.

Tisquantum had earlier been taken captive by Captain Hunt, and sailed to England as Hunt's servant. Tisquantum had lived and worked in both Spain and England, and thus escaped the plague that killed his tribe. The two men told the Pilgrims that the great Chief Massasoit was encamped nearby, and wished to meet with them. The Pilgrims agreed to meet with the chief, and an agreement with Massasoit was soon concluded over a hearty meal and some strong drink, which caused the chief to sweat profusely all during the meeting.

When spring finally arrived, the planting of some 20 acres of corn, wheat, and peas was undertaken in the native manner using alewives (American Shad), which clogged the streams and rivers of New England each spring, as fertilizer. The Indian Squanto stayed with the Pilgrims, and proved to be an invaluable source of practical knowledge.

In the late summer, a young boy from the settlement became lost in the woods and could not be located by search parties. Word eventually came to the settlement that the boy had been picked up by the Monomets and taken to the Nanset village to the south. The Nansets were the tribe who'd attacked the Pilgrims in their first unfriendly encounter, and it was feared that they might do harm to the boy. A group of ten armed men from the settlement was therefore sent out by boat for Nanset, accompanied by native interpreters, in order to safely retrieve the young child.

Their trip was interrupted by a severe thunderstorm however, and the group sought refuge in Comoaquid (Barnstable) harbor. The Comoaquid chief, Iyanough, agreed to accompany the Pilgrims on their trip to the Nanset village. They arrived at Nanset late in the day, and native interpreters traveled to a small nearby village to inquire about the boy. The Nanset chief Aspinet returned with about a hundred of his tribe and delivered the boy safely to the Pilgrims. It was said that the boy had wandered for five days before being picked up by the Monomets.

Aspinet told the Pilgrims that a sachem named Corbitant was plotting with the Narragansetts against the Pilgrim settlement, and that he had taken the great Chief Massasoit prisoner, and also Tisquantum. The Pilgrims were greatly disturbed by this news and decided to immediately undertake an expedition to Namasket to rescue both Tisquantum and Massasoit.

The Pilgrims sent a party of ten armed men to Namasket. The men arrived late in the evening and found Tisquantum alive and well. They shot and killed a few of the Namaskets, causing Corbitant and his followers to flee into the woods. Tisquantum was able to calm the rest of the tribe, and the Pilgrims left a warning that Chief Massasoit must be returned unharmed. They also warned the villagers that any natives found to be siding with Corbitant would be hunted down and killed.

The balance of the summer went very well for the Pilgrims, and their first harvest in the New World was truly a bountiful one. In October the governor of the settlement declared that a great feast of Thanksgiving should be held to thank the Lord for all their good fortune.

Hunters from the settlement were sent out to shoot wild turkeys and waterfowl for the great feast. The women gathered in large quantities of grapes and plums, and the local natives were also invited to attend. The natives brought along with them great baskets of clams, oysters, native pumpkins and popping corn. Even the great chief Massasoit attended with about one hundred of his men, and provided five deer for venison. The great feast of Thanksgiving continued on for more than three days, and was heartily enjoyed by both natives and Christians alike. And so Thanksgiving was thus officially established as the first Christian holiday celebrated in America.

Through a policy of Christian fairness, honesty and mutual respect, the Pilgrims were finally able to establish a peace with, and among, the various native tribes in the area. Many of these tribes had formerly warred with one another, but now a state of peace prevailed throughout the land, and it was possible for any man, Christian or native, to travel the forest trails in complete safety. The natives freely visited the homes of the Pilgrims, and great knowledge was passed on concerning native customs, foods, and medicines.

The colonists had applied their Christian principles to create a peaceful and positive change in a people who had for thousands of years been suffering in war and ignorance. Never before had these native tribes lived in such a state of peace and mutual respect for one another. The Pilgrims educated many of the native sagamores on the teachings of Jesus, and native emissaries were sent out amongst the tribes to spread the message of Jesus Christ.

It was a truly happy time for the Christian Pilgrims in this new land of plenty. God had paved the way for them with a plague upon the savages, and had also led them to settle upon the only twenty-mile section of coastline in the entire New World unclaimed by any native tribe. They would now be able to spread the message of Jesus to all the heathens of the New World. Truly the Lord does work in mysterious ways.

News of the Pilgrim colony's success, in light of earlier failures by similar colonies from Maine to Virginia, was received with great delight by wealthy merchants in England. Funding was soon made available for a new settlement of

English Puritans in the area of the Massachusetts Bay (Agawam) colony.

The milk of human kindness however, did not flow within the hearts of many of the Puritans, who held no great regard for the rights of heathen savages, and paid heavy bounties for Indian scalps. The Puritans referred to white men as "man," and native Americans as "mankind." There were many disagreements as to whether these inferior races could be educated to become free Christians.

When England's former Catholics, now known as Episcopals (Anglicans), settled America's south, they imported black slaves from Africa to work their farms. This race question would remain unanswered until the mid 19th century, when a man named Abraham Lincoln would be provided by God to settle the issue.

Within a short time the Puritan settlements had grown to over 10,000 members, including merchants, lawyers, and other business interests, all intending to reap huge profits from the enormous quantities of natural resources now made available to them through the sufferings of the original Christian missionaries of the Plymouth Colony.

CHAPTER 25

EASTER

"And (Thomas) Morton became lord of misrule, and maintained a school of Atheism. They also set up a May-Pole, drinking and dancing about it many days together, inviting the Indian women for their consorts, dancing and frisking together like so many fairies (or furies rather), and worse practices."

William Bradford - Governor, Plymouth Colony

The Easter holiday is still celebrated each spring by Christians honoring the resurrection of Jesus Christ. Easter is therefore one of the most meaningful of all the Christian holidays. Easter is commonly celebrated with Easter bunnies, Easter chicks, Easter eggs, and Easter sunrise services. Easter is also preceded by a period of fasting known as Lent.

The tremendous symbolism of the Easter holiday still remains a mystery to most Christians, but it is important for modern Christians to explore that symbolism if Easter's true origins are to be revealed. The Easter celebration was passed down to us from the traditions of the Holy Roman Church of Europe. The Catholic Church rose in consort with the Holy Roman Empire, which was originally formed through a union of the Roman Empire and the Christian Church. This union was formed around 312 AD, when the Roman emperor Constantine struck a deal with Christians to have Romans accept the Christian faith.

In the year 312, at the battle of Milvian Bridge, it is said that Constantine saw a vision in the sky of a cross bearing the words "In Hoc Signo Vinces" (by this sign thou shalt conquer), and claimed that it was God who had led him to victory.

At the time this deal was originally struck, the Roman Empire was in a state of serious economic decline, and Constantine had to act quickly to strengthen his hold on the European continent. The Christians had made huge inroads into northern Europe, and also controlled a major portion of the Roman Empire itself. Constantine therefore decided it was in his best interests to form a union with the Christian Church in order to prevent his empire from crumbling.

In 323 AD Constantine held his famous "Council of Nicea" in order to officially establish a new "Holy" Roman Empire. As part of this agreement, the Roman Church agreed to change its official Sabbath day from the seventh day of the week, to the first day of the week. The Bishop of Rome agreed to this compromise in order to accommodate the wishes of his pagan Roman sun-worshippers.

The Christian Sabbath therefore, was officially changed from Saturday to Sunday, the Roman day of the sun. In exchange for this compromise, the Church would benefit from the protection of the Roman government, and church bishops would be made official magistrates of the Roman Empire.

The divinity of Jesus, which until this time had not been established, was also declared to be an official fact. The Father and the Son were now declared to be of one and the same spirit, much to the pleasure of the pagan Romans, who had always wanted to worship God Himself, and not merely His son. This new doctrine declaring the "Father, Son, and Holy Spirit" to be one and the same entity, did not sit well with Arius, head bishop of the Holy See at Alexandria, who decided to break away from the Roman See (see: Arianism). This new concept of a "Holy Trinity," would later be exposed and attacked by many men, including the great scientist Sir Isaac Newton.

It was advantageous for Constantine to strike this doctrinal deal with the Christians, because it extended the boundaries of his empire into the farthest reaches of barbarian Europe, where the Church held great power. The Church wielded a great deal of influence with the pagan Germanic tribes of the Danube River region of Europe. The Romans had long been warring with these German barbarians.

The German people were known as the "barbarians," or "bearded-people," of Europe. They were sometimes also referred to as the "people of Ister." Ister was the Roman name for the Danube River. This name was originally derived from a celebration held there every spring by these pagan Germanic tribes in order to guarantee the fertility of their summer crops. This celebration, known as Ister, (Babylonian Ishtar) was held every spring to honor Ishtar, the Babylonian goddess of fertility.

These blond-haired, blue-eyed, full-bearded people from the upper Danube region, whose children often possessed platinum-blonde hair, were thought to be direct descendants of the Caucasian (white-skinned) peoples of the Caucuses Mountains of southern Russia, also known as the "Russ." These "Russ," for whom "Russia" was originally named, migrated northward and westward from the Caucuses across the lands of Sythia, Sarmatia, and Saxony, to populate Germany, the Baltics, Scandinavia, Britannia, and a few even extended their influence eastward across the steppes of Russia. Their long beards, tartan plaids, coats of arms, boat axes, witches hats, and sturdy little ponies can still be found today in societies extending all the way from the Shetland Islands of England, to the plains of northern Mongolia. Even the great Mongol leader Genghis Khan, was known to be a Turkic Caucasian. These people are still popularly known in the field of archeology today as the "longheads."

This Caucasian race that once lived under the rule of the ancient Assyrians and Babylonians, had ascended northward through ancient Media and the Caucuses Mountains of Russia into their new northern European homeland. Unfortunately they also carried their Babylonian gods and customs along with them. Their path through history can be easily traced by the peculiar habit of their males of wearing skirts. They were recorded as wearing these skirts when they were with the Medes in what is now Armenia (Ar-Media), and again many years later in the Danube region of Germany as the "Sigynnae," as noted by the Greek historian Herodotus.

The Ister holiday was celebrated by these pagan Germanic tribes every spring, and was based upon astronomical positions of the sun and moon. The Ister holiday was always celebrated on the first Sunday after the first full moon, after the spring equinox of the sun. This astronomical date, originally set by ancient Babylonian astrologers, is still the date on which Easter is celebrated today.

The original Easter (Ister) celebration was held all over northern Europe by pagans seeking to guarantee the fertility of their summer crops by paying tribute to Ishtar, the Babylonian goddess of fertility. The Ister celebration was held in every German village and town, and included the consumption of copious quantities of beer and wine by the male elders of each village, who would then seek out the village "virgins" for a little fun and merriment.

This "virgin" portion of the celebration was marked by a formal dance around the village May-Pole by unmarried females, who would dance in a provocative manner in order to stimulate the interest of their male suitors.

When the May-Pole dance was completed, the virgins would flee off into the woods, pursued by their drunken male suitors. This reverse form of "Sadie Hawkins Day" ® often established new bonds for future marriages in the village.

The many familiar Easter fertility symbols were also a necessary part of every Ister celebration. Rabbits and chickens, noted for their prolific propagation abilities, were ritually sacrificed to Ishtar, daughter of Sin, the Babylonian Moon-god, and then consumed by all the celebrants. Children were sent into the forest to hunt for decorated Easter eggs, and got to eat and enjoy their prizes. It was also a pagan custom to bake little cake offerings to the "Queen of Heaven" (Ishtar)(Jer.7:18). These little cakes were the forerunners of our modern-day "Hot Cross" buns, baked by modern Christians for their Easter celebrations.

Many libraries still contain paintings and illustrations of these early European Easter orgies. If you've ever wondered why European males are often pictured wearing tights, these paintings leave no doubt that their purpose was to accentuate the lower portion of the male anatomy, just as modern-day women's clothing is designed to accentuate the upper portion of the female anatomy. In those days, European males were apparently not very shy about their maleness.

When Catholic priests first ventured into the forests of Europe to witness these pagan orgies, they tried to discourage the sexual orientation of the celebrations, but met with fierce resistance from village elders. They then decided instead to negotiate with the pagans in order to lend a Christian air to the festivities.

Since Ister was held every spring to celebrate the resurrection of green plants from their winter death, it was agreed that the celebration would also be used to commemorate the resurrection of Jesus Christ from death.

The Catholic priests found this compromise technique quite useful in extending their influence into the farthest reaches of the Holy Roman empire. Prevailing opinion was that the village elders would eventually die off, thereby allowing the priests to educate the younger generation into accepting the principles of Christianity.

This plan however, never quite materialized, and today the Church still retains all the original pagan fertility symbols, including rabbits, chicks, and eggs, in its Easter celebrations. Easter sunrise services are also still a vital part of the Easter morning mass, reflecting pagan worship of the rising sun.

Our Christian God is an invisible God, but the pagans needed a God that they could both see and touch. They therefore steadfastly refused to give up their idols and statues. One statue that was central to the Ister celebration was the statue of the Babylonian goddess Ishtar, represented by the faceless, naked, pregnant female body. This statue celebrated the female anatomy in its most fertile state.

Catholic priests quickly took advantage of this statue by telling the pagans that it could be used to represent the pregnant body of the Virgin Mary, mother of Jesus. This change in focus from Jesus Christ to the Virgin Mary ultimately resulted in the early Church often being referred to as the "cult of Mary."

All in all, Catholic priests were quite successful at compromising their way into pagan philosophy. They were also successful in their efforts to turn the spring Germanic pagan celebration of Ister (Ishtar – Eoster) into our modern-day "Easter" celebration. This compromise technique was also used on the pagan Romans as well. Through many such compromises, the Catholic Church was ultimately able to place itself into a very powerful and secure position in Europe that guaranteed its existence for the next 1700 years.

The prophets tell us however, that God does not permit His people to compromise, and that it is every Christian's responsibility to continually examine his personal behavior to make sure it conforms to God's strict laws. Down through history, God's people have strayed from His laws many times and taken up the worship of pagan gods and idols. In every case, they were severely punished for their behavior.

Many modern Christians celebrating Easter today probably do not realize that their Easter celebration is rooted in Babylonian pagan tradition. Christians however, by their own tenets, are expected to study the Holy Scriptures carefully, and to be wary of pagan influence in their religious celebrations.

CHAPTER 26

THE CHRISTIAN CHURCH

"And he (Simeon) came by the spirit into the temple, and when the parents brought in the child Jesus to do him after the custom of the law, then took he him in his arms and blessed God and said, Lord, now lettest thou thy servant depart in peace according to thy word: for mine eyes have seen thy salvation which thou hast prepared before the face of all people. A light to lighten the Gentiles, and the glory of thy people Israel."

Luke (2: 27-32)

Approximately two thousand years ago in the land of Judea, in the middle of the month of June, an unusually bright star was observed in the midnight sky. This star was also seen by astrologers in nearby Persia, who determined it to be a sign from God heralding the birth of a new Hebrew messiah. These Persian wisemen hurriedly gathered up their belongings and prepared to journey into the distant land of Judea in order to personally honor this newly arrived "king of the Jews."

Approximately three decades later, this same child would establish the beginnings of what we now know as the Christian Church. The Church from its very beginnings was resigned to surviving outside the limits of so-called "civilized" society, because its very existence threatened the authority of established government. The Roman government in fact persecuted its Christian masses, and greatly enjoyed feeding Christians to the hungry lions in its Colosseum in Rome.

The followers of Jesus Christ of Nazareth were thus forced to flee into the forests of northern Europe, where their religion would flourish, mainly due to the kindness and understanding it always extended toward the poor and destitute castoffs of organized society.

The government of Rome lived off the spoils of its military conquests, but ultimately the limits of those conquests were reached. And when there were no more spoils to be had, the economy of Rome slowly began to falter, as witnessed by the slow but steady decline in the silver content of its coinage.

It is a well known fact that world conquering governments often survive off the backs of the poor, and invariably fail when their demands become too great for the common man to bear. As the Roman government continued to persecute its Christian masses, the number of poor grew steadily, along with the membership of the Christian Church.

By the year 300 AD, the Empire of Rome was in a state of serious economic decline, and could no longer even feed its own citizens. The empire had broken up into two alliances, one in the West under the emperors Maximian, Maxentius and Constantine, and one in the East under the emperors Galerius, Maxinian, and Licinius.

The young emperor Constantine, who'd recently inherited his empire when his father passed away at York, Britain, quickly worked his way up through the ranks of the Roman army, and soon was a formidable candidate for taking control of the entire Roman Empire. After the emperor Maximian fell to the evil hand of his son-in law at Marseilles, and Galerius died of an unknown illness, Constantine decided to lead his army against the effeminate Maxentius of Rome.

In a historic battle known as the "Battle of Milvian Bridge," Constantine claimed to have seen a vision in the sky of a cross with the Greek words "Ev rourw vixa" (Latin: In this, conquer). Constantine then adopted this phrase as his motto, and would later use it to strike a deal with the Holy See of Rome in order to prevent his newly won Roman Empire from falling into complete ruin.

A few years later, in 323 AD, Constantine held his famous "Council at Nicea" in order to officially establish the tenets of his newly formed alliance with the Christian Church. This infamous council marked the beginnings of a series of negotiations between the Roman government and the Roman See, in which the doctrines of Christianity would be severely compromised.

Roman church officials agreed to form an alliance with the Roman government, thus creating a new "Holy" Roman Empire. As a part of this agreement, Church leaders agreed to change their official Sabbath from the seventh day of the week to the first day of the week, Sun-day, in order to please the pagan sun-worshippers of Rome. In turn for this compromise, the Roman government agreed that Church bishops would be appointed official magistrates of the Roman Empire.

The divinity of Jesus, which until this time had not been established, was also officially declared to be a true fact. The Father, the Son, and the Holy Spirit were now declared to be one and the same entity. This concept of the "Holy Trinity", greatly pleased the pagan Romans, who had always wanted to worship God himself, and not merely His Son.

These many alterations to established church doctrines did not sit well with Arius, head priest of the Holy See at Alexandria (established by St. Peter himself), who immediately rebelled against these outrageous heresies by the Roman See.

Arius and many other Christian bishops from other sees around the Mediterranean area refused to go along with these outrageous compromises agreed to by the Roman See. Arius was joined in his dissent by churches all around the Christian realm, and a new doctrine of "Arianism" was firmly established.

From this time forward, the basic tenets of Christianity would always remain a subject for great controversy, and the "Holy" Roman Empire, now led by a Christian Pope and a Roman Emperor, would never quite arrive at a complete state of harmony with its Christian masses.

With its power once again renewed, Rome and its armies continued to pillage their way across new lands, but now under the sign of the Christian Cross. The Roman Empire however, never quite regained its former status, and Constantine decided that it was time to expand his empire to the East.

After defeating the Eastern Empire of his brother-in-law Licinius, Constantine was able to declare himself sole emperor of the entire Roman Empire. Constantine then decided to build a new Christian capital city in the East named "Constantinople". But shortly after Constantine's death, Valens, a follower of Arius, became Emperor of the Eastern Empire, and decided to spread the doctrine of Arianism into the barbaric lands of northern Europe.

The Western Empire of Rome would still continue to exist, but for the next few centuries it was besieged by a host of Arian invaders from the north including the Goths of Germany, the Huns of Russia, the Vandals of Denmark, and other barbaric tribes. Most of these barbarians agreed not to spoil Rome and its many treasures, with the notable exception of the Vandals, whose brutal sack of Rome earned their name a permanent place in the English language.

The Eastern Empire eventually turned away from Arianism to again embrace Roman Catholicism, but an ongoing series of battles between the Germanic barbarians and the Eastern Empire for control of Rome ultimately reduced the great city to a state of complete ruin. And in the year 536 AD, the population of Rome, which normally numbered about 500,000, fell to a new low of only about 500 people. The city had been totally destroyed by a combination of war, disease, and famine. A "dry fog" of gloom was said to have formed over the entire Mediterranean region, as Rome reached its lowest point in history. The pope was removed from Rome, and many theologians marked this time as the "cessation of the daily sacrifice" in the Vatican.

In the lands to the East, the Arabs were not at all impressed with the blatant acts of immorality displayed by the Romans and their so-called "Christian" religion. They observed that the members of the Holy Roman faith openly engaged in gambling, alcohol, adultery, and almost every other form of carnal pleasure.

Around the year 600 AD, a Middle Eastern prophet named Mohamed introduced the religion of Islam to the Arab world, which eventually resulted in more problems for the Holy Roman Empire. Muhammad resurrected the old Mosaic Law, and commanded that his followers obey the Sharia, a system of Talmudic-like laws forbidding gambling, alcohol, public entertainment, and the eating of pork. To reduce the sexual temptation of men and other aberrant behaviors, women were required to cover their bodies and faces in public, and common criminal offenses were often dealt with very harshly. A man could now lose his hand for thievery.

The followers of the God of Abraham now found themselves divided into four religious sects, Roman Catholics,

Jews, Eastern Orthodox, and Muslims. The Jews existed everywhere within the other three realms, but were often discriminated against due to the perception that they tended to control the economies of their host nations. Around the year 655, Islamic forces would also threaten the Christian Church by sea, and make great conquests around the Mediterranean. The next five hundred years would mark a dark period in European history, with feudal times recording much human suffering and extreme poverty across the European continent.

Around the year 1000 AD, a series of military Crusades were launched from Christian centers in Europe to recapture the Holy Land from the Muslims, but after these many conquests, the Holy Land would nearly always revert back to Arab control.

The First Christian Crusade, launched in 1096 from Central Europe to recapture Jerusalem from the Muslims, was severely hampered by disease and hunger. When the Christian Crusaders left the pristine forests of Europe and entered into the hot, dry deserts of the Middle East, they quickly fell victim to the many diseases inhabiting the polluted water wells of that region. There also was very little food available in the hot desert environment, and it was difficult to store food in the hot desert sun.

The Christian forces however, were ultimately successful in usurping control of the city of Jerusalem from the Muslims. The Christian Crusades continued on for many decades and were not ended until 1444, when the Ottoman Turks decisively defeated an army of Christian Crusaders at the battle of Varna, on the shores of the Black Sea. The Muslims were now finally able to capture the great city of Constantinople and destroy the Christian Empire in the East. The Holy Land was now reclaimed for Islam.

The Holy Roman Empire however, managed to survive intact for more than a millennium, and finally celebrated it's Renaissance, or "rebirth," in the late 1500's. Church leadership however, again fell victim to the many temptations of the material world, and slowly began to align itself with the rich monarchies of Europe, in a campaign to raise itself to the same economic level as those monarchies. Its vows of poverty were ignored, as it gained the temporal power to own land, and began to construct many lavish churches and cathedrals. The Church and its leadership now began to demand more and more money from the struggling poor. In order to complete Saint Peter's Basilica in Rome, the Pope resorted to selling tickets into heaven, known as Indulgences, to anyone with enough money to purchase them.

When the Dominican friar John Tetzel was hired by the Pope in 1517 to sell indulgences in German Saxony, it was the last straw for the Catholic priest Martin Luther, who decided it was now time to speak out against the Roman See. This act of religious heresy by Rome had also infuriated many other Catholic leaders in northern Europe, who eventually sought to break off relations with the Vatican, and form themselves into a new "Protestant" alliance. Luther began to print and distribute copies of the Holy Bible that were able to be read and understood by the common man, thereby abolishing the need to obtain religious instruction solely from Roman priests. This action infuriated the Pope, who directed the armies of his Catholic League to kill and drive out all Protestants and Jews from the European continent.

A state of civil war now existed in nearly all of Europe, as Catholics and Protestants fought for control of the continent. Many Protestant sects, including Lutherans, Huguenots, Calvinists, Anglicans, and dozens of others, would now confuse the religious landscape of Europe for the next 100 years.

In England there were primarily three Protestant sects, Anglicans, Puritans, and Pilgrim Separatists. The Anglicans followed many of the original Catholic precepts, and the Puritans sought to purify the Church of all pagan doctrines. The Saxon Pilgrim Separatists however, decided to break off completely from the Catholic Church and receive their instruction directly from the Holy Scriptures. This distinction made them a subject of constant attacks and persecutions by the European government and Church officials.

A few free-spirited Christian Pilgrim Separatists eventually decided to flee to Holland and eventually escape Europe entirely to establish a new religious-based colony in the New World. They sought to create a new free society in which Christians would be able to freely interpret the truth of the Holy Scriptures for themselves.

And so the thirst for perfect knowledge held so deeply within the human soul for nearly a millennium and a half, could now finally be quenched by the message of the holy prophets of God, held within the Holy Scriptures. The Christian Church would now aspire to a new level, and the truth of the Holy Scriptures would be utilized to spread the message of God through His son Jesus Christ to all people of the Earth.

CHAPTER 27

THE STONE OF DESTINY

And Jacob rose up early in the morning, and took the stone that he had used for his pillow, and set it up for a pillar, and poured oil upon the top of it.

Gen. (28:18)

For centuries, men have been captivated by tales of ancient holy relics such as the Ark of the Covenant and the Holy Grail. These objects spawned numerous books and movies about their magical powers and prophetic mystique. The existence of these holy objects however, can only be confirmed by ancient legend. None of these objects has ever been located. There is however, one holy item that has survived into modern times. It is the famous "Stone of Destiny". This holy relic predates all others, and carries with it a history and a destiny that is truly the stuff great legends are made of.

The significance of the stone is deeply rooted in Bible history, for the stone is thought to carry God's blessing upon those who possess it, and was destined to follow God's people on their long journey through history. The story behind the Stone of Destiny is nearly 4000 years old, and I therefore thought you might enjoy reading about this holy object that really does exist, and still has a role to play in modern times. In order to discuss the stone however, it will first be necessary for us to discuss the blessing it carries.

We all know that in the beginning God created Adam, and that the bloodline of Adam still exists upon the Earth today. This Genesis story comes down to us through the ancient Hebrew Scriptures. These Scriptures also tell us that in the time of Adam, the sons of Gods gazed upon the daughters of men and saw that they were fair; and so the sons of Gods went in unto the daughters of men and bare them children (Gen. 6:2-6). Thus began the line of the great patriarchs, a superior race of men created through this strange union. These biblical patriarchs had the unique ability to live for ten times as long as normal human beings, but unfortunately they also carried with them the carnal nature of man.

The world of the patriarchs eventually developed into a world of great evil, and so God decided to destroy what He had created. There was however one patriarch named Noah, who was blessed with great goodness, and so God decided to save Noah and his family from the destruction of the great Flood. We are all familiar with the story of Noah's Ark and the great Flood, and how Noah and his family survived this great catastrophe. Noah was the first in a blessed line of men to carry God's special blessing into the modern world. God's blessing was passed down from father to son along a genealogical line that is very carefully recorded for us within the pages of the Bible.

After approximately thirteen more generations, God appears to the prophet Abram (father) and promises Abram that he will eventually father a great nation. Abram's name is then changed to Abraham (father of a multitude), for he is destined to father a blessed line of the Hebrew people. It is this same blessing that the Stone of Destiny still carries with it today.

The Stone of Destiny, also known as "Jacob's Pillow," was just another stone lying on the desert floor, until one night in

1950 BC, when Jacob (Abraham's grandson) used it as a pillow while on a trip from Harab to Bethel (Gen. 28:18). While sleeping on the stone, Jacob dreamed of a great ladder leading up to heaven with angels climbing up and down it. In the dream, the Lord spoke to Jacob, and told him that his children would be a blessing unto the world. When Jacob arose in the morning, he took the stone along with him, and thus the stone began its long trek through history.

Jacob's name was eventually changed to Israel (those cherished by God), and he fathered twelve sons who would be the progenitors of the twelve tribes of Israel. Jacob could only bestow God's blessing upon one of his sons, and so he sat his twelve sons down one day and told them of the ultimate destiny of their descendants in the last days (Gen. 49). Jacob decided to bestow God's special blessing upon his son Joseph, and so the blessing, and the "Shepherd's Stone," would follow the descendants of Joseph until the last days (Gen. 49:24).

The location of the stone remained a great mystery for many centuries. It was eventually traced to Great Britain, and now resides in Edinburgh Castle in Scotland. But because the Irish, the Scots, and the English so love to tell tall tales, there are quite a number of stories about how the stone first arrived in Great Britain. Probably the most interesting of all these stories is one involving the biblical prophet Jeremiah.

It is said that around 580 BC, when the Babylonians were sacking Jerusalem, that Jeremiah removed the stone from the Great Temple in Jerusalem and fled south into Egypt, taking with him Tea Tephi, the daughter of King Zedikiah of Judah. Jeremiah then traveled by sea to Ireland where the stone was used to wed Tea Tephi to the Irish king, Eochaide the Heremon, thus preserving the bloodline of David upon a world throne.

From that day forward, all Irish Kings were required to be enthroned in the presence of the holy stone. The stone was kept at Tarah, in Meath, and followed the line of the Dalriadic kings down through Irish history. Even Saint Patrick is said to have blessed this holy stone that followed the descendants of Erc, first king of the Dal Riata tribe of Antrim.

Around 850 AD, Fergus is rumored to have borrowed the "Lia Fail" (Stone of Fate) from his brother, King Muisceortagh of Ireland, in order to use it at his coronation in Alba (Scotland). Fergus however, never returned the stone to his brother. The stone remained in Scotland, and eventually found a home in the city of Scone (pronounced "scoon"). This "Stone of Scone" was then used to enthrone all subsequent kings of Scotland. The last Scottish king to be enthroned in the presence of the holy stone was John Baloil in the year 1292.

When Edward I of England invaded Scotland in 1296, Baloil surrender the stone to Edward, and abdicated the throne. Edward then transferred the stone from Scone to Westminster in England.

In 1301 the English built a "Coronation Chair" to house the stone, and this chair was thenceforth used to enthrone all subsequent British monarchs.

Then, in the year 1328, the Scots formally won back their independence from England with the signing of the Treaty of Northampton by Edward III, who promised to return the stone to Scotland. The stone however, was never returned. And so on Christmas day in 1950, a group of young Scottish students from Glasgow decided to reclaim the stone from Westminster Abbey and return it to Scotland. They broke into Westminster Abby and removed the stone from beneath the Coronation Chair. They then placed the stone in the trunk of their car and spirited it off to an unknown location.

Scotland Yard finally located the stone many months later in Arbroath Abbey in Scotland, and it was formally reinstated in Westminster Abbey in February of 1952. In 1953, the stone was used at the coronation ceremony for Queen Elizabeth II. During the anointing ceremony for the new queen, the Archbishop of Canterbury recited the following prayer:

"Oh Lord and Heavenly Father, exalter of the humble and the strength of thy chosen, who by anointing with oil, didst of old make and, consecrate kings, priests, and prophets, to teach and govern thy people Israel. Bless and sanctify thy chosen servant Elizabeth, who by our office and ministry is now to be anointed with this oil."

The stone still remained a source of great controversy however, and in 1996, Elizabeth II finally agreed to allow the stone's return to Scotland with the stipulation that it be made available for any future coronations.

According to ancient prophecy, the Stone of Destiny will follow an unbroken line of monarchs from the original throne of David, until the Lord's return. We know from the record of history that this sacred stone was indeed used to enthrone a long line of Irish, Scottish, and English monarchs from 580 BC to 2000 AD, and may assume that the prophet Jeremiah delivered it to Great Britain for this express purpose. This is a truly amazing case of ancient prophecy still operating in modern times.

There are many curious links between the ancient Hebrews and the people of the British Isles, particularly the Scottish people. It seems that the ancient Israelites were also known to wear skirts, or kilts, displaying the plaids of their various tribes.

Also, the bagpipes used by modern Irish and Scottish pipers are almost identical to the ancient Hebrew goatskin bagpipe that David played while guarding his sheep. And ancient Hebrew mason guilds were employed by many other civilizations whenever stone buildings or monuments needed to be erected. There are some who insist that this masonic link extends even to the original formation of the United States of America in 1776. The famed Washington Monument that sits at the very center of the Capital Mall in Washington DC, is in fact a masonic obelisk, and was erected by the members of the guild of the ancient Scottish rite.

There are some who still doubt that the British Stone of Destiny is in fact Jacob's Pillow, but the British Crown continues to observe this ancient rite. This is just one more example of ancient prophecy still operating in modern times.

CHAPTER 28

OUR LADY OF FATIMA

"The war (WWI) is going to end soon, but if people do not cease offending God, a worse war will break out under the pontificate of Pius XI."

Our Lady of Fatima

History records for us many interesting and prophetic events. Some of these events are recorded within the pages of the Bible, but some have also occurred in modern times as well. Often these modern prophetic events come under intense public scrutiny, and a few have even been exposed as frauds. Occasionally however, a prophetic event occurs that defies all reasonable explanation, and thus gains credibility with the masses. The following story recounts just such an event.

In the year 1916, a prophetic event occurred in Europe that was destined to affect the lives of the world's Catholics for the next century. In the tiny village of Fatima, Portugal, three young children, Lucia de Jesus Santos, 9 years old, and her two younger cousins, Francisco and Jacinta Marto, ages 8 and 6 respectively, were watching over their flock of sheep when an angel suddenly appeared to them. This angel identified himself as the Guardian Angel of Portugal. The angel appeared to the children a total of three times, and asked them to pray for more angelic appearances.

The children, captivated by the appearance of this angel, dutifully prayed as the angel had requested, and the following year another angel appeared to them as they tended their sheep in a field near their small village. The children described this second angel as a beautiful lady who informed them that the present war (World War One) would soon be over, but that a second and even more terrible war would eventually follow. The angel lamented to the children that the people of the world were not obeying God's laws, and therefore must suffer God's vengeance in the form of another world war.

The first time the children witnessed the appearance of "Our Lady" was on May 13th, 1917, followed by a second apparition on June 13th. Word of these miraculous visions spread quickly, and when the children visited the same field on July 13th, they were accompanied by nearly 5000 curious onlookers. Local government officials however, were becoming concerned about the large numbers of people flocking into the small town of Fatima, and in August the children were placed under arrest to prevent a public panic.

An August vision occurred anyway on the 19th of the month, followed by further apparitions on September 13th and October 13th. By the time of the October vision, the crowds of onlookers had grown to more than 50,000 people. Many people reported witnessing miraculous astronomical occurrences, including the sun cavorting about in the sky, and various colors appearing in the heavens.

"Our Lady" revealed a total of three prophecies to the children concerning future events. The story of these miraculous visions eventually found its way to the world's Catholics, and the tiny town of Fatima, Portugal became an object of intense interest for Catholics all around the globe. Ten-year old Lucia was the principal source of information concerning the prophecies. She dutifully related all that she had been told by "Our Lady" to a local priest, and the three Secrets of Fatima were eventually delivered into the vaults of the Vatican Library to be examined for authenticity. They were also submitted for official acceptance to Catholic Church hierarchy. The Secrets of Fatima could not be released to the general public without the express permission of the Pope himself.

The First Secret given to the children concerned a vision of human souls suffering in the fires of hell. Ten-year old Lucia describes what she saw in this first vision:

"Our Lady showed us a sea of fire, which seemed to be under the Earth. Immersed in this fire were many demons and souls in human form, like transparent burning embers, all blackened or burnished bronze, floating about in the conflagration, now raised into the air by flames that issued from within them together with great clouds of smoke; now falling back on every side like sparks in a huge fire without weight or equilibrium, amid shrieks and groans of pain and despair which horrified us and made us tremble with fear. The demons could be distinguished by their terrifying and repulsive likeness to frightful and unknown animals, all black and transparent. The vision lasted for but an instant. How can we ever thank our kind, heavenly mother who had already prepared us by promising in the first apparition to take us to Heaven, otherwise I think we would have died of fear and terror."

This frightening vision should be enough to scare the living daylights out of the most ardent of sinners. The thought of spending an eternity in this kind of hell would make the trials of everyday life seem a blessing.

The Second Secret of Fatima was thought to contain a warning about the coming of a second worldwide war. Lucia was told that if men continued to offend God, a second, and even more terrible war would occur during the pontificate of Pius XI. She was told that a strange light would appear in the skies over Europe as a warning, and then God would again punish the world with war, hunger and pestilence, even punishing the Church, and the Pope himself.

During the First World War, in addition to the 9 million war deaths, a great pestilence known as the Spanish Flu spread across the world, killing over twice as many people as had died in the war. Unfortunately, young Jacinta and Francisco were destined to become victims of this great plague. When Lucia later asked Our Lady what had happened to her two friends, Our Lady answered that one of them was in heaven, and the other in purgatory.

This vision of Catholics burning in hell, and another of God punishing the Church and even the Pope himself, did not sit very well with the Catholic hierarchy, who much preferred a God Who forgave everyone for all their sins. The idea that God might punish the Church and even the Pope himself, did not do much to further the cause of the Church's acceptance of the three Fatima visions. The fame of Fatima however, continued to grow steadily, and ultimately the Church was obliged to place its seal of approval upon the Fatima visions in October of 1930.

The Second Secret of Fatima was rumored to contain a warning about another worldwide war that might occur sometime in the future. The Second Secret was officially released in 1941. Lucia describes this second vision given to her by Our Lady.

> *"You have seen hell where the poor sinners go. To save them, God wishes to establish in the world a devotion to my Immaculate Heart. If what I say is done, many souls will be saved and there will be peace. The war (World War One) is going to end soon, but if people do not cease offending God, a worse war will break out during the pontificate of Pius XI. When you see a night illuminated by an unknown light, know that this is the great sign given by God that he is about to punish the world for its crimes by means of war, famine and persecutions of the Church and of the Holy Father. To prevent this, I come to ask for the consecration of Russia to my Immaculate Heart, and the Commission of repentance on the First Saturdays. If my requests are heeded, Russia will be converted and there will be peace, if not, she will spread her errors throughout the world causing wars and persecutions of the Church. The good will be martyred, the Holy Father will have much to suffer, and various nations will be annihilated. In the end my Immaculate Heart will triumph. The Holy Father will consecrate Russia to me, and she shall be converted; a period of peace will then be granted to the world."*

On January 25th, 1938, an unusually bright Aurora Borealis was witnessed in the skies over the continent of Europe. Thousands of people telephoned authorities wondering if this was the end of the world. A short time later, Adolph Hitler invaded Austria. Then, on January 25th, 1939, exactly one year after the lights illuminated Europe's skies, Hitler issued his Jewish Policy edict, and the Second World War was officially on.

Lucia made a decision to go into the service of the church as a nun, and it was decided that no more secrets would be released until a much later date. Lucia recorded the Third Secret in 1943, but it was not to be released until a much later date. In the 1950's, the Prophecies of Fatima were a primary focus of attention for the world's Catholics, who desperately wanted to prevent a future war with atheist Russia. Shrines to "Our Lady of Fatima" were constructed in Churches all over the world as places where Catholics could go on Saturdays to light candles and pray for the conversion of Russia. Catholics everywhere dutifully prayed for this conversion. Every Catholic was thoroughly familiar with the prophecies of Fatima, and the still unreleased Third Secret was the subject of much anxious discussion in many religious circles.

The Third Secret of Fatima was rumored to contain a reference to the assassination of a pope. This Third Secret was scheduled to be opened and read by the Pope in 1960; but when Pope John XXIII opened and read the prophecy, he was so horrified by its contents that he refused to release it to the public. He placed the Third Prophecy of Fatima back into the Vatican's vaults, and the next 40 years witnessed interest in Fatima fading away from the minds of most of the world's Catholics.

Then, in May of the year 2000, Pope John Paul II met with Sister Lucia at the Vatican, and decided that it was finally time for the Third Prophecy of Fatima to be released. An official Church statement released along with the prophecy proclaimed it to be a "figurative representation" of the attempted assassination of Pope John Paul II that had taken place on May 5th, 1981. It should be noted however, that the appearance of the great light in the skies over Europe was not a figurative event; and the second prophecy concerning Russia's conversion from Communism, was also not a figurative event.

The Third Prophecy of Fatima describes a Vatican in ruins, littered with human corpses, and a Pope being held prisoner by the soldiers of an invading army. These soldiers march the Pope and his bishops to the top of a hill to pray in front of an old rugged cross. The soldiers then execute the Pope along with his bishops and a host of others. This haunting vision is very similar to one experienced by an earlier pope in the year 1909.

Pope Pius X is said to have awakened suddenly from a dream in 1909, and announced that he had just seen a horrible vision of a future pope exiting the Vatican over the dead bodies of his bishops.

This vision also matches that of Saint Malachy O'Morgan, an 11th century Roman Catholic priest from Ireland, who prophesied the coming of Peter the Roman, last Pope of the Roman Catholic Church. Peter witnesses the destruction of the seven-hilled city (Rome), followed by the arrival of the dreadful Judge, who comes to judge the nations of the world. Malachy places the papacy of Peter the Roman after that of Pope Benedict XVI.

Malachy's vision, if true, places us only one pontificate from the fulfillment of the Third Fatima prophecy. Many Church leaders in America also insist that this exact prophecy on the destruction of the Vatican is described within the pages of the book of Revelation. It is thought to be one of the last events before the Lord's return.

This is Lucia's description of the Third Secret as revealed to her by Our Lady so long ago in that field near her small village.

"At the left of Our Lady and a little above, we saw an angel with a flaming sword in his left hand, flashing, it gave out flames that looked as though they could set the world on fire, but they died out in contact with the splendor Our Lady radiated toward him from her right hand. Pointing to the earth with his right hand, the angel cried out in a loud voice, "Penance! Penance! Penance!" and we saw a great light that is God, something similar to how people look in a mirror when they pass in front of it. A bishop dressed in white, we had the impression it was the Holy Father, and other bishops, priests, and religious men and women were going up a steep hill, at the top of which was a big cross made of rough tree trunks, like a cork tree with its bark. Before reaching there, the Holy father passed through a big city, half in ruins, and trembling, in halting steps, suffering from deep pain and sorrow, he prayed for the souls of the corpses he passed along the way. Having reached the top of the hill, he knelt down at the foot of the big cross, and was killed by a group of soldiers who fired upon him. In the same way died all the other bishops, priests, and religious men and women, and also various lay people of different rank and position. Beneath the arms of the cross stood two angels, each with a crystal aspertorium in his hand, with which they each gathered up the blood of the martyrs, and with it sprinkled the souls that were making their way to God."

Might this chilling vision actually come true? The First World War began with the assassination of the heir to the Holy Roman Empire on July 28th, 1914, when Archduke Franz Ferdinand was assassinated by a young Serbian extremist, while riding in an open car through the streets of Sarajevo. It has also been predicted that the last world war will be initiated by the assassination of the Pope of Rome. It is very strange indeed that a prophecy such as this should come out of the Vatican's own vaults.

CHAPTER 29

SAINT MALACHY

"For to one is given by the Spirit the word of Wisdom; to another the word of Knowledge by the same Spirit; to another Faith by the same Spirit; to another the gifts of Healing by the same Spirit; to another the working of Miracles; to another Prophecy..."

I Corinthians 12:8-10

If indeed the prophet Nostradamus is the most recent of the 500-year Hebrew prophets, then the question logically arises as to who it was that proceeded him. The most likely candidate for this position seems to be a famous Irish Catholic prophet known as Saint Malachy. Saint Malachy O'Morgan was a Roman Catholic priest who lived in Ireland around the 11th century AD. We must be very careful of any historical dates arising out of this period in European history, as conditions in Europe at the time did not allow for the accurate recording of historical data.

Saint Malachy is said to have been born in Armagh, Ireland around the year 1094, and is thought to have been of noble birth. As a young man, he decided to dedicate his life to the service of God, and studied under the hermetic monk Imhar O' Hagan (who later became Abbott of Armagh). He was eventually ordained into the Catholic priesthood by Saint Celsus (Cellach) in 1119. Malachy was the first formally canonized Irish priest.

Saint Malachy continued his religious studies under Saint Malchus and was eventually promoted to the position of Abbott of Bangor in 1123. He then rose to the position of Bishop of Connor, and finally to Archbishop of Armagh in 1132.

While on a pilgrimage to the Vatican around the year 1139, Saint Malachy is said to have received an unusual series of visions involving the succession of the popes of the Holy Roman Church. Malachy's visions involved 112 popes, from his time until the end of time. His prophecy concerned the future of the Roman papacy from the reign of Pope Celestine II in 1143, until the end of the papacy.

Malachy's prophecies involve brief Latin phrases, usually consisting of only two or three words, that briefly describe some detail of the papacy of 112 popes from his time until the end of the Roman papacy.

Saint Malachy's predictions were quickly assailed as forgeries by many religious authorities of his time, who denied both their accuracy and their validity. St. Malachy's prophecies however, have survived intact into modern times, mostly due to their amazingly accurate references to many celebrated popes.

Malachy's prophecies were reportedly hidden away in the vaults of the Vatican Library for many centuries. They were not again revealed to the world until 1590, when the prophecies were published as "Proph, de la succession des papes."

Malachy's prophecies were again assailed as forgeries by many Church officials, but the prophecies did indeed seem to accurately describe the papacies of many celebrated popes. Some rather outstanding examples of their accuracy in modern times may be observed in their uncanny references to certain 20th century popes.

Pope Pius X, first pope elected in the 20th century, was labeled by Malachy with the Latin phrase "Ignis Ardens," or

"Burning Fire," and Pope Puis X perfectly fit that description. Acting more like a southern evangelist preacher than a quiet and somber member of the Roman papacy, Puis X was a zealous propagandist for the Catholic Church. He was ultimately responsible for expanding the influence of the Catholic Church throughout the Americas, and actively campaigned against the socialist forces of "modernists" who sought to alter long-standing Church doctrines. He also expelled any priests who promoted independence from Canon Law, and was quick to respond to the needs of the poor. He was truly the firebrand of the Roman papacy in the 20th century.

Saint Malachy next described the 1914 papacy of Pope Benedict XV with the Latin Phrase "religio depopulata," or "religious depopulation." And indeed Pope Benedict XV presided over the period of World War One, which witnessed a great "religious depopulation" taking place all across Europe. From 1914 to 1922, over 30 million people perished as a result of the effects of the war and also a devastating worldwide plague known as the Spanish Flu.

The following papacy of Pope Pius XI carried with it the Latin phrase "fidens intrepida" or "loyal and fearless." And Pope Pius XI did indeed demonstrate himself to be a loyal and fearless protector of the Catholic Church. He successfully carried the church through one of the darkest periods in modern history, enduring the rise of Nazism and Fascism in Europe. This period resulted in many severe threats to the future of the Catholic Church and its leadership.

"Pastor Angelicus" or "The Angelic Pastor" described the next papacy of Pius XII, who angelically led his faithful followers through the many hardships of World War Two.

A period of relative peace however, surrounded the following papacy of Pope John XXIII, who served from 1958 to 1963. Pope John XXIII's papacy was described with the Latin phrase "pastor et nauta," or "pastor and sailor." And when Pope John XXIII convened the World Ecumenical Council in 1962, he chose two very appropriate symbols for the official Council badge, a cross and a ship.

The next papacy of Pope Paul VI was described by Malachy as "flos florum," or "flower of flowers," and Pope Paul VI's family coat of arms clearly displayed three Fluer-de-Lis for all to see.

After the papacy of Pius VI came the rather unusual papacy of John Paul I. The papacy of John Paul I lasted only 34 days. Malachi described this particular papacy with the Latin phrase "de mediatate lunae" or the "shortened moon." It should also be noted that not only was the length of John Paul's papacy very short, but his given name was Luciani Albino, or "White Light," accurately describing the Moon's unique "white" luster.

After John Paul I, we have another very unusual papacy. The papacy of John Paul II marked the first time in over 450 years that a non-Italian was elected to the papacy. John Paul II was born in Poland, and spoke with a very heavy Polish accent. He was therefore viewed as an outsider by many of his Roman bishops. This fact may have had some influence on his decision to honor the papacy of his immediate predecessor by choosing the name John Paul II.

The papacy of John Paul II was marked by a great "falling away" from long-established church traditions by many members of the Roman Catholic faith. John Paul II however, demanded that his followers continue to obey longstanding Church doctrines, and steadfastly refused to accept such modern concepts as the ordination of women into the priesthood, and the killing of the unborn within the womb. St. Malachy described the papacy of John Paul II with the Latin phrase "de labore solis," or he who "works alone," and indeed, John Paul II worked in extreme solitude, carrying on his official duties as leader of the Catholic Church. John Paul II refused to bend to the wishes of those around him who sought to alter the supreme laws of God. In doing so, he alienated many of his immediate subordinates. Many of John Paul's own bishops openly circulated writings and opinions that opposed his own.

In Pope John Paul's ongoing battle to maintain his principles and beliefs against a relentless assault by those seeking to alter long-standing Church doctrines and traditions, he had by his side a loyal supporter in Cardinal Ratzinger of Germany. And it was Ratzinger who would eventually succeed John Paul II as Pope, thus fulfilling Saint Malachy's next prophetic Latin phrase, "de gloria olivae," or "the glory of the olives." For Ratzinger was a member of the Benedictine, or "Olivetan," order.

In the 6th century AD, it was Saint Benedict himself who predicted that it would be a Benedictine who would lead the church in its final battle against evil just before the Apocalypse. In June of 2005, Cardinal Ratzinger was officially elected to the papacy of the Holy Roman Church, and he chose as his title, Benedict XVI, reflecting his fierce loyalty to the strict laws of the Benedictines, or "Olivetans."

According to Saint Malachy's prophecies, there may be only one more pope elected to the papacy of the Roman Catholic Church. That's right, only one more papacy after that of Pope Benedict XVI. Malachy describes his last pope with the Latin words "Petrus Romanus," or "Peter the Roman." Malachy's prophecy on "Peter the Roman." reads as follows:

In persecutione extreme romanae ecclesiae sedebit
During an extreme persecution of the Roman church sits
Petrus Romanus, qui pascet oves in multis
Peter the Roman, who leads his flock through many
tribulationibus. Quibus transactis, civitas septis-collis
tribulations. This accomplished, the 7-hilled city will be
diruetur, et Judex tremendus populum suum.
destroyed, and the Dreadful Judge will judge His people.
Amen.
This is Truth.

The city of Rome has long been referred to as the "seven-hilled city." Could this prophecy be predicting the actual physical destruction of Rome? On a second pilgrimage to the Vatican in 1148, Saint Malachy fell ill while passing through the French city of Clairvaux, and died in the arms of Saint Bernard on November 2, All Souls Day. It is in fact Saint Bernard who is the principal source of most information concerning the life and prophecies of Saint Malachy.

St. Malachy was officially canonized by Pope Clement II on July 6, 1199, and his prophecies still remain a subject of great controversy within the Catholic Church concerning the future of the Church, and of the papacy.

For those interested in interpreting the rest of Malachy's prophecies, the following is a list of the many other popes (and anti-popes) referred to by Saint Malachy, from Pope Celestine II into latter times:

Celestine II - "ex castro Tiberis"
Lucius II – "Inimicus expulsus"
Eugene III – "ex magnitudine montis"

Anastasius IV – "Abbas Suburranus"

Adrian IV – "de rure Albo"

Vittore IV – "ex tetro carcere"*

Pasquale III – "de via transtibertina"*

Callisto III – "de pannonia Tusciae"*

Alexander III – "ex ansere custode"

Lucius III – "lux in ostio"

Urban III – "sus in cribro"

Gregory VIII – "ensis Laurentii"

Clement III – "de schola exiet"

Celestine III – "de rure bovense"

Innocent III – "comes signatus"

Honorius III – "canonicus de latere"

Gregory IX – "avis ostiensis"

Celestine IV – "Leo Sabinus"

Innocent IV – "comes laurentius"

Alexander IV – "signum ostiense"

Urban IV – "Jerusalem campaniae"

Clement IV – "drago depressus"

Gregory X – "anguineus vir"

Innocent V – "cancionator gallus"

Adrian V – "bonus comes"

Giovanni XXI – "piscator tuscus"

Nicholas III – "rosa composita"

Martin IV – "ex telonio liliacei Martini"

Honorius IV – "ex rosa leonina"

Nicholas IV – "picus inter escas"

Celestine V – "ex eremo celsus"

Boniface VIII – "ex undarum benedictione"

Benedict XI – "concionator pataren"

Clement V – "de faciis aquitanicus"

Giovanni XXII – "de suture orseo"

Nicholas V – "corvus schismaticus"*
Benedict XII – "frigidus abbas"
Clement VI – "ex rosa atrebatensis"
Innocent VI – "de montibus Pammachii"
Urban V – "Gallus vicecomes"
Gregory XI – "novus de virgine forti"
Clement VII – "de cruce apostolica"*
Benedict XIII – "luna cosmedina"*
Clement VIII – "schismo barcinoscum"*
Urban VI – "de inferno pregnani"
Boniface IX – "cubus de mixtione"
Innocent VII – "de meliore sidere"
Gregory XII – "nauta de ponte nigro"
Alexander V – "flagellum solis"*
Giovanni XXIII – "cervus sirenae"*
Martin V – "corona veli aurei"
Eugene IV – "lupa coelestina"
Felix V – "amator crucis"*
Nicholas V – "de modicitate lunae"
Cllisto III – "bos pascens"
Pius II – "se capre et albergo"
Paul II – "de cervo et leone"
Sixtus IV – "piscator minorita"
Innocent VIII – "praecursor Siciliae"
Alexander VI – "bos Albanus in portu"
Pius III – "de parvo homine"
Julius II – "fructus jovis juvabit"
Leo X – "de craticula politiana"
Adrian VI – "Leo Florentius"
Clement VII – "flos pilae"
Paul III – "hyacinthus medicorum"
Julius III – "de corona montana"

Marcellus II – "frumentum floccidum"
Paul IV – "de fide Petri"
Pius IV – "aesculapii pharmacum"
Pius V – "angelus nemorosus"
Gregory XIII – "medium corpus pilarum"
Sixtus V – "axis in medietate signi"
Urban VII – "de rore coeli"
Gregory XIV – "de antiquitate urbis"
Innocent IX – "pia civitas in bello"
Clement VIII – "crux romulea"
Leo XI – "undosus vir"
Paul V – "gens perversa"
Gregory XV – "in tribulatione pacis"
Urban VIII – "lilium et rosa"
Innocent X – "jucunditas crucis"
Alexander VII – "montium custos"
Clement IX – "sydus olorum"
Clement X = "de fulmine magno"
Innocent XI – "bellua insatiabilis"
Alexander VIII – "poenitentia gloriosa"
Innocent XII – "rastrum in porta"
Clement XI – "flores circumdati"
Innocent XIII – "de bona religione"
Benedict XIII – "miles in bello"
Clement XII – "columna excelsa"
Benedict XIV – "animal rurale"
Clement XIII – "rosa Umbriae"
Clement XIV – "ursus velox"
Pius VI – "peregrinus apostolicus"
Pius VII – "aquila rapax"
Leo XII – "canis ed coluber"
Pius VIII – "vio religiosus"

Gregory XVI – "de balneis Etruriae"
Pius IX – "crux de cruce"
Leo XIII – "lumen de coelo"

The prophecies of Saint Malachy represent just one more example of ancient prophecy still operating in modern times.

CHAPTER 30

AMERICA IN PROPHECY

And God blessed them, and God said unto them, Be fruitful, and multiply, and replenish the earth, and subdue it......

Gen. 1:28

Is America mentioned anywhere in prophecy? This is a question that Bible historians have been trying to answer for many decades. If we wish to thoroughly explore this question however, it will first be necessary for us to explore the history of the North American continent, its people, and its discovery and occupation by the early European colonists who first conquered and claimed it for Christianity. If we are to gain a better understanding of the unique heritage of America, we must first retrace its human history

Archeological records tell us that the North American continent did not originally host any human inhabitants. It was instead populated by three different native groups who began migrating here about 15,000 years ago, near the end of the last Ice Age. The first significant group of humans to arrive in North America came by way of the northeastern tip of Asia where it nearly meets the North American continent in the area of present-day Alaska. This was the shortest and most direct land route (the oceans were 300 ft. lower than today) from Asia to North America, for most of these early settlers of our continent. In testimony to this Asian-American link, today's

Alaskan Eskimos still clearly exhibit the oriental customs and features of their Asian ancestors.

Much later, a second group of newcomers arrived by sea to the western shores of South America, near present-day Peru. These immigrants (Aborigines and Malays) came by way of Australia and the islands of the East Indies, and were blown eastward by the trade winds that still blow today across the Pacific Ocean from the South Seas to South America. These new arrivals made their living from the sea, and possessed large vessels capable of enduring ocean voyages. As evidence of their arrival, they also brought along with them some unwanted stowaways in the form of marsupial rats (opossums), and marsupial mice. These marsupial animals are still thriving today on the American continents.

Then, many centuries later, a third and final group of immigrants arrived in Central America also by sea. But these people came from an entirely different direction. This final group of emigres had sailed westward across the Atlantic Ocean on the trade winds that still blow at us today from the western tip of Africa. This is the same route that our annual fall hurricanes take to arrive on the eastern coast of the United States. The people who came by this route (Caucasians and a few Black slaves) originally hailed from the Mediterranean shores of North Africa, and eventually became known as the "mound builders" or "pyramid builders" of the Americas.

The unique stonework of these pyramid builders can be accurately traced from its Mediterranean origins by many unusual archeological markers. Archeologists have discovered unique "doggy-bone" shaped metal anchor pins used to fasten the cornerstones of these great American pyramids. These corner pins, poured from molten metal, have also been found in the pyramids of Egypt and also in the remains of many classical Greek structures. Some other unique archeological markers include four-sided pyramids that are oriented toward the four cardinal points of the compass, and unique decorative headpieces on large stone statues.

All these native groups eventually melded together into one large native population that comprised the original group of Native Americans encountered by early European explorers when they first arrived on America's shores in the late 1400's.

The first Europeans to visit North America arrived in New England around 750 AD from the British Isles (although some earlier Europeans had crossed over during the Ice Age approximately 14,000 years earlier). These early Irish and Welsh adventurers attempted to settle on the northeastern coast of North America, but were not very successful in permanently establishing themselves upon the North American continent.

These early Celtic explorers were then followed by the Vikings (pronounced Vick-ings), who arrived around 1000 AD on the Eastern coast of Canada, which they immediately named "Vinland" due to great quantities of wild grapes they found growing there. The Vikings' first native encounters were with American Eskimos, whom they described as "skraelings" (little people) with round faces and large eyes, who paddled around in animal-skin boats. These early Vikings also attempted to establish permanent colonies near deep-water harbors on the North American seacoast, and eventually traveled as far south as Newport, Rhode Island. But their colonies failed miserably due to constant clashes with the native inhabitants of the regions.

The Vikings did manage to establish a successful colony of about 70,000 people in Iceland. On the American continent however, the Native Americans soon grew tired of the Viking brand of tyranny, and permanently destroyed the new invaders and their settlements. The Vikings' whaling settlement on the island of Iceland later met its demise through an epidemic of the bubonic plague that arrived from Europe around the year 1350, and was also later adversely affected by a period of sudden global cooling.

It is interesting to note that it was common practice for Native Americans to kill all the adult male members of the tribes of their enemies, and to take the women and children captive as slaves. This practice led to the eventual mixing of bloodlines between early European explorers and native tribes. Thus, many of the Indian tribes of Eastern North America and Canada were seen by later explorers to possess distinctly Caucasian features, including even blond or red hair. Some of these tribes, like the Tarentines of Bangor, Maine, absorbed so much Viking blood that they actually assumed Viking behaviors, and began sacking and pillaging other native tribes on the American continent. The Tarentines also enjoyed a limited immunity from certain European diseases due to their Viking blood.

Because the continent of North America was such an uncivilized place, and populated by "heathen savages," the continent did not receive much more attention until early European explorers began seeking new trade routes to the Far East around the end of the 15th century.

European trade with the Far East for spices, dyes, gems and other trade goods had been handled by the Genovese, who sailed through the Black Sea, and by the Venetians, who used a more southerly route through the Red Sea. Both these bodies of water were much deeper in those days, allowing free passage for large sailing vessels.

When the Ottoman Empire captured the city of Constantinople however, the Genovese were forced to find another route to the Far East. A forward thinking Genovese entrepreneur by the name of Christopher Columbus convinced Spain's young Queen Isabella to finance his wild scheme to reach the Far East by sailing West.

In 1492, Captain Christopher Columbus sailed westward across the Atlantic Ocean and finally landed in what he thought was the land of the "Indies" to establish first contact with the "people of the East". Columbus named these native people "Indians," because he thought he'd sailed half way around the world and landed on the coast of India. By the time the truth was finally revealed, it was too late to change the name of the American "Indians", who had by now been permanently labeled with this misconceived title. Columbus returned to Europe with many new finds such as tobacco, casava, cotton, and a new disease called Syphilis, that his Spanish and Italian sailors had acquired through their consorts with the native women.

It was not until 1501 that the explorer Amerigo Vespucci finally demonstrated that this new land was not India after all, but a newfound continent. It was therefore Amerigo Vespucci who got to place his name upon the newly discovered continent of "America" (A-mer-rica / across-the sea-riches).

Then, around the year 1520, Magellan sailed around the tip of South America to discover the Pacific Ocean, and Balboa also viewed the Pacific from a high mountain in Panama. Early Spanish explorers attempted to establish small settlements in the Americas, but these settlements never flourished because they were never truly accepted by the native people, and ended up as little more than hostile intrusions of the continent. The Europeans were ultimately able to establish a trading relationship with the Indians for such things as furs and gold, but the few bits of cloth and trinkets traded with native tribes did little to earn their trust.

Small European colonies were soon established all over the Americas by the Spanish, the French and the English, but none were truly successful. Later Spanish conquistadors like Cortez and Pizarro, would loot and destroy the Mayan, Aztec and Incan empires in desperate attempts to uncover gold and other treasures.

In the year 1620 however, a small group of Christian Protestant Separatists from England arrived in Plymouth, Massachusetts, to establish the first successful Christian colony in the New World. These religious Pilgrims came to the New World fleeing religious persecution by the Holy Roman Church of Europe. Their intention in coming to America was to establish a new free Christian society on the North American continent, and to introduce the heathen savages of North America to the teachings of Jesus Christ.

Early Spanish and Portuguese priests had also sought to convince their governments that the Native Americans should be educated in Christianity and treated as free Christians, but they were overruled by rich European business interests who sought instead to use the Indians as common mine laborers, and plantation slaves.

The Pilgrims of the Plymouth Colony viewed America as a land of great opportunity where Christians could expand their religious base in a free human society, and find refuge from the tyranny of the Roman Catholic Church. They viewed America as a land that could provide unlimited opportunities for those willing to work hard to make their dreams come true. America was considered to be the "New Israel" for God's loyal followers.

The Pilgrims of the Plymouth Colony were ultimately able to convert many Native Americans to Christianity, and to establish peace between formally warring Indian tribes. Their success however, caught the eye of rich European business interests, who responded by sending over more Christian colonists to exploit the New World and its many treasures. These new Christian colonists however, were Christian in name only. The so-called "Christian" Puritans for instance, were known to pay high bounties for Indian scalps.

The Pilgrims and Puritans still numbered only about 20,000 people by 1640, and in 1651 were joined by about 500 more Scottish freedom fighters sent over by Oliver Cromwell (after his Dunbar and Worcester campaigns). In 1685 about 1,000 more Protestant Huguenots arrived, due to the revocation of the Edict of Nantes, and in 1719 another 500 or so Scotch-Irish families arrived in New England. As late as 1800 however, there were still only about 50,000 Protestant colonists in all of North America.

When the true potential of America's "well of plenty" was finally realized, many English religious colonists began to believe that America might actually be "Israel," the final resting place for the "10 Lost Tribes". This theory was quite common among many early American colonists.

When President Thomas Jefferson first sent the explorers Lewis and Clark into the wilds of the interior of the American continent, he instructed them to carefully record all the various spoken dialects of the native people they found there. Jefferson knew that the descendants of Seth, who'd built the pyramids of Egypt, had also built pyramids in the Americas, and believed it was possible that the "10 Lost Tribes" might still be living somewhere on the North American continent. He wanted to see if any of the native Indian tribes still spoke the original Hebrew tongue.

This "Lost Tribes" theory was formed out of the Masonic and Philo-Israel movements, which traced their roots back to the ancient Hebrews of the Holy Land. It was known that in ancient times Israel's 10 Lost Tribes, or "Lost Sheep" (Matt.10:6), had been relocated by the Assyrians to the northwest of Assyria in the Caucuses Mountains, where they became known as "Caucasians," due to their white skin, blonde hair, and blue eyes.

The story of the wanderings of the mysterious 10 Lost Tribes was similar in many ways to the biblical story of the Prodigal Son. This Bible story may be found in the book of Luke, Chapter 15.

Jesus was a very clever storyteller who often had a deeper message to convey with each story he told. He generally told his stories in the form of allegories that were thought to be prophecies of things to come. Jesus' disciples were very careful to record these stories for posterity, even though the disciples themselves often had no idea as to the actual meaning of the tales. These stories were passed down through the Holy Scriptures to us today, in the hopes that their meaning might eventually be understood in the last days.

The story of the Prodigal Son involved a father who had two sons. The older of these two sons was a typical eldest son, remaining loyal to his family in the hopes that he might someday inherit the family fortune. The younger of the two sons was also a typical youngest son who, being somewhat wild and impetuous, wanted to set off on his own to see the greater world.

One day the younger son asked his father for his portion of the family inheritance, so that he might go forth into the world to seek his fortune. The father begrudgingly granted his son's request, and the boy set off to see the world. Eventually however, the young boy was drawn to the many attractions of the big city, and squandered all his money and possessions on the material pleasures made available to him within the sinful city environment. He soon found himself penniless, and forced to live within the sin and squalor of the city.

One day, after considering his plight, he decided that he'd taken the wrong path in life, and longed once again to return to the family fold. With his head hanging in shame, he set off for his father's house with intentions of asking to be taken back in as a servant, so that he might eventually work his way back into his father's favor. But as he approached his boyhood home, his father saw him coming from afar off, and was overjoyed that his youngest son had finally returned. The father ordered his servants to slaughter a fatted calf and prepare a great feast to welcome home his long-lost son.

The eldest son, after toiling all day in the fields, returned home that evening to find a great feast being held. He asked his father's servants why they were holding this great banquet, and was quickly informed that the celebration was in honor of his younger brother's return. The eldest son immediately became furious, and asked his father how he could do such a thing, since his brother had run off and squandered the family's wealth, while he, the eldest, had remained loyal to his father and toiled all these years in the field. His father replied that his son, who was once dead, was now alive again, and that this was certainly a reason for all to be joyful.

The meaning of this story was often interpreted by early Catholic priests as illustrating the point that we should all be forgiving of those who've sinned against us, and then come to repentance. But is it possible that this story contains a deeper and more literal truth? Was it perhaps a prophecy of an event to occur in the last days?

Many early American colonists thought that the story of the Prodigal Son was a prophecy foretelling the final return of the 10 Lost Tribes to the dominion of God, especially the blessed tribe of Joseph. Could the story of the Prodigal Son be a prophecy of a last days event?

The Bible reveals that there was a time in history when the Almighty Father did indeed have two sons. One of these sons was named Israel, and the other, Judah. History tells us that around the year 1000 BC, Jacob's children decided to split themselves into two separate groups. The 10 northern tribes (Israel) broke off from the two southern tribes (Judah) in order to form themselves into a new nation. The two southern tribes remained loyal to the Almighty Father, while Israel decided to leave the family fold to seek its fortune in a secular world.

The 10 northern tribes of Israel felt they could become a great nation if they could just break away from the many restrictive laws placed upon them by the Father. Their older brother Judah however, chose to stay within the family fold, remaining loyal to the many laws and traditions that had long provided it protection from its many enemies.

The northern 10-tribe nation of Israel eventually did grow into a modern progressive, city-based state, while the southern 2-tribe nation of Judah remained loyal to the Father, living off the land as nomadic sheep herders.

Israel did develop into a rich and powerful society, but soon began to suffer from the moral and social decay normally associated with a society giving in to the carnal desires of an overindulgent citizenry. Israel quickly fell into a state of godlessness, ignoring the religious laws and moral principles that had once made it strong. This angered God greatly, and so

He sent the Assyrians down out of the north to war against the Israelites and punish them by taking them into captivity. A few centuries later, the now-weakened nation of Judah also fell under Ishmaelite rule.

After a long period, known as the "Babylonian Captivity," the sons of Isaac, now held captive by the sons of Ishmael, eventually came under the influence of a benevolent Persian emperor named Cyrus, who decided to allow the Hebrews to return to their homeland. The nation of Judah did in fact return to Jerusalem, but the 10 northern tribes of Israel decided instead to travel northward across the forests and steppes of Europe and Asia to seek their fortune in a new land. Israel thus began its long trek through history, setting historians and theologians on an unrelenting quest for the whereabouts of the mysterious "10 Lost Tribes."

The reason that the final resting place of the 10 Lost Tribes was so important, was that one of these tribes, the tribe of Joseph, carried with it God's blessing for the inheritance of the Hebrew people. The early colonists of America were therefore also searching for the whereabouts of these 10 Lost Tribes.

The early Christian Protestants who first settled America were a deeply religious people, who were constantly attempting to rightly discern the truth of the Holy Scriptures. They felt that the Bible had been infected with many pagan doctrines by the Roman Catholic Church, but knew that the ancient prophets who originally recorded this information were clever enough to provide protections against that truth ever being totally lost. They were therefore deeply involved in an effort to rightly discern the truth from the Holy Scriptures.

America's early colonists dutifully read and studied their Bibles in great depth every evening in an effort to uncover that truth. These early Christian colonists would then gather together in their churches every Sunday to discuss what they'd discerned from their readings. For many centuries in Europe, the best scientific minds had also been trying to uncover these same truths, but the Catholic Church committed itself to hunting down and persecuting anyone who dared to question its teachings. For many centuries, great scientists like Galileo, Kepler, and Newton had risked Church condemnation to reveal those same truths. Now, in America however, people were finally free to read the Scriptures and express their thoughts and words freely, without fear of government or church retribution.

For many years, historians and archeologists had been attempting to follow the wanderings of the mysterious 10 Lost Tribes of Israel after they left their homeland in the Caucuses Mountains of southern Russia, but the evidence of their wanderings was not easy to follow.

We do know that the 10 Lost Tribes trekked off into the forests and steppes of northern Europe and Asia, but the exact route of each of the 10 tribes is very difficult to follow. It is possible however, to track them by their rather unusual customs, appearance, clothing, and music, and also by their unique stone-building talents and abilities.

Their white faces, long beards, blond hair, blue eyes, kilts, bagpipes, pointed witches hats, megalithic stones, and sturdy little ponies, served as unique ethnic markers that followed them about wherever they wandered. Their great stoneworking talents left a clear trail for historians and archeologists to follow. Many of these unique ethnic artifacts are still being uncovered today in cultures stretching all the way from the Shetland Islands in England, to the Gobi Desert in China.

But where did the 10 Lost tribes, and particularly the mysterious tribe of Joseph, finally settle? Was President

Thomas Jefferson right? Could America be the final resting place for the 10 Lost Tribes, or at least for the blessed tribe of Joseph? Could America be the Prodigal Son who left the family fold to seek his fortune in a new land?

The Bible had long prophesied that the tribe of Joseph would father two children, Manasseh and Ephraim. Many early American colonists believed it was possible that the English-speaking people of England were the Hebrew tribe of Manasseh (Forgetful), and that the English-speaking people in America were their younger brother Ephraim (Fruitful). They believed it was the destiny of the Christians of North America to become the "rock formed without hands," or the most powerful God fearing nation on the face of the Earth, thus fulfilling Jacob's prophecy for the final destiny of his blessed son Joseph.

Is America actually the blessed tribe of Ephraim, the youngest son of Joseph? Will England and America eventually exert their influence over the entire world? And will they both someday agree to return to the Father to once again obey His laws? History may someday provide us with an answer to this confusing riddle.

The following are Jacob's prophecies from Chapter 49 of the book of Genesis, on the unique destiny of each of his twelve sons:

THE FATE OF THE TEN TRIBES OF ISRAEL:

Joseph – Joseph is a fruitful bough, even a fruitful bough by a well, whose branches run over the wall. The archers have sorely grieved him, and shot at him, and hated him, but his bow abode in strength and the arms of his hands were made strong by the hands of the mighty God of Jacob; (from thence is the shepherd, the stone of Israel). His children are Manasseh and Ephraim (England and America?).

Reuben – possessing strength, dignity, and power, but unstable as water (the French?).

Simeon and Levi – these are brethren. Instruments of cruelty are in their habitations. I shall divide and scatter them amongst Israel.

Zebulun – shall dwell in the haven of the sea.

Issachar - is as a strong ass couching, a servant under tribute

Dan – shall be a serpent by the way who biteth the horse heels so the rider shall fall (the Danish?).

Gad – a troop shall overcome him, but he shall overcome at the last.

Asher – his bread shall be fat, and he shall yield royal dainties.

Naphtali is a hind let loose. He giveth good words

THE FATE OF THE TWO TRIBES OF JUDAH:

Judah – the lion's whelp, his hand shall be on the neck of his enemies, and the scepter (God's laws) shall not depart from him – (Orthodox Jews?)

Benjamin – Benjamin shall ravin as the wolf; in the morning he shall devour the prey, and at night he shall divide the spoil.

CHAPTER 31

ASTEROID!

"That day is impending when people will admit the pure truth within the book of nature, as well as in the Holy Bible, and rejoice at the harmony between these two revelations."

Johannes Kepler

Some people say they go through life feeling like a duck in a shooting gallery. Well, this statement may be truer than many of us realize. In some earlier chapters of this book we established that America's early colonists believed that weather, and all other natural events, were controlled by God, and that God often used these natural disasters to deliver His vengeance upon mankind whenever men strayed from obeying His laws.

We later learned from the Fatima prophecies that God also uses war and pestilence to deliver similar punishments upon mankind. The largest and most devastating natural disaster of all however, was not mentioned in any of our previous stories. It's an event that has been the subject of some best-selling books and videos in recent years. This most frightening of all natural disasters is the deadly asteroid or comet strike.

The idea that an immense asteroid might suddenly and unexpectedly strike Earth, has been a frightening reality for scientists and astronomers for many years. The void of outer space is filled with many small objects that spin around in our solar system in widely eccentric orbits, and some of these objects occasionally pass by very close to our planet.

Most of the video productions made about these giant space objects involve plots concerning someone saving the Earth from certain destruction by sending out a team of astronauts who use a nuclear missile to blow up the asteroid or knock it off course. Just how real is the possibility that an asteroid or comet might strike Earth? Well, let's take a look at that question to see if we can find an answer.

There are two common types of roving objects that normally travel through space and threaten the planets of our solar system; they are comets and asteroids. Comets are huge balls of loosely packed space debris that move rapidly through space and give off light due to the reflection of the sun off their vapor trails. Comets are therefore quite easy for us to spot if they approach Earth. Since comets are so easily seen, we would at least have some time to react if a comet were to pose any real danger to our planet.

Just how dangerous are comets? Well, in the summer of 1908, a small comet exploded in the atmosphere over the forests of Tunguska, Siberia, causing massive devastation, and felling trees within a radius of 20 miles in every direction from the epicenter of the explosion. It is estimated that this small comet had a diameter of less than 150 feet, and was traveling at a speed of approximately 40 miles per second. It was however, able to generate an explosive force equivalent to roughly 10 times that of the Hiroshima bomb. That's right, it was like setting off 10 Hiroshima nukes in one place at one time!

Luckily, this tiny comet struck in one of the most desolate places on our planet. If it had struck near a major city, it would have exploded with a force capable of destroying the entire city and its human population.

In 1994, Earth's astronomers witnessed a large comet striking the surface of the planet Jupiter. This comet, called Shoemaker- Levy 9, was captured by Jupiter's gravitational field and orbited the planet briefly, before breaking up into 21 pieces and crashing into the planet's surface. The largest piece of this comet was estimated to be almost 2 miles in diameter. Scientists said that if this same comet had crashed into Earth, it would have destroyed all civilization on our planet. The planet Jupiter however, is a thousand times the size of Earth, and therefore did not suffer unduly from the collision.

Another space object that poses a much greater danger to us, is the asteroid. The reason asteroids are so dangerous is that they do not give off any light, and are therefore very difficult to see in the blackness of space. Asteroids may therefore strike Earth without warning.

The myriad of craters visible on the surface of the Moon, were created over the millennia by thousands of asteroid strikes. The Moon has no atmosphere with which to generate the rain and wind necessary to erode these craters. Earth has been struck just as many times by asteroids from outer space, but most of the craters created by these impacts have been completely eroded away due to the effects of wind and water.

Asteroids, or meteors as they are sometimes called, have struck Earth many times. Actually, hundreds of tiny meteors strike the Earth every day. They are the familiar shooting stars we see each evening in the sky. Very few meteors are large enough to punch through Earth's atmosphere and reach the ground intact, but some do.

In modern history there have been a few celebrated incidents involving meteor strikes. In 1954 a meteor actually struck a woman in the State of Alabama. A meteor weighing approximately 8 pounds crashed through the roof of the woman's home, ripped a large hole in her ceiling, and bounced off her console radio, eventually striking her on the hip while she was seated on her couch, leaving her with a large bruise for the experience.

Another famous asteroid incident involved an incredible coincidence where two separate meteor strikes occurred on two separate homes located about a mile apart in the small town of Wethersfield, Connecticut. One home was struck in 1971, and the other home was struck a decade later in 1982.

Then, another decade later, on the night of October 9th, 1992, a giant fireball was witnessed in the skies over the town of Peekskill, New York. When a local resident heard a loud crash outside her home, she went outside to investigate the noise, and found that a meteor had pierced the trunk of her daughter's car that was parked in the driveway. The meteor left a large gaping hole in the pavement underneath the car. Oddly enough, if you trace this woman's family name back through the genealogy charts, her name can be traced back to its original roots in the 1600's in the small town of......you guessed it.....Wethersfield, Connecticut!

In the many movies and videos produced about large asteroid strikes, Earth's astronomers generally discover the asteroid as it is approaching Earth, and sound a general alarm. The government then initiates a hurried plan to destroy the asteroid before it actually crashes into our planet. In real life however, this situation is not quite as secure as described in these science fiction fantasies. Actually the chances of us ever sighting an asteroid in time to plan a coordinated response, are very small.

In March of 1989, a 1500-foot asteroid just missed Earth, and was not spotted until it was 650,000 miles past our planet, going away! If this asteroid had struck us, it would have delivered an explosive punch equivalent to 3000 nuclear warheads!

Since asteroids often travel at speeds of about 30 or 40 miles per second, they can cover a distance of 500,000 miles in as little as 3 or 4 hours. Even if we were lucky enough to spot one of these asteroids at this great distance, there would be very little time for us to react.

In 1932, 1936, and 1937, three huge asteroids named Apollo, Adonis and Hermes, all passed within about 500,000 miles of our planet. These asteroids were true giants, each one packing an explosive force roughly equivalent to 50,000 nuclear warheads. If one of these asteroids had struck our planet, it could have marked the end of civilization as we know it. Oddly enough, it seems that scientists in those days were much more watchful of the skies than our modern-day scientists. The Hermes asteroid was spotted by astronomers in Heidelberg, Germany many days before its arrival.

Approximately 65 million years ago our planet was struck by an asteroid almost 8 miles in diameter. This collision is thought to have been responsible for the extinction of Earth's dinosaurs. This asteroid strike created so much dust in Earth's upper atmosphere, that our planet suffered over three years of winter. The large, cold-blooded dinosaurs could not easily adapt to this sudden shift in air temperature, and quickly succumbed to the freezing conditions. Only the smallest cold blooded creatures were able to hide and survive the disaster. Earth's warm-blooded creatures however, were better equipped to handle this abrupt temperature change, and therefore survived to re-populate the planet.

Over time, these huge asteroids have been observed to strike Earth with a predictable frequency. Small asteroids tend to strike the Earth quite often, while larger asteroids generally strike only about once every 50 million years or so. The chart below will give you a rough idea of the strike frequency and explosive force of these huge space monsters.

DIAM.	MEGATONS	STRIKE FREQ.	CRATER
200 ft.	10	1,000 yrs.	10,000 ft.
1500 ft.	3,000	10,000 yrs.	5 miles
½ mile	30,000	100,000 yrs.	15 miles
1 ½ mi.	500,000	1,000,000 yrs.	30 miles
8 miles	60,000,000	100,000,000 yrs.	80 miles

Since Earth is estimated to be about 3 billion years old, we can assume that it has been struck 40 or 50 times by the largest asteroids during its long existence. Asteroid strikes capable of causing major changes in Earth's climate are rare, but as recently as 500 years ago, there was a major climatic change aided by an asteroid strike in the Pacific Ocean near Australia. This asteroid was nearly a quarter mile in diameter, and its effects were felt all around the world.

Asteroids have had major effects upon animal populations on Earth. Approximately 30,000 years ago, a large asteroid struck in the North Atlantic area and nearly wiped out the Neanderthals of northern Europe. Another asteroid strike approximately 13,000 years ago put an abrupt end to many Pleistocene mammals like the Woolly Mammoth, the Woolly

Rhinoceros, and the Saber-Toothed Cat. Their freeze dried remains are still being revealed today as a result of the approaching peak of our current global warming cycle. It is also thought that a large asteroid near miss in 2500 BC may have been responsible for the biblical Flood.

Every moment that ticks by places us one step closer to another asteroid strike. It is just a matter of time until one of these giant space rocks arrives to wreak havoc upon our world as we know it.

In God's great arsenal, there are few natural forces that compare to the power of the asteroid. If a truly large asteroid (1 mile or more across) were to land in one of our oceans, it would create a tidal wave large enough to wipe out many coastal cities, and if it struck land, it could throw our planet into an Ice Age. We would be unable to grow any food, or heat our homes in this type of situation, and our cities would almost certainly perish. Civilization as we know it, might even cease to exist.

Has modern science gotten any better at spotting asteroids before they arrive? Apparently not, because on June 14th, 2002, another Apollo-sized asteroid passed by Earth about one third the distance to the moon, and it too was not spotted until it had already passed us and was heading away!

There are few natural forces in God's universe that can match the destructive force of the largest comets and asteroids, and it is only through the grace of God that we have thus far avoided this threat to our very existence.

CHAPTER 32

THE MASONS

"What we have done for ourselves alone, dies with us: What we have done for others and the world, remains, and is immortal."

Albert Pike, 33rd Degree Mason

It seems to be a common human trait for men to fear what they do not understand, and perhaps no organization has been more feared and misunderstood than the secret society of the Masons. When discussing American history however, it would not be possible to adequately address the subject without also exploring the many significant contributions made to America's history by this rather secretive fraternal order.

We normally define the word "mason" as a tradesman who works in brick or stone, but the roots of the modern craft of masonry actually extend as far back as the history of civilization itself. The ancient pyramids of Egypt still bear witness to the amazing skill of the master stonemasons who originally designed and built these great stone edifices. From the Tower of Babel, to Solomon's Temple, the skill of the ancient masons in the science of geometry was clearly demonstrated in many of their great monuments all throughout history.

The roots of modern masonry in the United States can be traced back to the 17th century stonemason guilds, or unions, of Scotland and England. The word "guild" comes from the old

German/Saxon/Hebrew word meaning "to pay," referring to the payment of monthly union dues. European trade guilds were generally incorporated within specific townships, and workmen from these guilds were not normally allowed to pursue their "craft" outside the borders of their specific township. The masons however, were unique from other trade unions, in that they were allowed to work outside town limits. This was mostly due to the sheer size and complexity of many of their massive construction projects.

These great stone projects often involved European castles or cathedrals that required the quarrying of vast amounts of stone from far away places, and the utilization of large numbers of skilled craftsmen, often exceeding the number of laborers available within any specific township. The masons were therefore free to ply their trade in any place where their services were required. They thus became known as the "free" masons.

The two most powerful governmental entities in Europe during the Middle Ages were the Monarchy, and the Roman Catholic Church. The people of the working class were constantly subjected to the many capricious whims and fancies of these two powerful governmental powers, and had virtually no say in their own leadership. The European labor unions however, did enjoy a certain amount of influence in government and church circles, and the largest and most powerful of these trade unions was the masons.

The masons often acted as the voice of the commoners in Europe when there was no other place for the common worker to go with a grievance against a particular government or church decision. The masons therefore eventually came to represent a third source of authority within the European governmental system.

The ancient masons built lodges or "logges," which were huge wooden log structures with thatched roofs that served as workplaces during the day, and sleeping quarters at night, for their many members who had to travel far from home. They would gather together in these lodges every evening to fraternize and discuss their common concerns. This custom eventually gave way to more formal clubs and lodges that formed into larger groups capable of exerting a powerful voice in the public arena.

No matter how rich or famous one became in the community, it was simply not possible for the common man to break into the Monarchy or the Church. It was possible however, for him to join up with the masons, who often welcomed the rich and famous into their organization.

As the power of the mason guilds grew, they began to be viewed with much fear and suspicion by authorities from within both the government and the Church. When major social issues arose within a specific community, it was the masons who would hold their secret meetings in order to discuss the matter. Secrecy was a priority in order to prevent government and church infiltrators from spying on their meetings. It was therefore destined for the masons to become a secretive group of free men, dedicated to the protection and the welfare of the common man, in a world controlled by the government and the Catholic Church.

Masonic secrecy also contained a mystical side that recognized, and celebrated a direct a relationship between man and God. The Masons saw in their stonework, a relationship to God that was reflected in the ancient structure of the Great Pyramid itself, whose perfect form and geometry encompassed all earthly knowledge. Their Great Pyramid symbol can still be seen today on dollar bills, portraying at its pinnacle the great eye of God, forever watching over His Earthly garden.

Another great Masonic icon is the tall, crystal-shaped obelisk, symbolizing the perfection contained within the mystical structure of the quartz crystal. And it was indeed the magical quartz crystal that was responsible for almost all modern technological miracles. From the quartz crystal radios of the early 1900's that could receive and amplify radio signals without batteries or tuners, to the intentionally polluted quartz crystals of today that give us the transistor and modern silicon computer circuits, it was the magical silicon crystal that was responsible for all modern electronics.

The miracles contained within the quartz crystal also allowed us to receive and process radio signals, produce electricity in solar cells, prismatically diffuse light into its primary colors, convert light into a single powerful wavelength in lasers, and control the flow of electricity through miniature silicon circuits. Small wonder then that the geometric perfection of the crystal was enshrined within Masonic symbolism.

The masons had carried their unique heritage through ancient Saxony to Brittany, and then to England. From England they then moved on to the New World. When the first settlers of the New World began to arrive on America's shores from western Europe. It was the Masons who were primarily involved in the effort to create a new form of government operating in the best interests of the common man. In fact most, if not all, of the original founders of our nation were Masons. Some of these Masons were open and active members of the society, while others kept their membership a secret in order to avoid problems in the public arena.

It remains a fact however, that the original formation of the government of the United States of America was mostly due to the actions of a group of Freemasons determined to create a new form of government based upon the concept of individual freedom for all God-fearing men. In this newly formed Republic, the God-given rights of every free individual would be clearly defined under public law.

The Masons believed that the Almighty had given every individual the right to "life, liberty and the pursuit of happiness." These exact words were in fact enshrined within the original document used to found the United States of America on July 4th, 1776. It was mason Thomas Jefferson who personally authored America's new "Declaration of Independence," and he borrowed these immortal words from George Mason, another member of the secret order who'd originally recorded them in his Virginia Bill of Rights. The Masons were deeply involved in nearly every aspect of the original formation of the radical new Republic known as the United States of America.

It was mason Patrick Henry who uttered the famous phrase "Give me liberty or give me death," and mason Paul Revere who made that famous midnight ride through Concord, Massachusetts to warn us that the British were coming. And it was mason Robert Newman who lit the lamps in the Old North Church.

Mason Henry Knox bravely participated in both the Boston Massacre and the Battle of Bunker Hill, and it was his cannons, hauled all the way from Fort Ticonderoga in New York state, that finally drove the British out of Boston. The Bunker Hill Monument that stands today in Boston commemorating that city's famous struggle against the British, is in fact a Masonic obelisk.

Even Philadelphia's famous Independence Hall, where the Declaration of Independence was first signed, and the Liberty Bell once rang, was originally built by members of the secret order. It was mason William Adler who donated the land used to build the structure, and Grand Master Benjamin Franklin who presided over the cornerstone laying ceremony for the building.

Even the famous Liberty Bell, which once rang in Independence Hall, was cast by mason Paul Revere, and, when it cracked in 1799, it was tolling to mourn the passing of mason John Marshall, first Chief Justice of the United States Supreme Court.

It was mason George Washington who crossed the frozen Delaware River on that stormy Christmas night in 1776, and turned the tide of the Revolutionary War. And even America's famous Statue of Liberty that now stands in New York Harbor, was originally designed and built by the famous French mason, Frederic August Bartholdi.

The Washington Monument, centerpiece of our Capital Mall in Washington D.C., is a Masonic obelisk erected by members of the secret order. It is a little known fact that nearly every great event in American history revolved around a famous mason.

The original territories of the continental United States were claimed by many nations. The French controlled the central portion of the North American continent from their seaport in New Orleans, that catered to the gambling, alcohol, and carnal interests of sailors frequenting the city. It was the famous expedition of masons Meriwether Lewis and William Clark that eventually led to the purchase of the Louisiana Territories from the French, making New Orleans into a U.S. city.

The Spanish likewise held claim to much of the southwestern portion of the United States, but their interests were mainly to exploit the territory for gold and slaves. When a group of young Americans and Hispanics in Texas decided to declare allegiance to the United States of America instead of to Mexico, masons Davey Crockett and Jim Bowie took a brave stand against overwhelming odds at the famous Battle of the Alamo. Their actions eventually led to the claiming of the southwest territories as a new addition to the United States of America.

It is not well known that even the first man to walk on the moon was mason Niel Armstrong. Masons also played an important role in the American military as well. It was mason John Pershing who bravely led America's Expeditionary forces in the First World War, and mason Douglas MacArthur who presided over the signing of the documents ending the Second World War. Masons were in fact deeply involved in nearly every aspect of the American experience.

In music, it was mason Francis Scott Key who wrote our National Anthem, and mason John Philip Sousa who composed those famous marching tunes still played today in American parades, and masons George M Cohan and Irving Berlin who wrote many of America's great patriotic ballads.

Americans will never forget the musical contributions of masons like Louis Armstrong, William "Count" Basie, and Nat King Cole, whose songs are still a part of America's rich cultural heritage today.

The many greats in the entertainment field included masons John Wayne, Clark Gable, Douglas Fairbanks, Will Rogers, Al Jolson, and W.C. Fields. These famous men, and the masons who help them become famous, like Louis B Mayer, Adolf Zucor, Darryl S Zanuck, and Cecil B. DeMille, will always be remembered as an important part of America's cultural history.

In the fields of business and commerce, America's great mason industrialists and entrepreneurs Samuel Colt, John Jacob Astor, Charles Hilton, J. C. Penney, Henry Ford and Walt Disney, also managed to establish themselves as icons in the world of American business enterprise.

It can be truly said that no organization has contributed more to the establishment and perpetuation of the God-given rights of all free men than America's Masons. The followers of the ancient rite have always believed it was their manifest destiny to carry on the work of the ancient Hebrew masons of Egypt who left their mark on nearly every great civilization in history.

The ancient Masonic Scottish rite, and the famous "Stone of Destiny," had followed God's people all the way from the Hebrew Temple of Solomon in Jerusalem, to Edinburgh Castle in Britain. Jacob's blessing on his son Joseph was faithfully carried down through the centuries by the Masons to its ultimate destiny in the New World. The Masons believed it was their duty to carry on the work of the Hebrew sons of Seth, and establish the most powerful nation on Earth, thus helping to fulfill the ultimate destiny of God's people in the last days, as described within the pages of the Holy Scriptures.

Now in the last days, the Masons are regarded with suspicion and fear by many people. Many organizations, including even the Christian churches themselves, have undergone many changes in our modern "progressive" world. But the contributions of the Masons to America's original goals as a free society cannot be denied.

CHAPTER 33

ENERGY

"And a river went out of Eden to water the garden."

Gen. 2:10

The ancient Bible prophets warned us that in the last days, Satan would control the power of the air. And that prophecy has clearly manifested itself in the world of television and mass communications. The minds of the American public are now routinely manipulated by a daily bombardment of entertainment, opinion, and commercial advertising, efficiently distributed through the airborne media.

In the 1950's, America's parents were frightened nearly to death by the wildly gyrating hips of rock and roll idols spreading "heathen music" to America's youth through the twin media of television and radio.

By the 1960's a disease called Alzheimer's, formerly limited to business executives using aluminum-based underarm deodorants, was now spread to blue collar workers as well through television ads promoting the need for everyone to smell good.

In the 1970's, media hysteria was redirected toward a looming "Energy Crisis" that would cause the world to run completely out of oil in 20 years. Of course that never happened, but fuel oil prices managed to increase by a factor of ten.

In the 1980's, the public's attention was focused upon a dangerous and biologically inert fiber called asbestos that could be breathed into the lungs. It was immediately, and very expensively, replaced by another biologically inert fiber made of glass, that could unfortunately also be breathed into the lungs.

In the 1990's something called "Y2K" caused mass hysteria all around the globe, as billions of dollars were spent trying to save the world from a total computer meltdown on January 1st, 2000. Of course, that meltdown never happened.

Around the year 2000 the media would also prove that it was possible to achieve deception by omission. When American mothers began committing psychotic acts such as murdering their own small children, and teenagers began mass murdering their classmates at school, it wasn't revealed to the public that these psychotic acts may have been the result of unforeseen adverse reactions to seratonin-altering brain medications that had been previously prescribed for the treatment of mental health issues.

By the year 2000, the power of the airwaves had been clearly demonstrated to be a powerful tool for influencing public opinion. Programs were soon initiated to address new issues such as "Global Warming," supposedly caused by carbon emissions, which had caused the world's oceans to rise an inch or two since the year 1990. The whole world obediently accepted this new theory in spite of the fact that in 1100 AD a Solar Maxima had raised the world's oceans by over 100 inches, allowing Arab sailors to map the ice-free coast of Antarctica, and also allowing the Vikings to develop their warm "Greenland" paradise.

The American public had been so often deceived that it was now induced into quietly cutting off its own blood supply.

With energy being the lifeblood of America, television programming had now directed the public's attention toward developing new high tech energy sources such as deep-sea oil and natural gas supplies, and also wind-power and ethanol.

This caused the American public to totally ignore the dependable power source that had fueled its energy needs for the previous two centuries. What source was that? Why water power of course!

With modern society's ever increasing demand for more clean energy, there has been a desperate effort on the part of many to find and develop new high-tech sources of energy production in order to replace the familiar hydroelectric dam that has so reliably supplied America's power needs for countless decades.

But with every new high tech source of energy production, there were always drawbacks that could never be successfully eliminated. Nuclear energy for instance, which seemed to hold such great promise so many years ago, has now proven to be too dangerous to be entrusted into the hands of unscrupulous business interests, who often cheat on the maintenance of their nuclear facilities in order to save money.

Coal and oil supplies have likewise helped to fuel America's economy for many years, but are now running short in supply, and are also polluting our air and environment at a frightening rate. Unfortunately, wood and alcohol production place too great a demand on open land for their relatively small yield, and of course nobody wants an ugly wind farm in their neighborhood.

While it is true that no invention from the Industrial Age has been viewed with as much disdain as the modern hydro-electric dam, it is a fact that these dams were the main source of power that fueled America's Industrial growth.

Unfortunately however, these same dams have also served as barriers to populations of spawning wild fish, and also threatened human populations living downstream from these dams during periods of excess rainfall, when such dams have occasionally been known to burst.

The modern American lifestyle has now produced even more issues for the owners and operators of hydro-electric dams. We presently have liberal weekend kayakers demanding unimpeded access to river rapids, and liberal ecologists constantly complaining about the disturbance these dams cause to the delicate river ecology.

Hydro-electric dams are now therefore being abandoned at an alarming rate, and new programs have been initiated by liberal ecologists to permanently remove them from rivers where they have stood for a century or more. With our present energy shortage worsening so rapidly, it might now be time for us to take a second look at the hydroelectric dam to see if there might be some better solution to this unfortunate situation.

What if it were possible to build a hydroelectric dam that was not a barrier to spawning wild fish populations or kayakers? Is that possible? Well, believe it or not, it is actually possible.

Have you ever heard of the Granger Ecological Dam? Exactly what is the Granger Ecological Dam? Well, it's an ecologically-friendly hydro-electric dam that actually improves river ecology. That's right, it actually benefits the natural river ecology by working with the forces of nature, instead of against them.

The Granger Ecological Dam you see, is built to extend only half way across a river, instead of all the way across. At this critical half-way point, the wall of the dam then takes an abrupt 90 degree turn upstream, and continues upriver to a point where the level of the river water reaches a desired relationship to the water level at the generating portion of the dam.

In this way, half of the river's total volume is allowed to freely bypass the dam, thereby allowing free passage for wild spawning fish, boaters, kayakers, and any other ecologically sensitive interests.

The Granger Ecological Dam also benefits river ecology in many ways. First, the top of the Granger Ecological Dam is constructed twenty feet wide or more, thereby providing ample room for generating equipment to be housed completely within the structure. This eliminates the need for additional nearby structures to house the generating machinery.

The top of the dam is fenced in on both sides, thus permitting safe and unimpeded utilization of the top of the dam for recreational purposes such as viewing river ecology, or fishing. Trees may also be planted on top of the dam to improve shade, thereby lowering the temperature of river water. These trees can also provide ample shade for people using the dam for recreational purposes. In larger cities the dams could serve as quiet places for office workers to relax during lunch breaks and view the natural river ecology.

Since the Granger Ecological Dam extends only half-way across the river, multiple dams could be built along a river's entire length, thereby benefiting wild fish populations by providing deep-water sanctuaries at strategic points along the river, and supplying much needed aeration for river water during stagnant periods. This can provide fish and many other aquatic creatures with safe havens during times of drought or reduced river flow, and additionally creates many safe breeding areas for spawning fish. Multiple dams could help to provide additional aeration for river water during periods of reduced water flow. Multiple dams built at regular intervals along a river's entire length can be designed and fitted with fire hydrants to supply emergency water for use by local fire departments when battling nearby house or forest fires.

The design of the base of the Granger Ecological Dam includes overhangs placed at strategic heights above the river bottom, with screened-in areas for small fish fry, thereby providing a safe haven for immature fish to avoid being eaten by larger fish, thus improving fish survival rates.

The inlet of the Granger Ecological Dam is protected by a floating, angled skimmer/diverter for redirecting floating river debris out into the main channel in order to reduce cleaning at the generating portion of the dam.

The design of the Granger Ecological Dam can also be modified as land topography permits, by the addition of gated "holding ponds" constructed off to one side of selected dams at strategic points along the river. These holding ponds can serve as overflow areas during periods of peak river flow, and can also be used to augment river flow during periods of drought or reduced rainfall activity. They can also serve as sanctuaries for waterfowl and other wild creatures that depend upon wetlands for food or survival.

In these times of ever increasing dependence upon foreign oil and other finite sources of energy such as coal and gas, the Granger Ecological Dam could provide a clean source of non-polluting electric energy, and at the same time improve upon existing conditions in the natural ecology of many U.S. rivers. A large natural waterfall in a major river for instance, can act as an impassible barrier for spawning fish. The Granger Ecological Dam could easily correct such a condition, to the benefit of both man and fish.

The Granger Ecological Dam was originally designed in 1965, shortly after the infamous Northeast electric power outage, but the dam was far ahead of its time, and unfortunately not recognized for its ecological and economic benefits at that time.

Now, in the 21st century however, the Granger Ecological Dam could help to solve many ecological issues, and provide modern America with a clean, inexpensive, and Eco-friendly source of electric power. It can also provide an opportunity for altering, instead of removing, many existing hydro-electric installations around our nation.

The hydro-electric generating capacity of the average river far exceeds that necessary to supply the needs of the citizens living around it. The rivers of America alone contain enough potential energy to easily power the entire world for many decades to come. It is a terrible shame that this enormous untapped reserve of clean, non-polluting energy is not only being attacked by liberal activists, but is actually being systematically disassembled and destroyed right in front of our eyes.

CHAPTER 34

THE END OF TIME

And the Lord said, My spirit shall not always strive with man, for that he also is flesh: yet his days shall be an hundred and twenty years.

Gen. 6:3

One of the most fascinating concepts in God's universe is concept of time. Time is something that we all take for granted as we live out our everyday lives, and no one ever questions its dominance over us. We view its negative effects on our bodies every day, and use it to govern our every activity. It tells us when to get up in the morning, when to go to work, when to eat, and when to go to bed at night.

In the religious world however, time is viewed from an entirely different perspective. In fact, in modern Christianity, we are taught that time will someday come to an end. Exactly when this momentous event is expected to take place, and what form it will take, still remains a mystery for most Christians. I therefore felt it appropriate for us to explore this question in the very last chapter of this book.

This somewhat intriguing concept of the "end of time," also variously referred to as "The Last Days," the "Return of the Lord," and "Judgment Day," has historically caused much fear and anticipation among Christians all around the world. We've all seen the familiar cartoon drawing of a homeless man walking down a big city sidewalk carrying a sign announcing that "The End is Near." Could it be that "The End" really is near, or are we just worrying about nothing?

In previous chapters we traced the history of civilized man through the last six millennia by examining a plethora of Bible and historical facts. Bible records do seem to indicate that someday all things are eventually scheduled to come to a screeching halt.

At the very end of the book of Daniel for instance, we find the following phrase: "Go thy way Daniel, for the words are closed up and sealed until the time of the End."

In previous chapters we carefully traced the long history of the many great world-conquering empires that were created by man in vain attempts to achieve the perfect human society. Those empires spanned a space of approximately 6000 years, from ancient Egypt until the end of the modern Nazi era in 1945, thus fulfilling Daniel's famous prophecy concerning the end of the "last of the transgressors."

Since we've so carefully documented the existence of all these great world-conquering empires throughout history, we should expect that the date of the end must indeed be growing very close. The most important question we need to answer however, is exactly when this event is scheduled to take place.

It has long been held that the end of the world would occur near the change of a millennium, and history does indeed record a period of great social unrest occurring just prior to the change of the last millennium 1000 years ago.

In 1000 AD, people from all over the Christian world crowded into their churches and cathedrals in anxious anticipation of the arrival of the coming Day of Judgment.

Of course the great Judgment Day did not take place on December 31st, 999 AD, but the Catholic Church did make a large bundle of money on the many treasures delivered into its coffers by anxious Christians hoping to purchase their redemption in the glorious hereafter.

Recent history records for us a similar period of emotional hysteria occurring just prior to the turn of the year 2000 millennium (Y2K), when the entire civilized world was expected to come to a screeching halt as computers around the globe shut down at exactly midnight on December 31st, 1999.

This event also witnessed a great period of mass hysteria and renewed interest in "Last Days" prophecy. In fact, more Nostradamus books were sold at this time than at any other time in history, as nuclear missiles were expected to be launched at the stroke of midnight by "fail-safe" computerized control systems.

Of course the world did not come to an end in the year 2000, much to the embarrassment of many of the world's greatest scientific and political authorities, who'd been sucked into the hysteria of the moment. And of course there were many people who also took in great quantities of money during this apocalyptic episode as well.

But before we dismiss "the end" as just another example of political and religious fanaticism, we might take note of the fact that a large body of prophetic evidence does indeed seem to indicate that "the end of time" might soon be approaching.

There is a popularly held religious theory stating that God's "creation" of man would occur over a 6000 year period, or six biblical "days" (II Peter 3:8). And according to the calculations of Bishop Ussher (1580-1655), the Genesis event occurred around the year 4000 BC. If this is true, then the year 2000 represented roughly the 6000-year point of man's civilized existence here on Earth.

The Bible states in II Peter 3:8 that one day is to the Lord is as if a thousand years to man. Using this Bible code, many people have calculated that God allowed 6000 years, or six "biblical days" for the development of mankind here on Earth, and will return around the seventh millennium, or "seventh day" to harvest the results of His efforts. Could this be God's master plan for mankind?

The evidence supporting this hypothesis can be graphically illustrated by examining the record of human history. If you were to draw a 60 inch long horizontal line on a wall representing a graph of the history of civilized man, and then trace the history of almost anything you wish on that graph, the graph would remain relatively flat for nearly its entire length. It is only within the last hundred years or so that any activity at all can be shown on such a graph.

That's right, for nearly all of man's civilized existence here on Earth, very little has been accomplished. It is only within the last century or two that anything of significance can be shown to have actually taken place. In the year 1800 for instance, the world's population had still not reached the one billion mark, but now, only two hundred years later, it stands at over 6 billion, and is still growing at an exponential rate.

It doesn't matter what you attempt to trace on this 60 inch long horizontal graph, you can record statistics for world population, world economics, technology, scientific achievement, medical advances, or almost anything you wish, and nothing of any consequence happens until you reach the far right end of the graph.

If the graph were drawn using one inch to represent 100 years, it is only within the last two inches on the far right hand side of this 60 inch long graph that any significant activity could be shown. In fact, the line of the graph, after remaining flat for nearly all of its length, would then suddenly take off in a nearly vertical direction and disappear off the top of the graph. Was it mere coincidence that all of mankind's major achievements occurred at the exact point when the Scriptures predicted they would?

The Bible makes some very specific references to the "time of the end". In Daniel 12:4 for instance, we read about the "time of the end: when many shall run to and fro, and knowledge shall be increased." Many religious scholars insist that this is indeed an accurate description of the hustle and bustle of today's modern world, where people can now routinely travel anywhere on the globe in a matter of hours.

We should also take note that the Bible traces the history of the eight great civilizations of western society over the same 6000 years, and the history of these eight great civilizations of the western world now seems to have come to its end. The Egyptian, Babylonian, Persian, Greek, Roman, Holy Roman, Napoleonic and Nazi eras have all passed by, thereby leaving us very close to reaching the close of the 6000 years of events prophesied in the Holy Scriptures.

The events yet to occur are very clearly defined within the pages of the Scriptures, and also referenced by two modern-day prophets, Saint Malachy (1000 AD) and Nostradamus (1500 AD). And their predictions do seem to be occurring right on schedule, thereby placing us very close to the conclusion of things.

Even the ancient Babylonian prophecies recording the order of the planets in our solar system, seem to be coming to their ultimate fruition. The Sun, the moon, and the eleven stars (planets) spoken of by Joseph (Gen.37:9) are now rapidly being located and identified by the world's astronomers. The invention of the telescope allowed the five known visible planets to be joined by Uranus in 1781, Neptune in 1846, and Pluto in 1931. Modern computer driven telescopes are now revealing the existence of the rest of the planets in our solar system. The prophets have dictated that all of these planets must be discovered before "the end" can take place.

The great scientist Sir Isaac Newton also stated that the "end of time" would occur prior to the year 2060, and the great prophet Nostradamus stated that the world ends in 3757, but of course that is a coded date.

But exactly what form will this event called "the end of time' actually take? You've no doubt heard the old saying that there are two things in life that can always be counted on, death and taxes.

Most of us take these two things for granted, and never question their inevitability. In fact, we spend most of our lives saving for retirement, and dutifully making all those monthly life insurance payments so our loved ones will be well taken care of after we've gone.

But what if the limitations of time could be removed from our future? What if we didn't have to die? That's impossible, isn't it? Well, don't be so sure about that until you first check with the Bible to see what it has to say on the subject. You might be very surprised by what you find.

In the book of Genesis for instance, we read that sometime before the Great Flood, God decided to fix the lifespan of man at 120 years. This reference can be found in Genesis Chapter 6, Verse 3. At the same time God limited the age of man however, the biblical patriarchs were living for much longer than 120 years. Noah in fact, lived to be 950 years old, and Adam lived to be 930!

The biblical patriarchs were able to live for ten times as long as normal human beings. But how was that possible? Death comes as a result of aging, doesn't it? And we certainly can't stop the aging process, can we?

Well, it turns out that aging is caused by a tiny genetic timeclock that ticks away inside of every living human cell. This genetic timeclock is fixed within the genetic code of each and every one of our body cells. But remember, the patriarchs were not so very different from humans.

If you read a little deeper into the book of Genesis, you'll find that it tells the story of the beginning of the world, and also of the creation of man. It is interesting to note that in the book of Genesis, written over 3400 years ago, the Bible tells us that man can only expect to live for a maximum of 120 years. That's somewhat surprising, since at the time of the writing of the book of Genesis, the life expectancy of the average human being was less than 30 years. Was it mere coincidence that allowed the writer of the book of Genesis to get this fact correct?

Of course there are one or two people who claim to have lived for longer than one hundred and twenty years, but a thorough examination of their birth records leaves much to be desired. The overwhelming pattern of human longevity indicates a maximum life expectancy of exactly 120 years.

The real question for mankind is, can we alter our genetic timeclocks in such a way that we can live for longer than 120 years? The book of Genesis does indeed seem to indicate that this is possible.

When Adam and Eve were first created in the Garden of Eden, they were warned by God not to eat of the two trees in the center of the garden. One of these trees was known as the Tree of Knowledge, and the other, the Tree of Life (Gen. 2:9).

Eve was duped by the Serpent into partaking of the fruit of the Tree of Knowledge, thus condemning mankind to 6000 years of trying to create a perfect human society with that stolen knowledge. After Eve committed that act of original sin,

God banished both Adam and Eve from the Garden of Eden so they would not also partake of the Tree of Life, and live forever as gods do (Gen. 3:22).

So the Bible does seem to indicate that it is possible for men to live forever, if they eat from the Tree of Life. Now there's a frightening thought! Could it actually be possible for the genetic code within our cells to be altered so we can live forever as gods do? This intriguing question brings up the subject of the curious genetic condition known as "Progeria".

Progeria is an illness in which the genetic timeclock of the human cell has been accidentally altered. The word Progeria comes from the Greek *pro*, meaning "advanced", and *geria*, meaning "aging." Progeria is a genetic condition that causes the premature aging of its victims.

Progeria sufferers can age at ten times the normal rate for human beings. They can actually die of old age when they are only ten years old!

In this rare genetic condition, the timeclock inside the human cell has been genetically altered, and ticks at almost ten times its normal rate. A Progeria victim who is only nine years old, appears in every way to be a ninety-year old person.

Only a few people on Earth suffer from this rare genetic disorder, and the condition occurs without respect to the race or gender of its victims. This disease however, provides us with living proof that it is possible to alter the genetic timeclock inside the human cell!

Could it be possible that there are also some people on Earth who've had their genetic timeclocks altered in the opposite direction? We haven't heard from anyone with such a disease yet, but if you could live to be 1200 years old, you might not be telling anyone about it. After all, what would society do with all those unemployed life insurance salesmen?

Since the members of our scientific community seem to be so determined to fool around with our genes, might it be possible that they will someday locate this particular genetic code, and alter it? Or perhaps a more appropriate question might be, would God ever allow such a thing to happen?

BIBLIOGRAPHY

The many sources of information used in the creation of this book are so numerous that it would be impossible to list them all. The following is a list of a few of the more important books and videos that may help the reader to reach a better understanding of the many historic events that contributed to the ultimate destiny of God's people throughout history.

THE HOLY BIBLE
British and Foreign Bible Society, 1905
Oxford University Press, London

THE LEADING FACTS OF AMERICAN HISTORY
D. H. Montgomery, 1900
Ginn & Company, Boston, MA

DANIEL AND THE REVELATION
Uriah Smith, 1897
Pacific Press Publishing Assoc., Mtn. View, CA.

THE GREAT PYRAMID
WHY WAS IT BUILT & WHO BUILT IT
John Taylor, 1864
Longmans, Greene, London.

THE WORKS OF FLAVIUS JOSEPHUS
William L. Whiston, 1830
Armstrong and Plaskitt, Baltimore, MD.

THE OXFORD HISTORY OF THE AMERICAN PEOPLE
Samuel Eliot Morison, 1965
Oxford University Press, NewYork, NY.

THE HISTORY OF HERODOTUS
Rev. William Beloe, 1791
Leigh and Sotheby, London, England.

A STANDARD DICTIONARY
OF THE ENGLISH LANGUAGE
Isaac Funk, 1893
Funk & Wagnalls Co., New York, NY.

HANDBOOK OF NORTH AMERICAN INDIANS
VOL. 15 NORTHEAST
Wm. Sturtevant, 1978, USA.

THE LIFE OF PASTEUR
Rene Vallery-Radot, 1937
Sun Dial Press, NY.

HISTORICAL STATISTICS OF THE U S
Colonial times to 1970
C. B. Rogers, Sec.
US Dept. of Commerce, USA.

BENJAMIN FRANKLIN
Carl Van Doren, 1938
The Viking Press, NY.

THE LIFE AND DEATH OF ADOLF HITLER
Robert Payne, 1973
Praeger, New York, Washington.

THE BASIC WRITINGS OF THOMAS JEFFERSON
Philip S. Foner, 1944
Willey Book Company, NY.

THE MAN WHO SAW TOMMORROW
THE PROPHECIES OF NOSTRADAMUS
Erika Cheetham, 1974, Berkley, NY.

A TIME FOR ASTROLOGY
Jess Stearn, 1971
Coward, McCann, & Geohegan Inc., New York, NY.

NAPOLEON
Emil Ludwig, 1926
Garden City Publishing, Garden City, NY.

OUR INHERITANCE IN THE GREAT PYRAMID
Charles Piazzi Smith, 1864
Royal Astronomer, Scotland.

THE PILGRIMS FIRST YEAR IN NEW ENGLAND
Nahum Gale, 1857, Boston, MA.

EVIDENCE FROM SCRIPTURE AND THE
HISTORY OF THE SECOND COMING OF CHRIST
William Miller, 1842
Joshua Himes, Boston, MA.

CASELL'S FRENCH DICTIONARY
1962, Macmillan Publishing Co.
New York, NY.

THE COLUMBIA HISTORY OF THE WORLD
John A. Garraty & Peter Gay, 1972
Harper & Row, New York, NY.

THOMAS JEFFERSON
Fawn M. Brody, 1974
W. W. Norton Company Inc., New York, NY.

CASELL'S LATIN DICTIONARY
1959, Macmillan Publishing Co., New York, NY.

EVERYDAY LIFE IN ANCIENT TIMES
Gilbert Grosvenor, 1951
National Geographic Society, Washington, D.C.

THE PEOPLE'S CHRONOLOGY
James Trager, 1994
Henry Holt & Co., New York, NY.

THE AUTOBIOGRAPHY OF SCIENCE
F. R. Moulton & J. J. Schifferes, 1960
Doubleday & Co., New York, NY.

A DICTIONARIE OF THE FRENCH
AND ENGLISH TONGUES
Randall Cotgrave, 1611
Adam Islip, London, England.

THE COMPLETE PROPHECIES OF NOSTRADAMUS
Henry C. Roberts, 1949
Nostradamus Inc, Stratford Press, New York 13, NY.

THE GREAT REPUBLIC
The Master Historians, 1902
Copyright J. B. Lippincott Company
Copyright R. S Belcher Co., New York, NY.

WEBSTER'S ENCYCLOPEDIA OF DICTIONARIES
John Gage Alee, PH.D., 1958
Literary Press, Ottenheimer Publishers Inc., USA.

THE STORY OF PROPHECY
Henry James Forman, 1916
Farrar and Rinehart Inc., New York, NY.

THE COMPLETE WORKS OF ABRAHAM LINCOLN
John G. Nichols and John Hay, 1905
The Tandy & Thomas Company, New York, NY.

THE MARCH OF ARCHEOLOGY
C. W. Ceram, 1958
Alfred A Knopf, New York, NY.
Copyright Thames and Hudson Ltd., London.

INCIDENTS IN WHITE MOUNTAIN HISTORY
Benjamin S. Willey, 1856
Nathaniel Noyes, Boston, MA.

HISTORY OF NEW ENGLAND
John Gorham Palfrey, 1859
Little, Brown and Co., Boston, MA.
THE WORLD'S GREAT EVENTS
Esther Singleton, 1903
R. F. Collier & Sons, New York, NY.

THE MIDNIGHT CRY
Francis D. Nichol, 1944
Review and Herald Publishing, Washington DC.

THE RISE AND FALL OF THE THIRD REICH
William L. Shirer, 1960
Simon & Schuster, New York, NY.

LENIN – A BIOGRAPHY
David Shub, 1948
Doubleday & Co., New York, NY.

DESCENT OF MAN
Charles Darwin, 1896
D. Appleton & Co., New York, NY.

THE EVOLUTION OF MAN
Ernst Haeckel, 1896
D. Appleton & Company, New York, NY.

MYSTERIES OF THE UNEXPLAINED
The Editors, 1982
Reader's Digest Association, Pleasantville, NY.

THE PROPHECIES OF ST. MALACHY
Peter Bander - 1973
Tan Books Publishers, Rockford, IL.

THE MAN WHO KILLED LINCOLN
Philip Van Doren Stern, 1939
Random House, New York, NY.

MAN IN PREHISTORY
Chester S. Chard, 1969
McGraw-Hill Book Company, New York, NY.

MERVEILLEUX QUATRAINS DE NOSTRADAMUS
Colin de Larmor 1925
M. Lucien Dorbon/Dupas & Co. France

IMAGES: CC: Vladimir Pustovit, Mike Licht, Patriziasoliani

Made in United States
Orlando, FL
27 June 2023

34591606R00205